POSTWAR
PETERSFIELD

DAVID JEFFERY

SUTTON PUBLISHING

First published in the United Kingdom in 2006 by
Sutton Publishing Limited · Phoenix Mill
Thrupp · Stroud · Gloucestershire · GL5 2BU

British Library Cataloguing in Publication Data
A catalogue record for this book is available from the British Library.

ISBN 0-7509-4130-8

Title page picture: The Square, 1950s. (*The Petersfield Society*)

Cycle Speedway at Kimber's Field, 1950. (*Author's Collection*)

Typeset in 10/13 Novarese BT.
Typesetting and origination by
Sutton Publishing Limited.
Printed and bound in England by
J.H. Haynes & Co. Ltd, Sparkford.

Contents

Dog Alley, *c.* 1950. (*The Petersfield Society*)

Foreword & Acknowledgements

History is an elusive concept: a written or oral record of events is no guide to its authenticity and, even after the lapse of time (perhaps especially after the lapse of time), there is no guarantee that that original record is either accurate, non-tendentious or definitive. Whose perception of events are we relying on? What conditions prevailed at the time of recording those events? What role does nostalgia play in the reminiscence of those events? When historians attempt to define a 'Zeitgeist', this could be no more than a new perception of events, tainted by new prejudices engendered by subsequent 'history'. One solution to such dilemmas facing the recorder of events is to ignore them all and simply allow history to write itself (which it manifestly does!), then to comment upon it. However, at this point, other dangers lurk: what is the role of the observer-interpreter and how is his perception coloured by his own, possibly prejudiced, stance?

We can, of course, dismiss all this philosophical conjecture and rely entirely on 'face-value' history, or 'take-it-for-granted' history, the sum of which is more like a 'take-it-or-leave-it' account. It may not be ideal but, like a theatre director who encourages his actors to inject their own interpretation of a script, the historian-director can at least offer his reader the opportunity to interpret events for himself. What has to be accepted, however, is the uncontrollable nature of those events. History doesn't just happen, it lurches along in fits and starts, short bursts of civic or individual energy being punctuated by longer bouts of inertia, moments of elation alternating with periods of frustration. One family's achievements and advances are matched by another's setbacks and reversals. History abounds with 'hiccups' punctuating the flow of time and events, deceiving the optimist and slowing the pace of progress; momentum is relative. Local development has its own momentum and does not necessarily (indeed, rarely does it) correlate with the national.

The role of chance, the interaction between people and events, the catalyst of exterior forces, the intervention of government, the arbitrariness of decision-making, prevarication and delay, all play their part in forming the continuum of history and they have all performed a function in Petersfield's development. It is this inconstancy which I have tried to portray in my account of events. Petersfield has, by chance or design, pursued a policy of gradualism in its affairs in the postwar years, and this in itself has contributed to the overall character of our town. The impartial observer probably does not exist, but, since I am not a native of Petersfield myself, I hope at least to have been objective in my judgements and to have gained from the benefit or, more presumptuously, from the wisdom of distance – and thereby to have portrayed the town I have come to love as comprehensively and as dispassionately as possible in the pages that follow.

Pre-war Petersfield was, naturally, a different Petersfield. Commentators have described it as 'one of England's prettiest villages' with a quality of sleepiness, 'dozing tranquilly' between bouts of fervour on market days. The population was sufficiently small for most of its inhabitants to recognise, if not know, almost all their fellow townsfolk. The immediate postwar ambience was not too dissimilar: the physical environment was unchanged, the town having suffered virtually no damage in the war; the shops were those of pre-war days and remained in the hands of the same owners; families continued to make their own entertainment, unfettered by the universal availability of television or cars.

But, slowly, austerity has given way to prosperity, and that has changed everything. The first aim of this book has been to illustrate and interpret those changes that have taken place in the town over the second half of the twentieth century. However, since historical happenings do not adhere to convenient time periods, nor follow any logical pattern, references have been made to wider events, external forces at work on the community or a general appreciation of matters of national or international relevance.

The bulk of the material has been gleaned from the local press, which, while not perfect from the point of view of accuracy or historical authenticity, does provide a framework for comment and interpretation. Anecdotal material from individual interviews has been added to the core text with the aim of substantiating the press reports and to personalise the account. In addition, some historical detail has occasionally been added to give background substance and to place the events within the context of the overall story of Petersfield since the Second World War. Since 'living memory' accounts are such a valuable and indispensable commodity to the oral historian, I have concluded each chapter with a section dedicated to 'Departures', which, in their own way, indicate breaks with the past, while the 'Plus ça change . . .' tailpieces are there to remind the complacent that we can neither decide the pace of history nor expect too much from it.

I am indebted to a very large number of people for their contributions to my efforts: to the staff of Petersfield Library, to my colleagues at Petersfield Museum and to the undermentioned contributors and correspondents, all of whom have shared with me my fascination for the development of our wonderful town. I apologise for any inadvertent omissions or unintentional errors and, finally, thank my daughter, Anna-Louise, for reading the manuscript and making many helpful suggestions.

David Jeffery

CHAPTER ONE

Austerity
1945–52

VE DAY AND VJ DAY

As the seven members of Emanuel School's Windsor Rhythm Kings Jazz Band spontaneously clambered on top of the air-raid shelter in front of St Peter's Church on the evening of VE (Victory in Europe) Day, 8 May 1945, to play to the joyful crowds which were gathering around them, little did they realise that they were not only celebrating the end of six years of conflict in Europe, but also heralding the imminent emergence of a new Petersfield. The Emanuel boys formed part of a contingent of more than a thousand schoolchildren who had found themselves evacuated to Petersfield during the war years and who were shortly to leave the town that summer, thus reducing the town to its 'normal' size of about 5,000 inhabitants. The population of the town, which had taken a century to double in size since the 1840s, was about to treble in size in the next half-century.

On the day after VE Day, the front page of the normal Wednesday edition of the *Hants and Sussex News* carried a mundane report of the proceedings of the Petersfield UDC (Urban District Council), including information on respirators (gas masks) and hackney carriage licences; a warning about the local gas supply; and a short condemnation of the misuse of the children's swings on the Heath. A mere two column inches on page three were devoted to a bland acknowledgement of the end of the war in Europe. Lack of rapid technology in the news media had made it impossible, until the following week, to mention that 'the two days officially set apart for the purpose [of celebrating] were days of great joy and relaxation, the weather being for the most part favourable and pleasant, and in town and country alike, people generally kept holiday and were strengthened and refreshed for the great and continued effort which still lies ahead before world peace can be secured'. In the week following VE Day, the Petersfield (ex-services) Fund organised a programme of dances, a whist drive, a celebrity concert, a boxing tournament and an Empire Day Ball. There were also thanksgiving services in all the local churches.

Three months later, VJ (Victory over Japan) Day passed by relatively quietly, partly because the weather on the evening of 15 August had been too cold to attract people to dance in the open air; instead, the town hall was the venue for public dancing. The children of Petersfield had their own special jollification to celebrate VJ Day in September: the UDC arranged a party for more than 550 youngsters at the town hall, with music, tea, community singing and conjuring and Punch and Judy shows.

In 1946, the Clerk of the UDC announced that food gifts from the colonies were still being received in Petersfield: '150 tins of marmalade and grapefruit, a gift from the people of South Africa, have been distributed to 75 necessitous persons.' In June that year there were

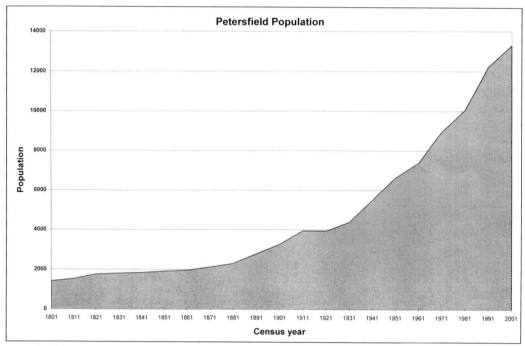

Petersfield population 1801–2001. (*David Brooks*)

celebrations to commemorate the first anniversary of the end of the war, with a cinema show at the Savoy, a fancy-dress parade, children's sports and a Punch and Judy show, dancing and community singing, and a tug-of-war and boxing displays.

NATIONAL AND LOCAL POLITICS

With the celebrations over, the task of conducting the 1945 general election preoccupied certain sections of the community, despite there being, according to the press, 'not much evidence of public excitement'. Polling Day was 5 July and, of the three candidates standing in Petersfield, it was General Sir George Jeffreys, the Conservative MP for the town since 1941, who won with a lead of more than 12,000 votes over his Liberal and Labour rivals. Shortly afterwards, he announced that he would not be standing in the next election and the Hon. Peter Legh was adopted as the prospective Conservative candidate; he was elected in October 1951 with a majority of more than 14,000 votes over his opponents.

   Local political interest centred around the immediate needs of the population, especially those of returning servicemen. There were calls for a maternity ward and an operating theatre at Petersfield Cottage Hospital and dedicated beds for patients recovering from illness or injuries sustained during war service. As elsewhere in Britain, there were vociferous demands for houses to be built urgently; for the moment, the projects suggested by the Advisory Committee of the Memorial Fund to provide public baths or a library for the town were rejected as of secondary importance.

Remnants of war – there had been very little material damage to the town in the war – included some Nissen huts on the Heath and air-raid shelters which were removed early in 1946. Some buildings used in wartime – Steep House, used by French Resistance workers as a safe haven, and Heath House, used as a sanatorium for evacuees since 1939 – were closed. The old library room at the town hall, given up at the outset of war to house the ARP office, now became the offices of the Surveyor's Department of the UDC because of their increased workload. The library had had temporary premises at the (Working) Men's Club in Station Road, but Harry Roberts, the ex-London doctor now living in Froxfield and supporting various Petersfield enterprises, suggested building a third storey on top of the town hall to accommodate the library and a reading room. His intellectual impetus was, as ever, matched by his financial generosity and he offered the first £100 towards this project 'to start the ball rolling'. Lord Horder, who lived at Ashford Chace, later contributed a further £100 to the scheme. Harry Roberts' concern for the town's future was expressed in a letter to the *Hants and Sussex News*.

> Petersfield's steady drift into a suburban status, which has lately begun and threatens to advance, is lamented by all who care for individuality, character, distinction and beauty. The normal population of Petersfield is rather too small for a vigorous market town possessing, as it should do, its theatre, art gallery and the rest; and one or two light industries, such as printing, bookbinding, furniture making, would go well to supplement the rural educational potentialities.

THE EDUCATION DEBATE

Of immediate priority for Petersfield was the provision of a site for a new secondary school, and the County Land Officer identified the Causeway Farm beyond the then gasworks (now the Tesco site) to be reserved for this purpose. Despite the determination of Miss Nora Tomkins, the Chairman of the Town Planning Committee, to put Petersfield on the map as a pioneer town in 'what education should be now and in the future', it was to be a further twelve years before her dream of a secondary school on this site was realised. The old (pre-war) senior and junior council schools in St Peter's Road had become woefully inadequate and, even with the use of temporary hutted accommodation, it was clear that a fresh look at educational provision in the town was long overdue. The school leaving age had been raised to 15 in 1947, and this put even more pressure on the authorities to seek a solution to the overcrowding then prevalent in the town's educational establishments.

Miss Tomkins had recommended to the Petersfield UDC that they ask the county council to consider provision for all educational needs at one location, from infancy to adult life, and comprising grammar, modern and technical sections in the secondary sector, in accordance with the provisions of the 1944 Education Act. She wanted Love Lane to be earmarked as this site for all the necessary buildings, but the UDC Chairman felt that the Causeway site would be preferable as it was much larger, could accommodate the school's own playing fields, as the UDC was not intending to offer them the continued use of the football pitch in Love Lane, and would allow for expansion in the future. This debate marked the start of a long, frustrating saga about the educational needs of Petersfield children which Miss Tomkins was not to see resolved during her period of office. She had been the first elected woman member of the Urban District Council and retired from it in November 1945 after nineteen years' service to the community.

The whole question of the type of secondary school to be chosen and where and when the building would take place, became the subject of considerable controversy and not a little prevarication for many years after the publication of the 1944 (Butler) Education Act. It was for this reason that the assumption was made that as Churcher's College was a grammar school, the old Petersfield Senior School would become the new secondary modern school, in line with the educational definitions of the 1944 Act. However, despite the tacit acceptance of the title 'Secondary Modern' – a school badge and a navy-blue and yellow uniform had even been created, although few of the children's parents could afford these – there was never an official naming ceremony and at various times between 1945 and 1957 the school was referred to as the Petersfield County School, the Petersfield County Secondary School, and even the Modern Secondary School. The pupils themselves knew it as PSM (Petersfield Secondary Modern), but the label (unfortunately for the children) carried with it a certain stigma, as it indicated a failure to obtain the 11-plus examination for entry to grammar school. In 1947, the Hampshire County Council added to the educational planning confusion which was unsettling the town by proposing an all-purpose (i.e. comprehensive) school for girls, and a secondary modern school for boys.

Yet another call for the building of Petersfield's new secondary modern school was made in the spring of 1951. In the original development scheme for the town's schools, the programme was to build a comprehensive school incorporating the Girls' County High School and the secondary modern school in one building. However, the County Education Committee had still not reached a final decision and it was more than likely that the new school would house the former Senior Council School in St Peter's Road and the local village schools. The former had a roll of nearly 400 between the ages of 11 and 15 and their classroom accommodation and playing space were hopelessly inadequate. As was the case in the war, supplementary halls in the town and the use of public grounds were hired to meet partially the educational needs of these pupils. A similarly desperate situation arose at primary level: the primary school had about 340 children in it and the roll was increasing year by year, with the result that, owing to lack of space, it was soon going to be impossible to admit any 5-year-olds.

Despite more calls by the parish councils for the building of a new secondary modern school for Petersfield, the project was again put on hold thanks to the restrictions on capital expenditure in the 1952 education budget, which forced another postponement. In addition to this setback, Mr E.J. Baker, the owner of the land, told the *Hants and Sussex News* that he did not intend to give permission for his land to be sold, as it would represent a loss to agriculture of valuable farming land. It was in the Causeway Meadows that it had been proposed to build the town's new secondary modern school and, beside it, the school's own playing fields, as the UDC was not intending to offer it the continued use of the future pitch in Love Lane. In the meantime, Mr E.C. Young was appointed Headmaster of the newly named Petersfield County Secondary School, and it was he who eventually saw the school through the difficult transition stage to its new premises in Cranford Road.

Churcher's College and Peter Symonds School in Winchester had both applied for Direct Grant status under the new regulations, but both had been refused by the Ministry of Education. There were no Direct Grant schools in Hampshire at this time. However,

Churcher's College was granted voluntary-aided status in 1949, thus enabling its own governors to control its curriculum, school and boarding policy while Hampshire County Council financed its maintenance and controlled its pupil entries.

It was perhaps coincidental, but also thereby historically significant, that many head-teachers of Petersfield schools retired immediately after the war: Mr A.H.G. Hoggarth had been associated with Churcher's College for thirty-five years, including eighteen years as its Head; Miss Emma Lowde had been the first and only Headmistress of the Girls' County High School since its opening in 1918; Mr Wilfrid Bennetts had joined the staff of Petersfield Senior Council School in 1911 and succeeded Mr W.R. Gates as its Head in 1942. He had also played an active part in the life of the town and served on the Urban District Council for several years. His wife, Mrs Emily Bennetts, had been the Headmistress of Sheet School since 1919 and she also retired in 1946. At Bedales, Mr Freddie Meier, who had taken over the headship from the founder, Mr Badley, in 1935, was replaced by Mr Hector Jacks in 1946. Mr Jack le Grice, Headmaster of Churcher's prep school under Mr Hoggarth, bought Broadlands in Ramshill and transformed it into his own Broadlands Prep School, preparing boys not just for Churcher's College, but also for other grammar and private schools. The school was to survive successfully until Mr and Mrs le Grice retired some twenty-five years later. Another Prep School, Winton House, closed at the end of the school year 1946–7 when its Headmistress, Miss G.M. Williams, retired after twenty-three years' service.

An educational era passed with the death in 1951 of Miss Annie Richardson who, with her sister Beatrice, had run Ling Riggs School in Sandringham Road for nearly half a century. They had come to Petersfield from London at the turn of the century and lived at 8 High Street, where their father was a bookseller. Thirty years later, the building was demolished by Woolworths for their new store.

Although Petersfield had lost two of its small private prep schools since the war, it shortly gained two more: Moreton House opened as a school in the old Hylton House in The Spain, and Dunannie began operating as Bedales pre-preparatory school in 1954. Dunannie, a large, partly seventeenth-century house between Petersfield and Steep, had become the centre of an experiment in friendship when young Germans and other Europeans had come to share their lives with young English students in 1948 under the auspices of The Friends Ambulance Group, which moved from London into the house as part of its relief work in postwar Europe. Dunannie moved 'across the road' into part of the Dunhurst premises in 1970.

The departure of evacuated children from the town at the end of the summer term in 1945 was as significant as it was sad. Emanuel School boys from London, who had far outnumbered the Churcher's boys they had shared their school with, had celebrated the 350th anniversary of their foundation in May. The Headmaster, Mr C.G.M. Broom, spoke then of the 'friendliness that had prevailed for six years between their hosts [Churcher's College] and themselves as guests in Petersfield'. Similar sentiments were expressed by Miss Dorothy Chadwick, the Headmistress of Battersea Central School for Girls, who had shared the Petersfield Girls' High School premises in the High Street and had held classes at Hylton House in The Spain and in various premises throughout the town.

In 1949, West Mark Camp School near Sheet Common, which had housed several hundred children evacuated from the Portsmouth area in the war, was chosen as the scene of a bold experiment in education. As a direct result of the successful wartime experience of bringing urban schoolchildren into a rural setting – for their own safety, but also enhancing their daily lives by giving them an appreciation of the countryside – ninety boys and sixty girls sent from the County of Middlesex arrived at West Mark Camp for a three months' stay. The principal aims were to develop the spirit of living together and to create a mutual respect between townsfolk and countryfolk.

West Mark Camp was one of thirty country estates owned by the National Camps Corporation and let by them for varying periods to local education authorities as an experiment in boarding education.

THE MARKET DEBATE

At the meetings of the Petersfield Urban District Council in the immediate postwar years, a good deal of debate arose over the state and the quality of Petersfield cattle market. Projects were discussed for a new site for the market (the so-called 'new market') as the accommodation currently afforded in The Square was said to be poor, particularly with regard to the conditions for the livestock. A new site was suggested near Borough Farm (in Borough

A sheep auction by Jacobs & Hunt in The Square, early 1950s. (*The News Group*)

Road), but, in the view of one correspondent to the *Squeaker*, 'this would lead the town to part with some of its ancient rights to a group of individuals who, having obtained that monopoly, proposed to exploit it for their private gain'. The council were prepared to discuss leasing the livestock rights. The auctioneers Hall, Pain and Foster and Hewitt and Lee abandoned the new market plan because of the costs involved and the opposition they had encountered to it.

Sporadically during the history of the market there were allegations of cruelty to the animals, which remained tethered for long periods of the day; occasionally there were accounts of heifers or calves which broke loose and 'rampaged' through the town. One report in 1947 described a 'horrible exhibition of savagery' which ensued when a heifer broke free from its tether at the railings in The Square and was pursued through the market and town by a yelling mob of men and boys, who were smashing it across the head and face with heavy sticks. These allegations, however, were vehemently denied in the following week's *Squeaker*. Nevertheless, regardless of the accuracy or otherwise of such reports, it is clear that market conditions aroused feelings of anger in some onlookers and these strongly felt concerns marked the beginning of the eventual demise of the cattle market (which finally closed in 1962). The RSPCA also called for the market to be abolished; it talked of the 'shocking scandal' of the animals standing in The Square from 9 a.m. until 4 p.m. with no facilities for sheltering or watering them and with them tethered in overcrowded conditions.

Meanwhile, protests by Petersfield traders over the displacement of farmers and their livestock by stallholders led to their demanding that the UDC take immediate steps to earmark a more suitable site for the livestock market. Petersfield was, nevertheless, still predominantly an agricultural-based community with rural interests and, in the late summer of 1948, over 5,000 people went to Bell Hill (now the recreation ground) to see the biggest agricultural show ever held in Petersfield – and the first since 1938 – organised by the Fareham and Hampshire Farmers' Club.

Another rural era passed when the cultivation of hops at Seward's Farm at Weston ceased after 142 years. Traditionally, for a fortnight every September, 24 acres of hops were pulled from the vines by more than eighty families, the vast majority of whom came from Portsmouth. Christopher Seward's last crop at Weston after twenty-five years was picked in 1946. Hops were still grown at Buriton, however, and schoolchildren were still being given time off school to harvest the crop in September each year, just as they had done during the pre-war and war years. The main Petersfield hop farms brought into the district about £30,000 each season, the bulk of which went towards labour costs, but this sum does reflect the value of the whole enterprise to the community.

THE *SQUEAKER*

The *Hants and Sussex News*, known to all (and, in an ironic fashion, to itself) as the *Squeaker*, remained as visually austere in 1945 as it had always been – perhaps consciously following the example of *The Times*, which resolutely retained its spread of small advertisements on its front page until Winston Churchill's death in 1965. The *Squeaker* (as it will be referred to here) was a four-page broadsheet costing 1½d, with reports from Petersfield Petty Sessions and the two local councils (Urban and Rural) on the front page, small adverts on page two, announcements of forthcoming events on page three, and news articles and letters to the Editor on the back page.

Petersfield Post *mastheads. (Author's Collection)*

However, it was not to remain immune from the postwar evolution in local life: with a change of ownership to Mr A.D. Millard, a London book publisher, in 1945, the structure and look of the paper underwent considerable modernisation over the next five years. It reached a wider readership, increased its circulation figures and published a short leading article each week. In 1946, its austere aspect and solemn prose gave way to larger front-page headlines, bolder typography in its page two advertisements and a wider reporting of news from Midhurst and 'Round the District'. Its first lurid headline ('Ran to girl with knife in his back', on the stabbing of a boy in Liss by a sailor) and its first photograph (of Kathleen Money-Chappelle at the closure of her 'Home from Home' canteen) appeared and, in 1947, linotype was adopted, more pictorial adverts started to feature and the paper increased in size from four pages to six. In 1948, under its new Editor, Hardiman Scott, the *Squeaker* appeared in a new dress. For sixty-five years the front-page title of the newspaper had been printed in heavy Old English Gothic type. The new type adopted saved 7in of space as the lines were set closer together. The paper expanded to six pages in 1949, and its price rose from 1½d to 2d that year. It began to carry half-page advertisements and banner headlines of a whole page width. Many more photographs began to adorn not only the front, but also the inside pages.

It became more of a campaigning newspaper too. For instance, it called for a referendum on the future of Petersfield market, adopting the stance that change might be for the better now that cattle were being transported to and from further afield on market days. Also in 1947, the *Squeaker*'s new Comment column, dwelling on the attraction of Petersfield as a visitor town, suggested that 'we would do well to give them a bigger welcome'. It felt that, without sacrificing any of its present charm, the Heath could be more tempting, and suggested the creation of a small beach and a paddling pool on the north side of the Pond, a tea house nearby, and greater publicity for the town's summer sports of cricket and golf, both established favourites on the Heath for generations. Furthermore, the local amateur dramatic societies could be encouraged to provide outdoor entertainment on the Heath, with Shakespeare given 'an open airing', concerts by the Victoria Brass Band, and more attention drawn to the town's historical and architectural beauties. To promote all this, a greater use of advertising was needed in neighbouring towns.

The *Petersfield Weekly News* had begun life in 1883 and had become the *Hants and Sussex News* in 1891 when Frank Carpenter became its Editor and the business was taken over by Mr A.W. Childs. Later, it removed to premises at the bottom of the High Street (now Your Move), then to Childs bookshop site (now Somerfield). The pre-war paper was known well outside the town for its intelligent and literate reporting. Indeed, it was also known as far afield as Africa: the first Mrs Rowswell, who had opened her newsagent's in the High Street in 1916, passed on ownership of the shop to her two daughters, one of whom had a daughter living in Southern Rhodesia and who received the newspaper weekly. She in turn passed it to the natives who used it to roll their cigarettes in, as it had such fine, combustible paper!

PETERSFIELD IN THE MEDIA SPOTLIGHT

During a programme in a BBC radio series entitled *Thank You for Your Letters*, broadcast on the General Forces Network in 1946, a commentary on Petersfield described the town as 'prosperous and bustling'. The Heath, Charles II, the Jolliffe family, Churcher's College and St Peter's Church were all mentioned in a series of brief verbal pictures.

Three years later, the broadcaster Brian Vesey-Fitzgerald was considerably more negative in his book *Hampshire and the Isle of Wight* in which he describes Petersfield as 'a pleasant, rather sleepy town, which gives me the impression that it missed success centuries ago, and has been waiting ever since for another chance to turn up'. He called the statue of William III 'quite the most ridiculous statue in England', the manners in its tea shops and cafés 'leaving much to be desired', and he doubts if Petersfield would ever be considered a 'first-class season' town.

However, under Hardiman Scott, Frank Carpenter's successor as Editor of the *Squeaker*, Petersfield's association with the media was particularly favourable. This was exemplified later in 1949 when it was learnt that after only one year in the post, Mr Scott was leaving to join the staff of the BBC Midland Region. He had been in Petersfield since the end of the war and had identified himself closely with the cultural life of the town in that time. His talents as a poet, novelist and, above all, as a broadcaster were to ensure that his name became a household word in Britain during the 1950s. It may not have been entirely coincidental that it was Hardiman Scott's *Squeaker* which had provided the information and pictures of the town from which two film companies would select their locations for two films to be made in the autumn and winter of 1949 and 1950.

In the autumn of 1949, many Petersfield schoolchildren played as extras in the film *The Happiest Days of your Life*, directed by Frank Launder and filmed at Byculla School in Rake, a private girls' school later named Little Abbey. The stars of the film were Margaret Rutherford and Alastair Sim. It is hardly surprising that the newly recruited, budding stars still remember being paid handsomely for the enjoyment of waving from the coaches as they arrived at the school, playing lacrosse, marching noisily around the building, then participating in a grand pillow fight in the 'dorms'! Churcher's boys even had some speaking parts. To cap their joy, they were taken to London to see the premiere in Leicester Square.

In February 1950, the Hollywood film star Robert Montgomery was in Petersfield Square to direct some sequences for the film *Your Witness*, in which he also starred. Hundreds of people thronged the Market Square and took part in the crowd scenes.

The same month, nearly five hundred people crowded into the town hall to watch and hear the BBC programme chairman Guy Mackarness and the producer Rupert Annand invite about forty local townspeople to answer questions on topical issues sent in by listeners. The recordings were destined for a thirty-minute programme entitled *Speak your Mind* to be broadcast later on the West of England Home Service.

Sixteen months later, Petersfield went on the air again: the town was chosen for the staging of the 100th edition of the BBC's *Any Questions?* Nearly seven hundred people were in the 'Large Hall' (Festival Hall) to hear Freddie Grisewood, the question master, open the programme and the panel of Ralph Wightman, Sir Steuart Wilson (a former Bedales Music Master), Sir Richard Acland and Sir 'Bob' Boothby (respectively Labour and Conservative politicians) answer the public's questions.

THE HOUSE-BUILDING PROGRAMME

Among the public works projects undertaken in the immediate postwar period was, of course, a substantial housing programme. The Urban District Council site in Cranford Road which it had purchased in 1945 from the two owners, Mr Ted Canterbury and Mr E.J. Baker, was designated in 1946 to receive a total of twenty-eight dwellings. The first few houses at the Causeway end of the road had been completed before the war; however, by mid-1947, only three of the new properties had been completed and occupied, as there were only twenty men working on the project and with an overtime ban in force. In the town, there were still some eighty German POWs, and these men were temporarily employed on the council's housing schemes to help with the building of streets and sewers; they – along with nearly half a million others who had been similarly detained in Britain after the war had ended – were eventually repatriated to Germany after spending ten months working in Petersfield. The general layout of the Cranford Road–Borough Grove–Grange Road estate was thought to be extremely wasteful by the infrastructure engineers, although of course it looked extremely attractive on the plan. In this respect, it resembled more a private development than a council project, with its central stream and ample green spaces and trees.

Despite Petersfield UDC's relatively slow start to the postwar house-building programme, due mainly to the policy of 'no pre-fabs', the 1948 change of heart and decision to order 26 'Reema' houses for Highfield Road took the total number of homes created by the end of 1949 to 80, with a further 34 under construction. By comparison, Biggleswade (Bedfordshire) had 248 (temporary or permanent) houses completed, Saffron Walden (Essex) 184 completed, and Stevenage (Hertfordshire) 160 completed. These Reema houses, built by Reema Construction Ltd, although prefabricated in their method of construction, were in fact considered to be permanent homes and were the subject of a compulsory purchase order by the Ministry of Health, thus intimating their approval. Construction on the Highfield Road and Borough Grove sites began in 1949 and was completed in little over a year.

The highest number of houses built in the UDC and RDC (Rural District Council) areas in one single year since the war was achieved in 1950, with 327 permanent homes completed, almost double the total number of those built between 1945 and 1949. The population of Petersfield recorded at the 1951 census (6,616) had also risen rapidly, by 22 per cent, since 1931.

By 1949, Petersfield felt that it was emerging well from the war and the UDC presented a note of success in its deliberations: the collective achievements of a new sports ground at Love Lane; a recreation ground at Bell Hill; an enlightened outlook on cultural activities which had produced grants for the Musical Festival and the repertory theatre; and the purchase of thirty-two Reema houses for Cranford Road exemplified the new optimism. Finally, a proposed boundary plan which merged the urban and rural areas outlined a possible new administrative

Reema houses in Borough Grove, 1980s. (*Petersfield Museum*)

convenience. In terms of population, it was expected that the town would double in size, and planning decisions were beginning to be made with this in mind.

In the Rural District, more than two hundred families were still living in requisitioned premises after the war and there were 475 families waiting to be housed. In the UDC area, the problem was not so acute: only 10 families were in requisitioned houses and 15 families in the huts at 'Oaklands Camp', built at the top end of Oaklands Road by the Ministry of Works during the war to house a civil defence unit. The first families of squatters had moved there in 1946 (where they shared the camp with the German POWs employed in building the Cranford Road estate), while they waited to be relocated in council houses. In fact, the UDC area house-building rate had slowed down by nearly a half by August 1952, there being a total of twenty-nine houses built between June 1951 and June 1952 owing to protracted negotiations for the possession of sites. By November 1952, however, the last house on the Cranford Road estate was completed and the link through to Borough Road effected, the biggest building scheme in the history of the Petersfield UDC. This substantial development was regarded as a 'model small town' with a shop incorporated into the estate consisting of a total of 219 dwellings and 68 Reema houses.

One feature of this period was the tight working unity forged between the UDC, the developers and the civil engineers who worked on the major projects around the town: as Borough Engineers and Surveyors, first Harold Longbottom, then, after his retirement in 1953, John Thomas, were responsible for water supplies (before the Wey Valley water company took this over), the market, highways, the Taro Fair and the Heath, sewerage and new housing estates such as the large Cranford Road–Borough Grove complex. It was John Thomas who introduced sodium street lighting to Petersfield (in the Causeway) in the 1960s, who rebuilt the sewage works in the 1970s, and who was responsible for alleviating the huge problem of flooding which had bedevilled the town for decades.

SOCIAL AMENITIES

Far-reaching plans for the future provision of social amenities in Petersfield were discussed by the Urban District Council in 1948: one proposal was for a children's recreation ground at Bell Hill, with football and cricket pitches, swings and a paddling pool; another was for a sports ground at Love Lane with rugby and football pitches, a swimming pool and a running track; a third facility was to be a car park and perhaps a bus station in the centre of town. About forty people representing Petersfield societies had also called upon the UDC to provide a community centre for the town, while an equally vociferous call was made for a youth centre.

One activity popular with local young men at the time was cycle speedway: Petersfield was represented by the 'Highfield Cobras' whose home track was at Kimber's Field (now Kimbers) and they had many hundreds of followers who went to their competitions against other teams from Hampshire and beyond. An annual cycle speedway match was held at the British Legion Fête in the Grange Field (now the site of The Petersfield School). With the return of Petersfield's newly demobbed servicemen, the town's former clubs and societies began to start up again. There were jobs available for the returnees too: the Post Office was a big employer, the Itshide rubber factory took on staff, the local council offered manual jobs, and some people went up to Longmoor to find work. It was as if Petersfield, unlike Horndean for example, was self-sufficient in labour supply and demand.

Charles Dickins, Scoutmaster of the Petersfield Troop, reported that three youth clubs had started since the war and had died out. It was Mr Dickins who had held the Scout troop together for thirty-seven years with a break of only three years during the First World War; he had been engaged on youth work for at least forty-two years during his lifetime and his belief was that, as the 1st Petersfield Scout Group (Lord Selborne's Own) had been formed in 1909, it must have been one of the oldest in the country. Their most recent achievement was the wartime collection and sorting of waste paper; the eighty or more boys had worked in relays on the organisation of the salvage, and had even bought a baler and two storage sheds, which were erected at the back of the Scout hut in Heath Road which the Scouts had moved into in 1915. An average of 2 tons of paper was collected each week during the war years.

The town library, which had moved premises three times since it had started in 1926, now took over Winton House in the High Street. Its first home had been above Mr E.J. Baker's butcher's shop (now Superdrug), then the Working Men's Club in Station Road, then a special room was dedicated to it in the town hall, until the demands of the war forced it to move back to the Men's Club. The Librarian, Mr Edgar Morris, had remained in his job throughout all these years of change and was now congratulated on his 'yeoman service'. A year later, the *Squeaker* joined those who were campaigning for a designated new library site in the town.

With the advent of the National Health Service in 1948, the old Petersfield Cottage Hospital became a state-run hospital. However, doctors in the district, who until then had consistently opposed the emergent National Health Service introduced by the Labour government of Clement Attlee, now decided to follow the advice of the BMA Council and join the service when it started in July of that year.

A further major consideration in these developments was the success of the Petersfield Cottage Hospital and how it was to cope under the new regime: the government had taken over the hospital and placed it within the scope of the Portsmouth Group Management Committee. However, Miss Bates, who had been Matron at the hospital for nearly twenty years, agreed that the hospital was running 'just as smoothly as ever', apart from the form-filling which had accompanied the change in management structure.

Meanwhile, the Petersfield Isolation Hospital in Durford Road (on the site of Home Way), which was closed in the middle of 1948, reopened in September 1949 as 'Heathside' with the aim of providing beds for up to forty chronically sick patients in three wards. Furthermore, in 1950, it was proposed to spend £2,500 on converting the old Public Assistance (or Poor Law) Institution in Ramshill (more generally referred to as the Workhouse) into a new Public Health Centre; but this project was later transferred to Swan Street on a site which had already been identified as a potential site for a fire station.

THE FESTIVAL OF BRITAIN

Despite its detractors, who branded it a colossal prodigality of money and effort, the national event which captured the imagination that year was the Festival of Britain, held on the South Bank of the Thames in the summer of 1951. Like other towns and villages throughout Britain at the time, Petersfield organised its own 'Festival of Britain Carnival' over two weeks at Whitsun. Despite postwar austerity, yards of bunting, hundreds of coloured lights and nearly two thousand tulips decorated The Square. Early preparations the previous year suggested that apathy was rife, but this was compensated for by the enthusiasm of the British Legion, the Petersfield Chamber of Commerce, the Victoria Brass Band and various youth organisations which worked hard from February until May that year. Under the chairmanship of Mr Charles Dickins, almost every organisation in the town contributed to the success of the fortnight which, as the advert showed, catered for all tastes. The Grand Carnival Procession drew about three thousand people into the town to see the half-mile of the procession with its floats of musical or dramatic displays, tableaux and equestrian sections, marching bands and a final dog show and evening of jitterbugging in The Square.

Perhaps it was in the same spirit of morale-boosting that a call was made later in the year to 'brighten up Petersfield': Mr R.H. Fielder spoke at a general meeting of the Chamber of Commerce about the need to enhance the four entrances to the town by erecting welcoming signs, that an illustrated map be placed in The Square, and that The Avenue approach to the Heath be improved for visitors. He generally complained about the poor state of railings seen around the town and called for a putting green to be created on the Heath.

1951 also marked the fiftieth anniversary of the founding of the Victoria Brass Band and of the Petersfield Musical Festival. The Victoria Brass Band had been formed by the youthful Fred Kimber and Mr Gale in 1901, although its survival had been precarious over the years; there was even a hope that a bandstand could be built for them on the Heath, but this was never realised.

The Musical Festival had had a steadier history, although it had not taken place during the First World War or in 1944. In 1947, the Petersfield Operatic and Dramatic Society had also been revived after lying dormant since pre-war days; its first production since before the war was Gilbert and Sullivan's *Iolanthe* in 1950. The same year, the Salisbury Arts Theatre Group brought its repertoire to Petersfield and the Musical Festival was going 'from strength to strength', according to its conductor Dr Sydney Watson. Famous names in the world of music came to the town to perform in the orchestral concerts, among them the oboist Leon Goossens and the pianist Nina Milkina.

At the end of the war, Kathleen Money-Chappelle had set up her school of music in her new family home at 24 High Street (now the *Petersfield Herald* office) where she gave private lessons in music, singing, speech and drama, preparing pupils for the Musical Festival and other competitions, examinations, theatre and TV productions, and plays for local drama groups, including the Petersfield Musical, Dramatic and Social Club, which she herself often directed. She kept the support of many who, like Lord Horder, had backed her highly successful wartime enterprise, the 'Home from Home' canteen for servicemen in College Street.

PLANNING PETERSFIELD'S DEVELOPMENT

The fire at Norman Burton's well-known drapery business in The Square in January 1947, which gutted the building and caused thousands of pounds worth of damage to its stock of clothing, furnishings and toys, seemed to be an almost symbolic act of destruction, not only to one of the most flourishing and longest-established businesses in the town, but also to the status of the town itself. In eliminating a centuries-old building and high-class enterprise in the town centre, the fire gave the appearance of having tolled the knell of 'old Petersfield', characterised by a clear-cut social class hierarchy which determined the shopping habits of its citizens. The strictly middle-class Burton's was renowned for its elegance: its polished wood cabinets and carpeted floors lent an aura of sophistication to the town, but it was not frequented by the working classes. It had,

The Victoria Brass Band, Walter Bone in the centre, *c.* 1950. (*Petersfield Museum*)

however, been very popular at the end of the war when it was the first shop in Petersfield to stock nylon stockings.

The Burton's fire episode smacked of a great portent – it occurred in the early hours of the morning, thereby sparing any human tragedy, but the snow which was falling (not for the first time during that memorably freezing winter) lent the whole scene a macabre atmosphere of unreal proportions. The subsequent press reports seemed to echo this feeling, with talk of a 'calamity', 'a fearsome and striking spectacle' and expressing the hope that the shop 'will rise again'. Thanks to the early discovery of the fire and the rapid intervention of the Petersfield company of the NFS fire brigade, the adjacent premises of A.G. Suthers (now part of Barclays Bank) and The Square Brewery were saved.

The harsh winter of 1946–7 brought with it a desperate shortage of fuel, shopping by candlelight, and the reliance on oil lamps and paraffin stoves in offices and homes. An ice storm ('only the second in living memory') plunged Petersfield into darkness for two days, electric power cables crashed to the ground and light industry and road and rail travel were paralysed. Ice-coated trees snapped and fell across roads, and vehicles left in the open were frozen to the ground. Some householders who kept chickens found that they had to dig them out of the snow in the mornings!

Festival Hall commemoration to Dr Harry Roberts, sketched by Flora Twort in 1947. (*Author's Collection*)

Under the terms of the Town and Country Planning Act of 1947, the Ministry was required to prepare lists of buildings which were to be preserved and could not be demolished or altered without permission. Petersfield's historic and architectural heritage was, it was claimed, to be preserved for all time, and more than sixty buildings in the town and its immediate locality were listed by the Ministry to this end. The list included both public buildings and private residences and a further list of seventy was drawn up which, while supposedly not of historic or architectural interest in themselves, were nevertheless deemed worthy of preservation because they added to the general group effect.

In its turn, the *Squeaker* rightly pointed out that it had for some time been stressing that the future prosperity of Petersfield stood or fell on the careful preservation of its

The Petersfield School of Music, 1950s. (*David Money-Chappelle*)

atmosphere of an old English country town. With the publication of the Ministry's document, therefore, it felt secure in proclaiming that 'barring accidents, and with the exercise of vigilance and good taste, there is a possibility of a steadily rising crescendo of prosperity in which all can participate' and 'Petersfield is quite exceptionally well placed for steady and well-planned development in the next decade'. The group best placed to maintain such vigilance over the town's development was the Petersfield Society, formed in July 1945 through the instigation of Edward Barnsley under the provisional title of 'Group for the Preservation and Improvement of Petersfield'. He had written:

> The town of Petersfield and its neighbourhood is one of the most beautiful in the South of England. It is a matter of the greatest importance that its character be preserved in future development. The postwar period will bring rapid changes and difficult problems, and if these are not carefully organised and controlled there will be grave danger that irretrievable damage will be done.

It will be interesting and instructive, but also tragic, to see just how these fine sentiments were disregarded and abused in the decade following the 1950s.

Discussions in the Petersfield UDC in 1949 over the use of land within the town showed some differences of opinion over the future of The Grange site in the Causeway and the Love Lane site. With the developing conflict over the market added to the picture, it was difficult to reach unanimity on how to handle all of these vitally important future developments. In addition to these problems, an offer from South Eastern Farmers Ltd to purchase council land in Frenchman's Road was rejected and the council now approached the Ministry of Health for permission to sell the site to J.B. Corrie (Flextella) Ltd who had acquired the old Flextella (part of the Portsmouth Steel Company) site in 1947 and who were seeking to double their capacity. This project, approved by the Urban District Council, marked the first step in their intention to expand Petersfield and to introduce more light industry into the town. Corrie's adopted Flextella's main product, aluminium chain-link fencing, which sold well for use on housing estates and parks, and to railway companies and coal mines; they therefore had a high priority with various government departments.

1952

The national event which marked the year was the death of King George VI in February. In Petersfield, as everywhere in Britain, there were memorial services in the churches, the Savoy cinema closed briefly, social life came to a standstill with the cancellation or postponement of dances, dinners and suchlike, and flags were lowered to half mast throughout the town. Shortly after 2 p.m. (it was a Wednesday market day) a special knell was tolled fifty-six times on the bells of St Peter's to mark the fifty-six years of the King's life. Business premises draped their windows with black and mauve cloth. At church services, congregations concluded their worship by singing 'God save the Queen' for the first time in over fifty years.

Earlier in the year, the statue of William III had officially become an Ancient Monument by being scheduled as such by the Ministry of Works. The practical effect of this legislation was to deny the UDC any right to do anything with the statue without the explicit permission of the Ministry, despite the fact that it was the UDC which had purchased it for the town in 1911, a hundred years after its first arrival as a gift from the Jolliffe family. It was renovated by the Ministry in 1957.

In his maiden speech in the House of Commons during the second reading of the Town Development Bill in March 1952, the Hon. Peter Legh, Petersfield's new MP, hit hard at the planners 'sitting in their offices in every county borough in the land, poring over maps and searching for little, inoffensive country towns upon which to pounce and to expand into what they like to call a balanced community'. In what, with hindsight, can be viewed as a foreshadowing of what the 1960s were to bring to Petersfield, he said: 'what a paradise there will be for [the planners] if they are permitted to expand a small town until they have achieved their idea of a balanced community'. Perhaps with an even greater sense of foresight, he spoke of 'a danger that new light industries in the expanded towns will attract labour away from agriculture and horticulture'.

By the end of 1952, there appeared to be some indications of a revival of spirits: another town carnival took place in the summer and crowds danced in The Square. One newspaper described the scene: a floodlight was trained on the statue of William and a huge silhouette of the mounted king was projected onto the wall of St Peter's Church in the background; the *Squeaker* predicted a cheaper Christmas for all, with big reductions in the price of children's toys and luxury foods, a plentiful supply of unrationed food and tinned fruit, and a better supply of fresh English fruit and turkeys. A Christmas tree, complete with decorations and fairy lights, was erected outside St Peter's Church. It was as if the postwar gloom had lifted the spirits and Petersfield, like the rest of the country, was preparing itself, in 1953, to welcome a new Elizabethan era.

DEPARTURES

Petersfield inevitably changed as its links with the past were being slowly but inexorably severed by the loss of some its local luminaries in the years immediately after the war. Until this time, it was not uncommon for people in public office to spend the best part of their lives (in both senses) in the service of the community.

The death of Dr Harry Roberts in November 1946 merited a lengthy tribute from the *Squeaker*, in which the distinguished doctor, writer and social reformer was remembered for

December, 1944.

DEAR SIR OR MADAM,

We are writing to you on behalf of the Officers and Committee of the Group for the Preservation and Improvement of Petersfield, which has recently been formed.

The Town of Petersfield and its neighbourhood is one of the most beautiful in the South of England. This beauty is not only a local asset but a national one, and it is a matter of the greatest importance that its character be preserved in future development. The post-war period will bring rapid changes and difficult problems, and if these are not carefully organised and controlled there will be grave danger that irretrievable damage will be done. Realisation of this danger and of the importance of the problems involved has led to the formation of this Group.

It is not possible, within the limits of a letter, to outline the full scope and intention of the Group, but the main objects may be set out briefly as follows :—

To develop and increase public interest in the beauty of Petersfield and its neighbourhood and in future planning within the area.

To focus this general interest and direct it into channels of practical work, in which members of the community may take part and contribute to Post-war Planning.

To build up a strong body of public opinion supporting the Planning Authorities in their difficult task of ensuring that building and development is organised to achieve the maximum possible degree of harmony. In short, to preserve and increase the beauty of the town and its neighbourhood.

As a beginning, there is now on show in the window of Mr. Dowler's offices in the High Street, the first of a series of displays of photographs and pictures to which we wish to draw your attention. Valuable and important work will be done by the Group if it develops as the Committee hope and expect, and they particularly invite your interest and support.

Yours truly,

EDWARD BARNSLEY, *Chairman.*
MARY WARD, *Hon. Secretary.*

Letter to the press announcing the establishment of the Petersfield Society, 1944. (*Petersfield Society*)

having had a great impact and influence on the people of Petersfield and, in particular, on the residents of Oakshott Hanger, where he had lived for the last thirty-eight years of his life. His cultural, intellectual and practical legacy for the town was visible in the bookshop he created at 1 and 2 The Square; in the Festival Hall; in his personal involvement in the Petersfield Arts and Crafts Society and the Petersfield Society; and in the youth club and darts club he supported in Hawkley. In a BBC broadcast in 1948 entitled *Western Lives*, the novelist and critic V.S. Pritchett described Harry Roberts as

a famous East End doctor, a politician of some pugnacity and, later on, a sort of saint in Stepney life. Half his week he spent in Hampshire, and there in corduroys and heavy boots he rode horses, gardened, hammered, read books, listened to music, botanised in his acres or sat writing in the largest and untidiest study I have seen in my life.

At the 42nd Musical Festival in 1948, the memorial plaque to Harry Roberts in the 'Large Hall' (now The Festival Hall) was unveiled by Sir Adrian Boult.

The deaths of Mr Percy Burley, Clerk to the UDC for thirty-three years, and of Mr Arthur Mackarness, the Clerk of the RDC after forty-four years' service to the community, not only deprived the two councils of their most experienced members and valued clerks, but it depleted the strong representation of the law in the town by removing two respected solicitors from their family firms, namely Burley and Geach, and Mackarness and Lunt.

Percy Burley, who died in 1947, had been Town Clerk and, like his father, W.C. Burley, before him, had filled many influential positions in the life of the town. He was particularly associated in an official capacity with Petersfield's schools, becoming the first secretary and vice-president of the Old Churcherians, Clerk to the Governors of Churcher's and Manager of the Petersfield and Sheet Council Schools. He was also a trustee and organist and choirmaster of the Methodist Church, Chairman of the Operatic Society, and one of the oldest members of the Petersfield Lodge of Freemasons. He was an earnest and strong supporter of the United Nations Association, superintendent registrar of births, deaths and marriages, a member of the committees of the Petersfield WI (Women's Institute) and YWCA (Young Women's Christian Association) and a director of many local companies.

The death in his 86th year of Mr A.J.C. Mackarness, in 1950, engendered the same feeling of great sadness and loss to the town. He had been Clerk to the Petersfield Isolation Hospital, registrar of the County Court and on the management committee of Petersfield Hospital for many years. Like Mr Burley, his hobbies included music and singing and he was a founder member of the Petersfield Musical Festival; also like Mr Burley, he was a keen churchman and was Churchwarden of St Peter's. He had been Chairman of the committee that eventually got the town hall built, was a district commissioner in the Boy Scouts and an active member of the East Hants Conservative Association.

Frank Carpenter was one of the best-known Petersfield characters of the pre-war, wartime and postwar years; he finally retired from the *Squeaker* in 1948 after fifty-six years as its editor. Public respect for him was so great that the UDC recognised his service to the community by opening a testimonial fund to him. He championed everything he felt to be of value to Petersfield and played a vigorous part in supporting Harry Roberts' call for the construction of a town hall in 1935. His participation in the life of the town was immense: he taught shorthand at Churcher's College and at evening classes; for half a century he was a member of the Petersfield Literary and Debating Society; he served as secretary of the Working Men's Institute; he was a senior member of St Peter's choir; and he captained the town's football eleven. But it was for his devotion to his professional duties as chief newspaper reporter that we owe him our deepest gratitude: Frank Carpenter saw it as his job to record the town's events for posterity and, thanks to this, his impeccably written reports have become the town's history.

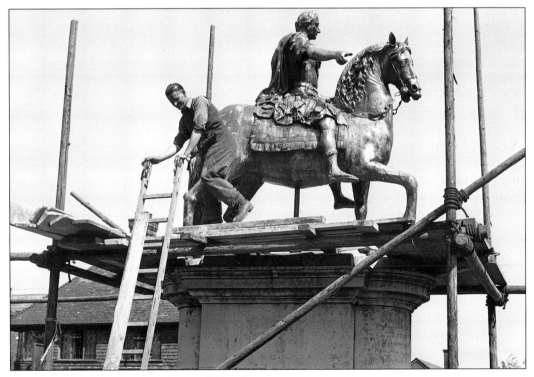

William III is repaired, 1950. (*The Petersfield Society*)

Two well-known Petersfield business people died in 1948: Miss Elizabeth Amey and Mr Victor Britnell. Miss Amey directed the fortunes of the Borough Brewery which had been established in Swan Street by her father Thomas Amey in the 1870s. Two young brothers at Emanuel School who were billeted with her in the war remember her as the spitting image of Queen Victoria, with her black dress buttoned to the neck and leather boots. She lived grandly, employing a butler, maid, cook and housekeeper. Mr Britnell had come to Petersfield in 1894 and later founded the motor sales and engineering firm Britnell and Crawter which traded in what is now the Folly Market. His home was in Love Lane and was the only private house to be bombed during the war; it stood close to the old Public Institution (known generally as the Workhouse) which took a direct hit from a lone German bomber in November 1940.

Two other well-known Petersfield personalities died in 1951. The first, Mr F.F. Wooldridge, was one of the chief pioneers of the National Farmers' Union in Hampshire and a manager of South Eastern Farmers Ltd, the Petersfield-based company which dealt with the farm collections, and the processing and bottling of milk at its depot in Station Road (opposite the station). It was a seminal company in the history of milk production, which eventually led to the creation of the national Milk Marketing Board. Mr Wooldridge became the Manager of United Dairies when it took over South Eastern Farmers.

Mr A.G. Suthers claimed to have made and sold the first wireless set in Petersfield; he was one of the town's best-known tradesmen and a member of many Petersfield clubs. An Old Churcherian, he followed an apprenticeship as an electrical engineer, then set up his electrical business in premises in The Square (now part of Barclays Bank).

In the churches of Petersfield, there were several changes of regime in 1946: the curate of St Peter's, the Revd H.D. Halsey, retired and at the Congregational Church, the Revd J.H. Milnes was inducted as their new pastor. At St Laurence's Church, the congregation was no longer to be ministered to by a member of the Benedictine Order when Father Ambrose Armstrong was replaced as priest-in-charge by the Revd Henry Clarke. Petersfield's Roman Catholic parish had its origin in the private chapel of Mr Laurence Trent Cave at Ditcham Park in the 1880s. Mr Cave then bought the present land in Station Road in 1890, had St Laurence's Church constructed and, shortly before his death in 1891, the church was consecrated and responsibility for serving it passed into the hands of the Benedictine monastery of St Laurence, Ampleforth.

At St Peter's Church, the churchyard was levelled and the gravestones replaced around the edge of it in 1950, the year the Vicar, Canon E.C.A. Kent, retired after twenty years' service to the church. Miss E.K. Matson, Headmistress of Petersfield primary school for twenty-three years, also retired in 1950.

Mr C.J.P. Cave died in December 1950. He was the son of Laurence Trent Cave of Ditcham Park and was a leading meteorologist of his day. He laid the meteorological groundwork for the research that led to the invention of radar (by Sir Ronald Watson-Watt, who described Cave as 'my father in meteorology'). He had the unique honour of being president of the Royal Meteorological Society for two terms, and was one of the pioneers of the meteorological service for aviation. In 1925 he turned to the study of architecture and his book on medieval churches is recognised as the standard work. His weather records for Petersfield date back to 1904. He was Vice-President of the Royal National Lifeboat

Institution and a Fellow of the Royal Astronomical Society, the Royal Photographic Society and the Society of Antiquarians. Locally, he was President of the Hampshire Field Club, sat on the Petersfield Bench as a magistrate for forty years, President of the Working Men's Club for thirty years, and was a Governor of Churcher's College.

The year 1952 saw the demise of several of Petersfield's most renowned tradespeople: Norman Burton, whose drapery business at 8 The Square had burnt down in 1947, retired in 1952 after thirty-two years' service in the town. After the fire, he had moved his business to Guard's outfitters at the bottom of the High Street, but did not enjoy his previous success with it.

After more than twenty-seven years in the Hampshire Constabulary, Sergeant Oliver Wilmot retired from the Petersfield Police Division in 1952. He was a familiar sight in the town, often seen walking with his tall, graceful Saluki dogs. He had been a considerable athlete in his youth and was also an accomplished photographer.

In 1880, George and Alfred Barnes, while still in their teens, founded a furniture and cabinetmaker's shop in Lavant Street, Petersfield. The brothers became probably the best-known traders in the town, before retiring in 1935. George died the following year, but Alfred survived until 1952, the oldest Old Churcherian in the town, aged 90. The reputation of A. & G. Barnes remained for years to come.

The sudden death of R.F.J. ('Bunny') Tew at the age of 35 following a horrendous accident in his Lagonda in 1952, brought tragedy to the Tew family, whose garage and motor engineering business in Lavant Street was familiar to all Petersfielders. 'Bunny' Tew was very tall and his large green sports car was usually seen parked outside the family premises (now Lambert's Estate Agents); he was a founder member of the Petersfield Motor Cycle and Car Club and the Petersfield Round Table.

Plus ça change . . .

'A letter to the *Squeaker* complained about "the intimidating cycling habits of young men who are old enough to know better, as well as of boys, especially in The Square, which is intermittently used as a trick-cycling arena, in and out and round about the parked cars".' (November 1946)

'At a meeting of the Petersfield Society, the Hampshire County Planning Officer discussed proposals set out by the National Parks Committee to establish a designated park area for the South Downs.' (March 1948)

'We who live in Petersfield are fortunate in that our town has an atmosphere and charm moulded by the centuries. It is therefore a pity that, with the approach of the evening hours, this tranquillity should be inevitably shattered for those who live near the centre of the community by the cat-calling and rowdy antics of "roughs". The fact is that our streets are becoming untidy with hooligans.' (June 1951)

CHAPTER TWO

Recovery
1953–9

THE CORONATION OF QUEEN ELIZABETH II

Posterity will probably define the coronation of Queen Elizabeth II in June 1953 as the beginning of a new era in our history. What is certain is that, by this time, the aftermath of the war was loosening its grip on our consciousness, bad memories were fading and people could see – or certainly wanted to see – a rosier future. In Petersfield, Queen's Road estate was being built, Buriton Woods were renamed Queen Elizabeth Forest and, only twelve days after her coronation, what the *Squeaker* termed 'Petersfield's Royal Sunday' brought thousands of local people out onto the (rain-soaked) streets to see her pass by on her way to the Spithead review of the Fleet. It was also the year of the conquest of Everest and the colour film (a novelty) of the expedition was showing at the Savoy cinema.

In an interesting re-enactment of Petersfield's past, when the town served as a staging post for people of all ranks – including Charles II who stayed at the White Hart (now Winton House and Twenty The High Street) – to break their journey between London and Portsmouth, the month of the coronation brought the Queen and the Duke of Edinburgh through the town. The royal entourage passed a smartly executed 'Present Arms' by 120 members of the Churcher's College CCF who were lining Ramshill, but then the royal Rolls-Royce with the royal standard came to a brief, unofficial but enforced halt in College Street because of a coach coming in the opposite direction (Tor Way did not then exist).

At about the same time, a royal train passed through the town bearing the Queen Mother and Princess Margaret. That same week, the Queen and the Duke of Edinburgh passed through Petersfield again, this time in the royal train on their way to Ascot.

CHANGING TIMES

That June, the *Squeaker* saw a changing mood in the town which it expressed in maudlin tones:

> The languid pace of life in Petersfield, happily free from the more glittering diversions of urban existence and as unspoilt today in its rural serenity as it was 500 years ago, has quickened perceptibly. This awakening has done nothing to despoil the character of the town, nor lessen the rewards that go with residence here. Rather has it brought a far deeper sense of municipal pride and a subtle enrichment that has lent greater profundity to the local scene, where latterly we paddled in the shallows of apathy.

This was the supposed new-found civic spirit which the *Squeaker* had witnessed in the greater harmony between the Petersfield UDC and local organisations to produce a programme of events to celebrate the coronation, a harmony and an effort which had not existed at the time of the Festival of Britain two years earlier. Coupled with this, there had been contested UDC elections that May for the first time since 1946, rather than 'the shameful legacy of unopposed returns' of the immediate postwar years.

The Petersfield Ratepayers' Association's work and the recent formation of an Old People's Welfare Committee and a Petersfield (business) Forum lent weight to the perception of the town as a more caring and harmonious community. The Petersfield Rotary Club was inaugurated in 1954. Symbolic of this new civic pride was the decision taken by the UDC to have the town mace cleaned and restored. The 1596 silver mace was a relic of the days when Petersfield had been a borough with its own town mayor; it had remained in the possession of several generations of the Jolliffe family, lords of the manor of Petersfield, during the nineteenth century, and it had been present at meetings in the Town Council Chamber until 1885. It was Harold Creedon, a former Clerk to the UDC and working for the solicitors Burley and Geech who, in 1923, discovered an old Charity Commission document of 1890 endowing the mace to the town; it was finally returned to the Council in 1927 after a petition was made by the UDC to the High Court to recover it from Lord Hylton (see p. 164).

Although 1953 saw the last of the horses for sale at the Taro Fair, that year's town carnival was especially grand: it consisted of the usual street procession followed by a fireworks display on the Heath, but there was also a water carnival on the Heath Pond with twenty decorated boats and rafts taking part, including one bearing the Victoria Brass Band in full swing. The Drama Festival flourished, not least through the participation of Kathleen Money-Chappelle's School of Music and Drama, which had opened after the war at 24 High Street (now the *Petersfield Herald* office).

However, although an emerging economic recovery was now being lauded, there were still pockets of social deprivation, especially in the villages, which needed addressing.

Educational provision in Petersfield, for example, was woefully deficient, especially for younger pupils, with the 450 children in the hugely overcrowded primary school working in thoroughly inadequate conditions; because of this, the old Workhouse chapel in Ramshill had had to be transformed into an overflow classroom. Secondary education was also still in the doldrums, but a new secondary modern school was at last within sight as the Ministry of Education had announced its plans for school building in 1955, after concerted protests from both the local councils and the neighbouring parish councils, helped by the support of Petersfield's MP, the Hon. Peter Legh.

The problems of occasional, severe flooding in the town, especially in the Winchester Road–Rushes Road–Frenchman's Road area, had still not been dealt with and there was a farcical situation for the inhabitants of Rushes Road, who had to move their furniture upstairs every time flooding looked likely to occur. 1953 was the worst year, with residents wondering if the council were ever likely to do anything to alleviate their suffering – or should they just sit tight and wait for the next deluge?

The Portsea Island Co-operative Society announced in 1953 that it would be rebuilding and expanding its stores in The Square. The old Co-operative Stores had been considered unsafe for a number of years and the new store, with a pseudo-Georgian frontage, would

The pre-1953 Co-operative Stores. (*The Petersfield Society*)

comprise many new departments and incorporate those which existed in the Co-op's Lavant Street and Chapel Street branches. At least the new store would provide the town's 15-year-old school leavers with the chance of a job; since self-service was still an unknown phenomenon on Britain's high streets, the more jobs available in shop work, the better the prospects of advancement in the retail trade and the less likely the need for youngsters to take uncongenial jobs in factories. As a result, there appears to have been virtually no unemployment in Petersfield at this time.

One sad result of the construction of the new Co-op building was the demolition, in 1953, of four small houses in Dog Alley situated between Rowswells and what is now a charity shop. Although dilapidated, they had survived for a century and were undoubtedly attractive and intimate, but any loss of such conveniently central dwellings in a town the size of Petersfield is a piece of wanton destruction (see the photograph on p. iv).

House building was a continuing problem and, although considerable progress had already been made in developing municipal housing schemes, more and more private buildings were being erected: Gloucester Court was one example, as was the rapid new expansion of Pulens Lane, where 135 houses and two new roads (Pulens Crescent and Rother Close) were built by the firm of W. Mould. The UDC was responsible for the development of twenty houses in Queen's Road. Nationally, local councils were slowly getting on top of the postwar housing crisis and, statistically, the nation's homeless were slowly being rehoused in Council accommodation. However, Petersfield represented one of the pockets of housing deprivation in Hampshire, where there were still 149 families on the waiting list in 1955. This was partly due to its stretched financial resources and partly to a reluctance to increase the general rate fund. A year later, the UDC was obliged to suspend all house-building programmes because of a government credit squeeze.

EDUCATION FACTS AND FANTASIES

Rumours about the fate of the Girls' High School abounded and there was a suspicion that it would close in the near future. In the meantime, work on the new secondary school in the Causeway had – at last – started in 1956, although it was still far from certain which pupils would be going there. Were the girls to be housed there? Was another school for boys to be built in the town? With 275 girls at the High School, couldn't another viable girls' school be opened somewhere?

West Mark Camp School in Sheet closed at the end of the war when the National Camps Corporation went into liquidation. A debate ensued about the future use of the premises. A suggestion that it could be used to educate disabled children was rejected by the Hampshire County Council. Given its potential as an educational site – it boasted good classroom accommodation for up to 185 pupils, plenty of open space for games, a swimming pool, staff accommodation and easy access from the A3 – it was even mooted that the Girls' High School could take advantage of its facilities.

The uncertainties, prevarication and sheer indecision on the part of the local authorities merely mirrored the greater national debate over the pros and cons of split grammar and secondary modern schooling, which the 1944 Education Act had deemed appropriate for the nation's schoolchildren. It was a case of sentiment versus experiment, with the children themselves caught up in the unedifying political tug-of-war.

The Hampshire County Council had already decided to replace the Girls' High School with a 'multi-lateral' school. Its arguments for closing the old school were understandable, if sad. They were clearly rejecting the idea of single-sex education for Hampshire in the future; the percentage of Petersfield girls at the school was a mere 14 per cent; many annexes to the school had to be found to accommodate all the pupils and this was educationally unacceptable; and, finally, the enlargement of Eggars Grammar School in Alton and the opening of a new grammar school in Havant in 1960 (both mixed schools) would allow local Petersfield girls to receive a grammar school education within reach of Petersfield. Inevitably, with the uncertainty surrounding its future, many girls had already left the High School and the resulting decline in pupil numbers had led to inefficiency in teaching and a deficiency in educational provision. At the same time, the governors of Churcher's College stressed that 'on no account could we possibly consider any question of co-education at Churcher's'. The Girls' High School finally closed at the end of the 1959–60 school year, much to the chagrin of the 200 girls still there, who hoisted a black flag over the school more as a symbol of mourning than of defiance.

The new Petersfield County Secondary School finally opened in April 1958, simultaneously, and apparently with the agreement of the County, eliminating the word 'Modern' from its name, although the press still referred to it as a County secondary modern school on occasion. What was certain was that, whatever its official label, the school operated virtually as a grammar school in outlook and achievement. The children were all well behaved, wore smart uniforms, and their teachers demanded the best of all of them – earning the grudging respect of the inspectors, who claimed that they were 'aiming too high'! The discipline exerted on the pupils was that of ex-RAF servicemen newly trained as teachers, who expected them to behave as recruits had done under their NCOs.

Mr E.C. Young, the Head of the secondary modern school in St Peter's Road, became the new Principal of the County Secondary School; his wife taught in the Junior Council School in St Peter's Road and his daughter had been his secretary there. Several other teachers from the St Peter's Road school also moved with the pupils to Cranford Road, so the transition was relatively smooth, but the larger catchment area of the school meant an influx of new pupils, who were bussed in from Liss, Longmoor, Blackmoor and Greatham as well as from Sheet and East Meon. Many local children could now cycle to school, although they had to take care to avoid the Causeway (the old A3). The pupils had moved from a rather claustrophobic, Victorian building in a narrow town street into a modern, light and spacious building with extensive windows, through which it was a great temptation to look outside – much to the annoyance of the teachers. However, it was claimed early on that the new premises were unable to meet all the requirements of the district, so the old Workhouse building and the Masonic Hall in Windsor Road continued to be used for 'slower children'.

THE MOUSE THAT ROARED

Frank Carpenter had been the Editor of the *Squeaker* from 1891 until 1948, and for the greater part of his editorship he had written almost the entire contents. He was his own reporter, sub-editor, commentator, local historian and editor. His perhaps rather wordy, but inimitable, style was reminiscent of the Victorian era in which he had grown up and learnt his trade; it was always careful, accurate, balanced and free of the sensationalism which he abominated. With his departure from the newspaper – although he continued to frequent the offices for many years after his 'retirement' – it was perhaps as much a conscious desire on the part of the paper to transform the 'house style' as it was a sign of the times that the *Squeaker* took on a new look in the 1950s.

Thus it was that the headlines of 1956 turned from their former more parochial concerns to ones of national import; likewise, the 'Comment' columns became campaigning outlets for local and national issues and the newspaper carried reports of Petersfield's MP, Peter Legh's, speeches to parliament and reviews of government policy. The paper did not shy away from expressing its own opinions on local issues such as the education debate or the need for new light industry to be encouraged in the town, and its front pages carried headlines and comment on, for example, the Cyprus war, the Trades Unions and the Hungarian Revolution of 1956. This last event was to have an immediate impact on Petersfield because it was to the empty West Mark Camp that incoming refugees were to be directed in the early months of 1957.

The Suez Crisis of 1956, during Anthony Eden's government, even caused the *Squeaker's* Comment column to pronounce (in bold type):

On the one or two occasions in the last ten years when the 'Squeaker' has ventured to comment on grave national issues, we have received one or two communications (mainly anonymous) branding us as 'a Red rag'. No doubt we shall receive them again. But nothing could be further from the truth. The simple fact is that we are sufficiently old-fashioned still to believe that figs don't grow on thistles and never can, and that in the long run it is righteousness alone that exalteth a nation.

The *Squeaker* adopted an anti-government stance on the war, and the above article provoked the following response from a reader: 'I consider the attempt of the *Squeaker* to launch itself into the field of national politics to be puny and ill-advised.'

It had become customary at this time for the *Squeaker* to print a 'Review of the Year' each January which not only summed up the events of the previous year – usually in pictures – but also gave the newspaper the opportunity to offer its views on the civic and social progress, or otherwise, which had taken place in Petersfield. In 1958, for instance, it offered the view that 'in a quiet way, the town had grown', citing the completion of the new fire station in Swan Street, the new Civil Defence Centre in Ramshill (now the Community Centre), the new Day Room at Heathside (geriatric) Hospital (where Home Way now stands), and the progress made on the flood prevention scheme for the town. The nucleus of Petersfield's fire brigade had been set up in 1884 with a hand-operated pump and a horse-drawn appliance, housed in St Peter's Road (now the public toilets); during the war, it had found temporary quarters in Heath Road, but there had been a project since the war to move it to a site in Swan Street where there would also be living accommodation for firemen.

Pride in the town and an acknowledgement of the role played by its leading personalities were also features of the *Squeaker* in the later 1950s: by publishing a series entitled 'Petersfield Personality', the newspaper made a strong contribution towards recognising a sense of community in the town.

The newspaper pointedly called for a removal of 'eyesores', 'derelict property' and 'higgledy-piggledy development' which abounded in College Street and Dragon Street and which smacked of town planning run riot. Barely four years later, there would be a general 'cleaning up' of the town's buildings which the *Squeaker* could perhaps not have intended, nor predicted. The *Squeaker* fully supported the proposals for the development of the town's commercial side and acted as a propagandist for Petersfield's advantages: 'There are areas west of the town which could be developed into a trading estate. Petersfield can offer industrialists not only first-rate sites but first-rate communications, not to mention pleasant surroundings in which to house their labour.'

THE NEW AGRICULTURAL V. COMMERCIAL BALANCE

In 1956, F.W. Tew & Sons, who ran a cycle, motorcycle and motor engineering works in Lavant Street (now the Bran Tub), gave the go-ahead for a £10,000 programme for a precision-tool engineering production works to be built in Frenchman's Road. It was the beginning of the more widespread move towards introducing small industry to the Frenchman's Road–Bedford Road area.

It was clear that the balance of trade in Petersfield was in the process of changing: as moves towards a light-industrial base for the town progressed, so the old farming community sensed its decline. With the doubts over the future of the cattle market and the associated trades it brought to the town, there began a gradual, but distinct, drift from the land. In the south of England generally, and in the east of Hampshire in particular, the agricultural labour force was shrinking: from 1955 to 1956 this decline was in the order of 6 per cent, compared with 4 per cent for the county as a whole. Many factors contributed to this phenomenon: the introduction of new industry, the lure of city (and town) life, low agricultural wages, poor public transport in rural areas and poor accommodation for farm workers.

Another nail in the coffin for rural Petersfield was struck when the Ministry of Agriculture, Fisheries and Food (MAFF) threatened to take away the certification of the market as a fatstock centre because of its lack of support from farmers. The farmers' (i.e. breeders', sellers' and buyers') market had been dwindling for some time and it was inevitable that eventually the MAFF would deem it uneconomic to provide a salaried fatstock officer. Hitherto, the town's prosperity and prestige had depended on the existence of the market and, according to the MAFF, it was up to the town authorities to see to it that it continued to exist by ensuring that there were adequate facilities for farmers when they visited the town. Partly as a consequence of this threat to their livelihood, the Petersfield Wholesale Meat Company carried out an extensive modernisation of their slaughterhouse (on The Grange site in the Causeway) in 1959.

But mechanisation also played a large role in the changing pattern of agricultural life: at Weston farm, for example, the introduction of new machinery displaced about thirty people whose families had worked for generations in bringing in the harvests, and brought an era of family-orientated and community-conscious work to an end. This sense of community was being slowly, and often brutally, lost in the agricultural sphere, just as it was to affect the commercial sphere in the years to come. Also as a consequence, unemployment in the Petersfield area in 1956 was up by 50 per cent on the previous year's figures.

Taro Horse Fair, 1948. (*Petersfield Museum*)

Indirectly linked to the agricultural scene was the fate of the Taro Fair: there were no horses for sale after 1953, although the Fair itself was larger. The first Heath Fair had taken place in 1820, when it was advertised 'for the shew of cattle' – and there were 1,400 animals present, half of which were sold. During the twentieth century, however, the cattle fair slowly dwindled and, during the First World War, the best horses were taken away for the war effort. Since the Seccond World War, the number of horses for sale had been dropping year by year – only five had been in the sale ring in 1951 – and there was even an attempt to save this unbroken tradition in 1953 by offering toy horses for sale! However, although no (real) horses were being sold by the auctioneers in the mid-1950s, a few dealers brought some into The Square, where private bidding took place.

As the commercial side of the town strove to expand, so the influence of the Chamber of Commerce made itself felt: in 1958, Mr R.H. Fielder, their Chairman, spoke of Petersfield's need for more light industry. 'We are very fortunate [in Petersfield] in having many proprietors who are not afraid to deal with their opposite numbers in the same trade and who will help each other.' In general, 1957 had been a hard year for traders, with higher rates and a shortage of money to develop businesses. Mr Fielder urged small traders to stand up to the large multiple companies.

Two factors emerge from this heartfelt plea to the town's traders: first, the recognition that there was a good deal of cooperation between traders and a friendly rivalry rather than the competitiveness which was to beset them in later decades and, secondly, that the pressure from the multiple stores would soon be exerting a constraining influence on the old family businesses in the town. This was Petersfield's defining moment as a town with a distinctive character and recognisably individual shops, an evolutionary stage whose repercussions are still felt today, over fifty years later. Town 'cloning' was not in the vocabulary of commerce then and the concept was clearly in its infancy; nonetheless, its impact – overt or covert – on a town like Petersfield would change the town more than any other factor.

Certain old-established businesses still thrived, of course, even if there had been a change of ownership. The Itshide Rubber Company, 90 per cent of whose shares were now owned by Charles Colston, the former Chairman of Hoover Ltd, kept Mr Moss Levy (brother of the founder) as its Managing Director. He had been with the company for thirty-eight years. All the shares of Petersfield Laundry Ltd, a company incorporated in 1899, were taken over by the Reliance Laundry of Alton and their new managing director was Mr Robert James.

George Bassett still kept his ironmonger's business in Swan Street, which he had opened in 1927 and where he was to trade for forty years. Nothing exemplifies the business practices of the town in the 1950s better than those of Bassett's. George Bassett was the archetypal individual trader through and through, for which Petersfield was renowned, with his philosophy of real customer service and 'proper' retailing (that is, offering his customers expert advice and choice, not simply taking money for the goods visible in the store). He had no cash till (merely an old wooden box), no Sellotape (just paper and string), almost nothing displayed (except saws, knives and scissors), and no electricity in the tin store-sheds at the rear of the shop. Some of his customers were used to paying their accounts (typical for private customers in this era) only once a year. But, despite the archaic aspect of the shop, Mr Bassett was a vital link between the local farmers, who came to him for their tools, and the town and its regular Wednesday markets. As with Martin and Triggs (now Haques) in Lavant Street, Bassett's had hardly changed in character and looks from pre-war days.

At 1 and 2 The Square, the home since 1918 of The Petersfield Bookshop and Workshops where Flora Twort had had her studio until 1949, Frank Westwood took over as the bookshop manager in 1956, beginning an association with bookselling in the town that was to last fifty years. At the time, the combination of a bookshop and a tea shop (known as the Buttery) was unique in Petersfield, although it was a formula to be reintroduced fifty years later in both individually owned bookshops and chain stores. In 1958, Frank Westwood bought the business (and its name) and moved The Petersfield Bookshop to 16a Chapel Street, where it was to become one of the finest and most well-known second-hand bookshops in the south of England.

The new Portsea Island Society's Co-op store opened in 1956: with its three-storey elevation, its pseudo-Georgian façade of Portland stone and its large loading bay off St Peter's Road, it represented all that was 'modern' for Petersfield. One immediate advantage was to eliminate the congestion in The Square caused regularly by its delivery lorries. On the ground floor, there was a self-service grocery and butchery (self-service was a novelty at that time, and this was the first store in Petersfield to offer it); on the first floor was a clothing and fashion department; and on the second floor there were furniture, hardware,

Edward Privett's, 1960s. (*Petersfield Museum*)

cycle and fancy goods departments. The Portsea Island Society, with a turnover of £10 million (1956 value) and shops spreading over an area of 600 square miles, was the biggest retailing organisation in the Portsmouth area.

WEST MARK CAMP

When West Mark Camp School finally closed at the end of the summer term in 1956, there were naturally some tears shed by the 140 children from Middlesex whose school it had been for seven years. The guest of honour, Mrs H.T. Tollemache, congratulated the children on their tremendous work connected with Sheet village functions; the Headmaster, Mr Graham Evans, said that the school's sports shields would be donated to the new Petersfield County Secondary School as a memento of what West Mark Camp had meant to Petersfield education; and the Middlesex Education Officer for Special Schools expressed his appreciation for what West Mark had achieved on behalf of the children.

It was only a matter of four months later that the Petersfield UDC made the suggestion that the now vacated West Mark site might become viable premises for the Hungarian refugees who were fleeing the revolution in their country which broke out that November. The government subsequently asked Hampshire County Council to implement this idea, assisted by Civil Defence, the British Red Cross, and the WVS (Women's Voluntary Service). West Mark was able to offer up to 250 places and some excellent facilities. It was renovated and refurbished that winter to be able to welcome the temporary exiles. The first batch of 170 refugees arrived in March 1957; however, the camp closed again after only eleven months, having accommodated a total of 840 Hungarians in that time, most of whom then left Britain for other countries. During their stay, the children had gone to Sheet village school.

In October 1958, it seemed possible that West Mark's next role would be as a detention centre for young men aged between 17 and 21 (detention centres had been established throughout the country in 1952). This news was met with some incredulity by three local residents (Mrs Alan Lubbock and Mrs Philby of Sheet, and Mr Basil Mould of Petersfield) who formed a syndicate with the intention of buying West Mark and offering it to a charity. After an indecisive local enquiry lasting two days, a public inquiry was forced upon the government and the idea of the detention centre was eventually quashed by the Home Secretary, R.A. Butler, in 1960.

PUBLIC ENTERTAINMENT AND LEISURE PURSUITS

The natural initial postwar desire for a safer and more prosperous world was felt on a national scale, of course, but the same feeling was reflected at a more local level by the quest for a

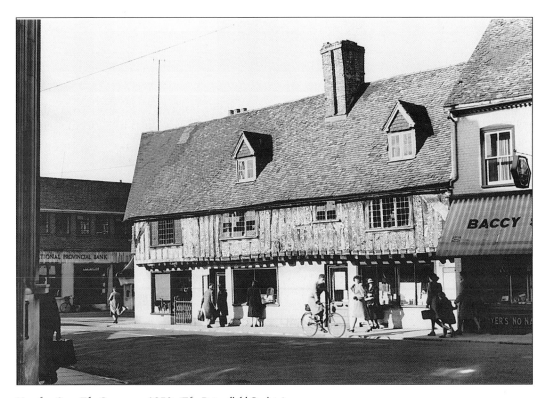

Number One, The Square, c. 1950. (The Petersfield Society)

more comfortable and pleasant lifestyle for individual communities. In Petersfield, people clamoured for the development of the Heath – a children's paddling pool, a miniature scenic railway, even a roller-skating rink and an ice rink were mooted, all of which schemes were subsequently rejected, partly as a result of the government demanding national economy, partly through strong local opposition. However, a 'children's corner' had been constructed, with swings taken from Bell Hill recreation ground, and Sam de Carte continued to provide rowing boats on the Pond, an enterprise started by his father, the licensee of the Sun Inn (now the Green Dragon) before the war. There were also some sailing boats on the Pond.

The Taro Fair, well patronised and a high point of the Petersfield entertainment year in the 1950s, had been run by the Wall family since 1936; it had even continued throughout the war – although the blackout had to be observed and no rifle shooting was allowed on the stalls! The Wall family have strong links with Petersfield: John Wall ran the Fair in the postwar years as his father had before him, and his son (also John), who was married in Petersfield town hall in 1966, would take over the business after him. 'Atmosphere' was the key to the success of contemporary entertainment: the Taro's immaculately kept traction engines for their motive power in the 1940s and '50s, the old pros challenging the brave or the foolhardy to their boxing booths, the now unthinkable freak sideshows with their tattooed ladies or 'smallest person in the world' to be gawped at.

The Wall family, left to right: 'Big' John Wall, his mother Doris, his son John and grandson John at the Taro Fair, 2004. (The News Group)

Entertainments of many kinds flourished, with several hundred people flocking to the town's carnival each July; a new sports pavilion was constructed at Love Lane; the successful and well-patronised Musical and Drama Festivals each lasted for four days in the spring and the autumn respectively; the Savoy cinema (now Vertigo nightclub) drew large audiences for its programmes, which changed three times a week. The BBC programme *Any Questions?* was broadcast from Petersfield town hall for the second time in 1957. That year too, the Chamber of Commerce purchased Christmas lights for the town (the first such decorations) and hung them in a criss-cross fashion over the High Street. Sadly for the town, the Victoria Brass Band, which had been formed in 1900, had to break up owing to a lack of new members.

As was the case before the war, young people still created their own leisure pursuits, where spontaneity was the order of the day, even if it upset some of the older order. In the 1950s, schools tended to accept the trend towards teenagers forming their own bands – hence the arrival of skiffle groups, aping the emerging television personalities of the likes of Lonnie Donegan. Within a matter of just a few years, this do-it-yourself music (played on a guitar, with tea-chest and broom handle 'bass' and corrugated metal washboard accompaniment), transformed itself into the first manifestations of rock and roll music.

The most ambitious scheme for the improvement of people's leisure in Petersfield was, however, the project to build an open-air swimming pool, which was first conceived in 1957 by the Chamber of Commerce, Round Table and Rotary organisations. Although no site was identified at the outset of the discussions, the UDC gave its blessing to the idea and even agreed to take over the management of the pool on its completion. Initially, it was proposed to build the pool with voluntary labour and to finance it with a mixture of voluntary contributions and public subscription. A year later, it was decided to use direct labour for its construction and a plan of the pool was exhibited in order to seek public opinion. The three organisations made a public appeal for £9,000 and the Ministry of Education promised a grant of £3,000 towards this sum, at the same time decreeing that it should be set up as a Charitable Deed to stop the UDC from ever selling it to finance other projects in the town. The UDC and, eventually, the Petersfield Town Council became its custodian trustees.

CONSTRUCTION AND DEMOLITION

Much larger building projects were either announced or called for: improved lighting for the town centre, a new ambulance station (to be built off Love Lane), a renewed call for a public library and the removal of the Ramshill railway bridge, for example. But these were minor operations compared with the proposed flood alleviation scheme (to cost £33,000) and, not for the first time, a plan for a bypass for the town, which suffered every summer from the thousands of cars travelling up and down the A3. In 1957, 3,600 cars an hour were passing through the town over the Whitsun Bank Holiday weekend in June. The flood alleviation scheme, paid for by both central and local government, covered over 2 miles of stream and involved levelling the gradient of the watercourse, installing new culverts and bridges, and straightening the watercourse at certain points.

One major development occurred which would sadden (but not surprise) many older Petersfield folk: the closure of the Midhurst railway line was announced in February 1955

The Midhurst branch line platform, Petersfield station, 1955. (*Author's Collection*)

and Petersfield's link with the West Sussex towns of Midhurst, Petworth, Fittleworth and Pulborough was broken after ninety years' service. The Meon Valley line was closed the same day. The future of public transport between these towns was assured by Southdown buses, but everybody regretted the loss of the beauty and the adventure of the rail journey along the Rother Valley. The closure also spelt the end of the functional loading platforms for the local industries of the South Eastern Farmers and Itshide both of which had had sidings and direct platform links to the railway system for their goods. The decision, taken by British Railways for reasons of economy, was inevitable.

It was not until four years later, in 1959, that the railway bridge spanning the A3 at the bottom of Ramshill was removed. The bridge was seen as a blot on one of the town's most pleasant entrances and it had always constituted a hazardous point for motor traffic, not to speak of the dangers for pedestrians and cyclists who were regularly soaked as they passed through the rainwater that had collected underneath it. Another common occurrence was the sight of a lorry jammed under the arch – and there were visible grooves in the brickwork where this had happened. The bridge finally came down in March 1959, not without some struggle; the *Squeaker* reported it thus:

It took the army and its explosives to demolish Ramshill Railway bridge after two 20-ton cranes had failed to do so. For three hours the cranes tried to lift the girder through the 80-year-old arch. From 11 p.m. on Saturday until 2 a.m. the next morning the crowds watched. But [it] would not budge and it was left to the Army to bring it to the end of its life. With traffic diverted, and the crowd huddled in raincoats, the Royal Engineers and the men working for the civilian demolition firm . . . started the final act of a drama which has already seen the end of many bridges spanning roads from Petersfield to Midhurst.

It was quite a spectacular disruption to the weekend: floodlights glared all night, families were evacuated to the Civil Defence Centre (now the Community Centre); and the arch finally crashed to the ground at 4 a.m.

NATIONAL AND LOCAL POLITICS

The Hon. Peter Legh, appointed an Assistant Whip in the Churchill government, was returned as Petersfield's MP at the 1955 and also at the 1959 general elections, with an increased majority of around 15,000 at the latter. He had held four posts since first becoming an MP in 1951. Born in 1915, both his grandparents had been Conservative MPs; he was educated at Eton and Oxford and had served in the Second World War, rising to the rank of major. He was President of the East Hants Young Conservatives, a Hampshire County Councillor and a Justice of the Peace for the county.

At the local level and as a result of the government's Local Government Act of 1958, there arose the question of whether there could be a merger between the UDC and the RDC. If Petersfield became a rural borough, then the parishes around the town would remain parishes and not become mere wards of the potential borough. The ramifications of the Act, however, were that it could lead to the absorption of smaller urban districts (such as Petersfield) into larger surrounding rural administrations, and it was felt that a strong case had to be made to retain Petersfield as a separate unit with its own identity.

At the end of 1959, the County Planning Officer was engaged in drawing up a draft map of Petersfield, with a view to discussing the optimum population of the urban district and its development potential. The *Squeaker* applauded the move, which it saw being of benefit to the town, as it would presumably lead to the creation of a trading estate, thus obviating the potential danger of what it termed 'innumerable back street developments'. The next edition of the newspaper carried the headline 'Town Population aim is 12,000' (the population in 1959 was approximately 7,200). The UDC had met and called for a 'steady, controlled development, coupled with the introduction of suitable light industry if possible'. The council were opposed to any measures which would lead to a rapid growth in the size of the town. Ironically, at the same meeting, five applications to develop land in Petersfield were submitted for housing developments: to the east and west of Pulens Lane; between Love Lane and Heath Road; and at Mill Lane, Sheet, a total of about 100 acres altogether. At a density of 6 houses per acre, this represented a population increase of around 2,000 in the immediate future and, at the same rate, an increase of 5,000 'in a very few years'. The Area Planning Officer therefore recommended refusal of the applications. However, the UDC was prepared to allow the town's population to increase to 12,000 and it felt that additional 'white' land should be released for that purpose, although it was generally known that some of the land had been acquired for the express purpose of preventing development. At a meeting in January 1960, Keith Gammon, the UDC Chairman, re-emphasised the council's commitment to 'a reasonably slow rate of expansion and [that] such expansion should not alter the character of the town'.

So where exactly was the town heading? How large and how fast would it develop? What constraints might there be in the future to limit rapid growth? What role did the UDC play in the decision-making process? To the suspicious, the cynical, or merely the highly observant, but perhaps also only with hindsight, the answer could be seen to be found in a small paragraph on the front page of the *Squeaker* of 25 November 1959, which stated that, at a public auction at the Welcome Inn (on the site of Meon Close), 25 High Street, the shop belonging to Gander's the butcher's (now part of Somerfield) was sold for £11,000 to a certain Group Captain Maurice Newnham of Liss, Chairman of a company called Raglan Property Trust. The sixties revolution was about to begin in Petersfield.

DEPARTURES

Three men, prominent in the town's affairs and instrumental in its development, died in 1955: Lord Horder, Arnold Levy and Charles Seward.

Thomas Jeeves Horder was born in Dorset, trained as a doctor at University College, London, and became one of the greatest diagnosticians of his age, specialising in cancer and in diseases of the heart and stomach. He was appointed to the post of Extra Physician to the Queen, having held a similar position with King George V, King Edward VII, King Edward VIII, and King George VI. Three prime ministers had also been his patients. He was knighted in 1918 and made a baron in 1935, taking the title of Lord Horder of Ashford, from his home at Ashford Chace. He took a great interest in local Petersfield affairs and was, among others, President of the local British Legion and the Horticultural Society, a keen follower of the Arts and Craft Society, and was Honorary Consultant to Petersfield Hospital. He was the author of numerous books, including one written jointly with his local friend, Dr Harry Roberts.

Arnold Levy, the Chairman and Managing Director of the Itshide Rubber Company Ltd was born in Eastern Europe, came to England as a boy, then went to seek his fortune in the USA, married there, and founded the ITS Rubber business in Petersfield on his return to Britain in 1919. Itshide was one of Petersfield's foremost employers and the wages were considered to be the best in town; the Levys were also respected as sympathetic and generous employers – the office girls receiving their first nylons from Arnold!

Charles Seward, one of Petersfield's most prominent and highly respected townsfolk, was an ex-Chairman of both the Urban and Rural District Councils, serving on the latter for forty-seven years. He was born in Weston in 1868, went to Churcher's College, then farmed Weston Farm and Borough Farm for most of his life, became a JP and received the OBE in 1939.

Plus ça change . . .

'Ten dissatisfied villagers walked 2 miles in falling snow to a meeting, so that they might put forward their views to gain the right to a bus service to Petersfield.' (March 1955)

'A new by-pass will "fly over" west Petersfield.' (August 1956)

'If we don't look out, the little shop will disappear in 20 or 30 years' time.' (March 1958)

CHAPTER THREE

Demolition
1960–5

'YOU'VE NEVER HAD IT SO GOOD'

The 1960s have been universally remembered by social historians as a watershed in Britain's postwar development, the decade which produced Swinging London, mini-skirts, the pill, liberated teenagers, Teddy Boys, fast food, drugs, The Beatles, new social-consciousness plays and films and, above all, prosperity. Bernard Levin called the decade 'The Pendulum Years', and among his many assertions as evidence of the emergence of this key decade was the statistically supported statement that a very substantial number of people began to live in conditions of material comfort absolutely unprecedented in the country's history. Indeed, Harold Macmillan, the incoming Prime Minister following the Conservatives' general election victory of 1959, exploited the new national sense of wealth and made political capital out of it.

As for Petersfield, it is not simply a chronological convenience to begin this chapter of the town's history in 1960, but rather a factual inevitability; for it was in that year that the town began its startlingly radical transformation from what many had described as a 'sleepy little town' into a developers' semi-paradise, remodelling the town with buildings which were, in the opinion of many, bold and brash rather that architecturally aesthetic. The *Squeaker* had already been upbeat about the town's development for a couple of years, calling 1957 'a year of progress' and 'the year of expensive projects', most of which it found commendable. In 1958, the new County Secondary School had opened at last and, in 1959, discussions began on creating a new central car park on the scrubby wasteland behind the High Street shops and a new telephone exchange (the old one still being housed in the Post Office) among other projects. In a leader of January 1960, the *Squeaker* echoed the sentiments of the Prime Minister, Harold Macmillan, talking of 'the prosperous times in which we live today'. But what, without a doubt, was to bring the most radical change to Petersfield between 1960 and 1965, was the drive to 'modernise' the town by the London development company, the Raglan Property Trust Ltd.

THE RAGLAN PROPERTY TRUST LTD

Virtually concurrent with the announcement of the purchase of Ganders butcher's shop, Raglan revealed its next plans – for a £50,000 office block in Swan Street, where the company had been buying property and land for several months, removing a row of old cottages in the process. Group Captain Maurice Newnham, Chairman of Raglan's, was said to be anxious to preserve the amenities of the town and to wish to choose architecture which

Swan Street, pre-1962. (*Petersfield Library*)

would merge, as far as possible, with existing buildings. The architectural design of the first office block (now Swan Court) was to be based on an existing building, ironically named Old Swan House, on the Thames Embankment in London, a feature of which were the mullioned windows. However, this design was abandoned in the planning stages for a neo-Georgian style block of nine offices. Opposite this building, which was later seen as a showpiece for the Raglan company, stood a high wall enclosing a nursery garden once belonging to Castle House; this land was also owned by Raglan and they intended to demolish the wall in order to open up a view of the Downs (Garden Court now stands on that site).

In March 1960, the death at the age of 93 of Mr E.J. Baker, the butcher of 13 High Street, brought a denial from the beneficiary of his will, Miss Ethel Broad, who had served as Mr and Mrs Baker's nurse, that she had sold the lease of the property to Raglan. In September, a 2½-acre site owned by Raglan in Frenchman's Road and twelve houses in Charles Street were among properties given permission for redevelopment. A letter to the *Squeaker* from Group Captain Newnham that month stated: 'we are completely opposed to unfair exploitation or developments which spoil the desirable characteristics of a town or locality'. Baker's shop is now Superdrug, although the upper storeys of the building have remained unchanged. In November, Raglan bought Clare Cross, a fine early seventeenth-century family house at 29 High Street, famed for being the surgery and home of Charles Dickins, the dentist and Scoutmaster of Petersfield. In December, Raglan acquired the neighbouring property, Petersfield's former Post Office at 31 High Street, which had served as a doctors'

surgery since pre-war days. In the space of a few short months Raglan had managed to grab
a good proportion of the south side of the High Street.

Raglan Developments Ltd were not a small firm at this time: in November 1960 they had
made a bid for control of First Garden City Ltd, the company which owned the Hertfordshire
town of Letchworth, the first of the experimental new towns and predecessor to Welwyn
Garden City, both built in the first half of the twentieth century, but whose concept was to
be reproduced in the new towns of the 1960s. Such was the (national, as well as local) need
for new housing or, at least, modernisation of existing properties, that development
committees were under enormous pressure to allow change to happen. The population of
Petersfield could easily have doubled in the 1960s if development restrictions had not been
applied as stringently as they were. For their part, developers used every possible means to
overcome this resistance.

Leader comments, articles and letters in the *Squeaker* showed the public concern at the
imminent transformation of the town: a conflict of opinions and interests manifested itself,
together with a certain amount of anxiety and not a little hypocrisy. In a leader entitled 'No
urgency' in February 1960, the *Squeaker* itself summed up the uncertainty:

> Slow development can be no encouragement to industrialists to establish light industry
> in the town; and the authorities tell us on the other hand that they would welcome more
> light industry. There are at the present time ambitious plans for the development of the

Swan Court, Swan Street, 1962. (*Petersfield Library*)

centre of the town with suites of offices and shops, but one cannot but wonder where the additional trade is to come from to support these projects. There is no indication that the present community is not pretty well served in this respect.

A month later, Ian Nairn, the campaigning editor of the *Architectural Review*, who had been described as 'the avowed enemy of all that is ugly in building and town planning' spoke to the Petersfield Society on 'The Future of Petersfield', warning the townsfolk that they had reached the moment of truth for their future. He called Petersfield

a happy place with an integrated community. There is a sense of purpose about everything that goes on. Everyone knows everyone else and those in authority are part of the community too. From the town you can walk straight out into the country. Once that no longer applies, and once you can no longer walk home with the shopping, then Petersfield will have lost its character and become a tiny industrial town. Population figures are no guide to the quality of a town. Petersfield is perfect in size and perfect in scale.

He quoted Basingstoke as an example of the 'horror' that could overtake a country town and urged South Hampshire to plan its total resources or risk winding up with a set of inferior replicas of Portsmouth.

Nairn's lecture rapidly became the catalyst for an unofficial 'Save Petersfield' movement. Admiral of the Fleet Sir Algernon Willis (a local resident) wanted to rouse everyone to take notice of the developers pressing in on the town and called for a deputation to the Ministry of Housing to include Petersfield in the green belt (projected for the area, behind the coastal towns); Lieut. Col. Michael Digby, the Liberal Party's prospective candidate for the area, talked of the growing realisation in the town that if Bordon, to the north, were developed, it would have a great effect on Petersfield's future; the *Squeaker* itself received an unprecedented number of telephone calls and letters on the subject of the town's future. But, in the same week, 'Spectator', a correspondent to the newspaper, warned townsfolk not to be smug or sentimental about their town, but to live in the context of their times: 'While it cannot resist progress or remain untouched, it can be blunt and say "There will be no jerry-building here."'

At a UDC meeting in November 1960, plans for the industrial development of Petersfield were called 'unimaginative, negative and, in part, farcical'. These comments were made by Mr Murray Urquhart and referred to a report prepared by the Area Planning Officer on the question of the industrial future of the town. The evident mismatch between the provision of housing and jobs in the town, coupled with the piecemeal location of suitable sites rather than the development of a larger site to house many industries, led Mr Urquhart to conclude that 'this is not town planning – it is just chaos'. Keith Gammon, Chairman of the urban development sub-committee, explained that their fear was that, by making available one larger site, they might attract one industrial giant, something Petersfield did not want. This clash of ideas was to be repeated over many years and it stemmed from the genuine fear of the UDC that the town might leave itself open to large-scale industrial development, which was anathema to the majority of councillors. If present-day Petersfield is grateful that such a development does not exist, then it is thanks to the Urban District Councillors of the early 1960s that the town was spared it.

Petersfield Market, 1946. (*Petersfield Museum*)

THE END OF THE CATTLE MARKET

Another major issue which overwhelmingly dominated the discussions of the first years of the 1960s was that of Petersfield's cattle market. The UDC asked whether it should be turned over completely to fatstock sales, suggesting the construction of permanent fixed pens in The Square and the provision of additional weighing facilities (a weighbridge stood outside the Market Inn). The consequence of this plan would be to oust the Wednesday traders from their traditional sites and the public would lose some of its car parking space (car parking in The Square was not prohibited until 1986). Meanwhile, the NFU (National Farmers' Union) called for a new market site and, at a public meeting, there was a general call for The Square to be abandoned by the cattle market. Keith Gammon, Chairman of the UDC, called for a 250 per cent increase in stock. As interim modifications to the facilities in The Square (demanded by the Ministry of Food) began, so did the search for a new market site in the town. Two other factors came into play at this point: meat was now derationed (after fourteen years), and the future of the Ministry-run Petersfield slaughterhouse at The Grange was also brought into question, with Sir Hugh Cocke, Chairman of the RDC, saying that the council preferred to see the continuation of their work, rather than the proliferation of smaller slaughterhouses in the East Hants area.

Part of the problem for Petersfield's cattle market was the government's wartime takeover of all cattle, sheep and pigs sent for slaughter, which had upset the process of the direct and private exchange of animals between farmers and auctioneers or between dealers and slaughterhouses. With the withdrawal of the Ministry from the operation, Petersfield market was set to revert to private enterprise; the Grange slaughterhouse was purchased by a local tradesman; farmers themselves were afraid that the meat trade would get into the hands of one or two big combines; and, finally, Guildford market was attracting more Petersfield farmers' cattle than was the town's market, which was said to be losing money. It was learnt later that the UDC had, in any case, no legal right to transfer its rights over the market to a private person or body.

The fate of the cattle market was sealed in 1962, when the Chamber of Commerce decided that it would take no further action to prevent the threatened closure. It described the final months of the poorly patronised market as a burden on the rates and pronounced that it should die. The mixing of tested and untested animals was also in breach of the Ministry of Agriculture regulations and it withdrew its support, not only from Petersfield, but also from other Hampshire markets. In Petersfield, the number of animals sold had diminished considerably and farmers seemed to prefer to sell their cattle direct to the slaughterhouse. All these factors played their part in deciding its fate and, after many years of slow decline and following a particularly harsh winter in 1962–3, the last market was held in The Square in May 1963. It was a symbolic moment for the town: a former auctioneer commented that the cattle market had made Petersfield – 'the town was the natural hub of the spokes of the farming wheel'.

The poultry market, for which Harry Jacobs was the auctioneer after the war, ran for a couple of years after the cattle had departed; it sold fruit and vegetables (often the surplus production from people's gardens) as well as hens, chicks (in boxes), cockerels, rabbits, turkey and geese (at Christmas) and was a natural attraction for young children in the town. As with the cattle market, however, the new regulations brought in to deal with outbreaks of foot-and-mouth disease (and, in the rabbit population, myxomatosis) had an impact on the numbers of animals for sale, and this rendered the business unviable. It had always been acknowledged that the poultry market's lifespan would be short because of the lack of space and purpose-built facilities; indeed, it was regarded as more of a street market.

INDUSTRIAL DEVELOPMENT

At the same time as confronting the enormous public anxiety expressed about the town's future, the UDC were giving a clear indication of the way in which they did want to encourage the town to develop industrially. Keith Gammon, who also chaired the finance and general purposes committee, mentioned the case of a Mr R.E. White, who sought to purchase land for the expansion of his lampshade manufacturing business, one to which the council would readily give encouragement and support. In fact, Edmund White Lampshades (now The King's Arms youth centre) became a very successful organisation in the postwar doldrums and stood as a positive example of how the town's industrial basis could develop cautiously in the 1960s. At the time, the town was quite clearly divided into two factions: those who wanted to preserve Petersfield almost precisely as it was, and those who wanted to see it healthily keep pace with the times, albeit at a modest speed.

Two other factors entered the equation: first, as Sir Humfrey Gale, Chairman of the Basildon New Town Development Corporation, pointed out in the *Squeaker* in May 1960, it was unfair to educate local children to a high standard but then give no regard to their future, preferably local, employment; secondly, Mr Aaron Wright, Deputy Chairman of the Itshide Rubber Co., complained that they had to recruit workers from outside the town and

Calibrated Papers (later UK Plastics), Swan Street, 1973. (The *Petersfield Society*)

the shortage of housing in Petersfield was adding to their struggles in finding labour. The company, the largest in Petersfield and, since 1958, part of the Colston Group, was now also manufacturing Colston dishwashers with great success.

The labour market looked optimistic, with the announcement that a new £180,000 poultry-packing station was to be sited at Penns Farm (two of the domed chicken houses are still there); a new factory for Calibrated Papers Ltd of 'honeycomb' design by local architects Salaman, McIver and Upfold was completed in Swan Street in 1961 (now Drum Mead), later taken over by the Spicer paper business; and 2¼ acres of land in Frenchman's Road were awarded to Raglan Facilities Ltd for light industrial purposes. However, the proposal for a 19-acre trading estate in nearby Durford Road with jobs for 500 people was rejected on the grounds that it represented a 'too big, too fast' development. This piecemeal selection of sites for industrial use across the town was described as 'an alarming tendency' and there was clearly some disagreement among councillors about the best way forward to create a coherent policy on industrial development for the town.

Far-sighted councillors were still calling for one single site to be identified as suitable for an industrial estate, but others preferred to adopt the piecemeal approach of offering smaller individual plots, fearing that a specific area designated as an estate would alter the town's character too much. This unfortunate, six-month long conflict between the UDC under its Chairman, Harry Jacobs, and its development sub-committee (consisting of eight out of the twelve full council members) under Keith Gammon, was seen as a 'planning

Bumbledom' by many. It inevitably led to the rejection of many planning applications for fear that the outcome might lead to an accelerated development of the town and in any case would contradict the agreed and stated view of the whole Council that Petersfield should only develop at a slow pace.

THE (CONTINUING) TRAFFIC PROBLEM

As Petersfield's traffic problems rumbled on during the early 1960s, some solutions were found to alleviate them. Two pubs were demolished in Dragon Street (The Fighting Cocks and The Crown Inn) to help traffic flow along the old A3; the central car park was extended considerably, theoretically to accommodate all the vehicles which currently lined the High Street (there were no parking restrictions in force at this time); finally, the Girls' High School, whose fate had focused attention on the future of the town more than any other single issue, was demolished in 1965, this being justified by the alleged need to widen the main road at that point.

Cars were taking 3½ hours to reach Petersfield from Hayling Island on summer weekends (eliciting the imaginative *Squeaker* headline 'No by-pass yet – jam today but jam tomorrow!'); as the queues increased the scene was described as being 'like a mechanical river in flood' and some motorists even got out of their cars and pushed them along the A3 a few yards at a time.

To alleviate the annual frustration for future motorists, the first plans were proposed for a partial one-way system in the town – a scheme which would eventually become Tor Way.

The hopes of those who had been calling for a bypass were thwarted again in 1962 when it was announced that one was 'not to be built for at least seven years'. The authorities had underestimated by about twenty-two years. In fact, a bypass had been mooted before the war and was again mentioned in the County Development Plan of the early postwar years (when the proposed route closely resembled the one we know now), but this was shelved owing to the economic plight of the country and the government's priorities of industrial development and the export trade.

The number of cars coming into the town on market days and other peak shopping periods had doubled since 1958 but, in January 1961, the new central car park opened, with spaces for 112 vehicles, having been paid for by money received from the town's transfer of its water supply undertaking to the Wey Valley Water Company.

ROTARY CLUB ESSAY CONTEST

In December 1960, entrants to this competition open to young people were asked to give their views on how they thought the town should develop, to keep pace with progress. Despite any preconceptions we may have on the generally natural conservatism of youth, it is both instructive and salutary to read what this generation had to say: the winner of the first prize in the senior competition, F.R. Bayliss from Churcher's College, for example, spoke of 'the well-kept streets and houses which are remarkably free from dust and litter which spoil so many towns'.

New buildings are being completed every day, and the High Street has a new look that is admired by all visitors. Indeed, there is no urgent need for drastic replanning. The cost of such a project would be astronomical, and a heavy burden on the ratepayers. . . . [With] reference to the proposal to set up light industries in the Petersfield area, . . . the fragrant beauty of the Petersfield countryside, including the enchanting lake, the lovely meadows, and the pleasant woodland, will not be spoilt by the suggested venture.

But Colin Gardiner, of Petersfield County Secondary School, who won second prize, was less sanguine:

Petersfield has remained the same for almost one hundred years. This is too long a time for progress to pass by, and in these days of rapid development, Petersfield would soon be turned into a forgotten town. . . . The average school-leaver does not expect to find employment in Petersfield, many have to go to outlying districts. . . . If this general exodus on the part of the younger generation continues, Petersfield will soon become a town of old people. [On the introduction of light industry], could not a compromise be formed so that light industry is permissible, providing the architecture of the factories and houses fits into the natural surroundings, and that there are adequate facilities for the education of the workers' children? In this way, the whole community would benefit.

Third prize winner, J.R. Francis of Churcher's, said that more industry was needed 'to give young people more opportunity than there is now. For industry will settle in Petersfield for the ease of communication with London by rail and road.' He wanted to see a slow but steady expansion of the town.

THE DEBATE INTENSIFIES . . .

Schoolchildren's views having been sought, it was now the turn of area planning officers to present their views on the future of Petersfield: whether it should become a bustling town with a rapid increase in population inside its present boundaries, or whether time would merely see a transformation of existing developments. Property speculation in recent years had made it certain that the town would inevitably change, although its physical dimensions might not be expected to increase a great deal. Alternatively, the decision might be made to use the town as a kind of pressure-release point for other places in the county which were being fought over by developers. Remarkably, this special report by planners was to remain secret for some months afterwards and a statement by the area planning sub-committee only made it more obscure. The *Squeaker* did not mince its words:

This quiet country town is going to see some startling changes in the next decade. This assertion is more than conjecture – it is fact. The majority of the deals which have made conversation have been the work of one company. A number of deals have made news. Others have attracted no publicity. Why is all this dealing going on? The local powers-that-be have set their faces steadfastly against industrial development. But the shrewd men who are investing their money in this quaint and charming old country town are not doing it for nothing. They see it as a potential goldmine.

Meanwhile, Harry Jacobs, Chairman of the Petersfield UDC, gave a clear hint in May 1961 that the council would be giving its blessing to developers who wanted to see Petersfield grow into a bigger and better shopping centre. He also indicated that the town must take care not to stagnate in other ways: 'we do not want to become little more than a village'. Despite these tussles over the town's future, the council's view was that it should develop slowly, but that more land could and should be allocated to house building.

At government level, Mr Henry Brooke, the Housing Minister, made this appeal to local councils in 1961:

> The public must be able to get regular information about what local authorities are doing. The main way of getting information is through local newspapers, so the relationship between the council and the press is of special importance. Council meetings should not, as occasionally happens, be merely formal proceedings in which proposals formulated and discussed in private are rubber-stamped without debate.

As if to heed the Minister's pronouncement on clandestine planning debates, a representative of Raglan Property Trust wrote to the *Squeaker* later that year, stating that 'the Raglan Board has no wish to be shrouded in mystery'. A list of their four directors published in this letter revealed for the first time that two of them were Petersfield residents: Group Captain Newnham – the chairman and Managing Director – and Sir Claude Holbrook. The directors were said to be 'anxious that development should take place without offending any ideas of beauty or traditional character and they believe that this can best be achieved by orderly planning rather than by a number of haphazard schemes by individual sponsors'.

In an extraordinary gesture, which was nonetheless good for public relations, these same directors (who had taken office ten years previously) told their shareholders that they were willing to take a smaller cut of the profits, as the company was doing so well. Profits had doubled in the previous year, a large proportion of which had come from securities dealing. It is clear, however, that their entry into the Petersfield property market had brought considerable wealth to them as a company: their annual profits had multiplied tenfold over the previous ten years.

RAGLAN EXPANDS ITS INTEREST IN PETERSFIELD

Within two years of the Raglan Trust's acquisition of properties in Swan Street and High Street, the company had completed Swan Court and a block of flats (Winchester House) in Winchester Road; had submitted plans for a three-storey block on the poultry market site (abandoned shortly after the demise of the cattle market); and had applied for permission to develop several sites in the High Street: the old Petersfield Girls' High School, the former Petersfield Post Office, a dark and dreary building which had housed the surgery of Drs. Panckridge, Jeffries, Campbell-Cooke and Hoey since before the war; and Clare Cross. The last of these properties was a listed building under Section 30 of the Town and Country Planning Act of 1947, but, despite this, Raglan intended to demolish their newly acquired properties to make way for a block of shops and flats (now Dragon Court).

Moves had been afoot to make profitable use of the old Girls' High School before it was eventually demolished. In 1962 it had temporarily served as a police station during the refurbishment of the St Peter's Road station, and Hampshire County Council now wanted to hold Further Education day and evening classes in it.

A flurry of articles and letters in the *Squeaker* in the first few months of 1962 testify to the enormous public interest generated by the Raglan company's plans for the development of Petersfield. First, a huge new precinct consisting of a hotel, shops, offices, assembly rooms and an underground car park, and costing five times as much as Swan Court, was proposed for the site opposite. It was estimated that, in the following decade, Raglan would spend more than £1 million on rebuilding the town. The Raglan Chairman wrote to the *Squeaker*: 'Apart from the quality of the district as a high-class residential area, the town's importance as a commercial and shopping centre is growing rapidly.' Raglan had also started work on its light industrial site in Frenchman's Road (now Paris House) and Winchester House was ready for occupation later in 1962. 'It is our firm intention,' he continued, 'to foster the inevitable growth which modern conditions demand of Petersfield in a manner which will ensure the approval and support of the townspeople.'

However, not everyone agreed with the liberal thinking of the *Squeaker*, which declared that:

In investing their money in the town, [the Raglan company] are using an imaginative approach. It would be idle to pretend that their motives are completely altruistic. They are running a business and they are running it to make profits. But at the same time there is a shape and purpose to their ideas which helps to lift their activities above money-making. Petersfield has grown haphazardly through the centuries. It has aspects of beauty. But there was also a great deal of decay around before re-development began.

Voices raised against this alleged distortion of the truth included that of Ian Nairn, who had visited Petersfield two years previously. Writing of Swan Court in the *Daily Telegraph*, he said that it was designed supposedly to harmonise with the traditional character of the town, 'yet the sad thing is that this design will strike a false note in Petersfield. In a country town which is still an unselfconscious mixture of true styles – Tudor, Georgian, Victorian – it simply looks like the twentieth century aping the eighteenth. The falseness will always show.'

John Wyndham, the novelist, wrote to the *Squeaker* to complain that development plans for Petersfield were 'apparently kept hidden from the public'. This statement appears to confirm the offensively patronising earlier declaration on the part of one top county planning officer 'that the re-planning of Petersfield was none of the town's business'. Wyndham continued:

'Development' of a town (which is simply builders' jargon for changing it to their own commercial benefit) is a matter of direct concern to the citizens of that town, and one on which they should be informed. Moreover, when the town is one which has in its nucleus managed to preserve character and unity, the proposal to alter it becomes of more than local concern. What appears to be intended is the arbitrary exploitation of the place as a commercial property, irrespective of any views that it and its neighbours may have. Many of the inhabitants of Petersfield choose to live there because they like Petersfield and the district; had they preferred the life of the dormitory-suburb, there are already more than enough that they could have chosen.

In May 1962, Flora Twort wrote a few suggestions to the Raglan Trust indirectly through the *Squeaker*. In summary, they were:

1. Tall buildings are out of scale here and we would like to continue to see the hills.
2. Keep the new buildings away from the old town around the church – The Square, The Spain, Sheep Street and High Street. Although old Petersfield means nothing to the Raglan Trust, we like it ourselves and so do the tourists who do not come here to look at anonymous blocks of offices.
3. If we must have a supermarket, please let us have shops for the small trader too. There is something very unattractive about the term 'self-service'.
4. If the Raglan Trust would use some of its large resources to give us what we really need (cheaper houses to rent or buy), and not what they think we ought to want, they could still make a considerable profit and earn a great deal of gratitude.

On Swan Court specifically, Helen Lubbock of Adhurst St Mary, remarking that rents were astronomically high and keeping the building empty of tenants, suggested it be renamed White Elephant Building, while the Vice President of the Design and Industries Association wrote: 'Let Swan Court be a horrible warning to us all!' Other correspondents, anticipating the consequences of Raglan's high rents, remarked that the company was forcing the town to run before it could walk, resulting in a loss of rate revenue for the council and leading Petersfielders to feel depressed about the future of their town. Swan Court, Petersfield's costliest building, was put up for sale almost as soon as it had been built, but it remained empty for a year. Raglan's plan to accommodate nine firms in this new business centre, yielding £12,000 a year in rents, was, instead, daunting commercial firms and contributing to the crippling of the local economy.

The industrial site in Frenchman's Road – where Raglan had hoped to build and lease four or five small factory units – was also being offered for sale. At the same time, the new shop at 25 High Street (now Somerfield) was progressing rapidly, Raglan applied to build four more shops at 29–31 High Street and sought approval for two shops with offices above at the old Poultry Market site. The saddest story attaches to 29 Clare Cross, the home and surgery of Charles Dickins, the dentist and town's Scoutmaster: the property having been sold to Raglan (Mr Dickins denied selling it directly, but he had in fact accepted cash for his very short lease), the dentist removed his belongings from the house where he had lived for fifty-four years and settled, temporarily, into the Scout hut in Heath Road. He died two months later in the new council bungalow which the council had found for him in Queens Road, just a few hours before he was due to receive a cheque for £160 as a testimonial marking his fifty years' service to the community and to the Scouting movement.

Amidst all the furore, the press announced that the Raglan Trust had become the new owners of the old Corn Exchange building; it is interesting to note, however, that that building was leased to Cubitt and West, R. Arnold, Smeed and Smeed (wine merchants), W. Pink and Sons (grocer's), and Rowswell's, three of which firms still occupy the same premises today. On the other side of the High Street, Raglan bought 26 High Street, which

Suter's advert, 1963. (*Author's Collection*)

also belonged to the Rowswells (now Portman Building Society). By 1963, Raglan owned more than half of the south side of the High Street and, in a deal with Alan Suter, the owner of a travel goods and shoe shop (until recently, Kenney's shoe shop), who had already negotiated the purchase of the old Punch and Judy tea rooms (now ASK restaurant) and the adjoining toyshop (now Bath Travel) from the owners, the Misses Mace and Hall, Raglan swallowed up yet another property dating from the late sixteenth century. Luckily for Petersfield, Raglan stated that the old Punch and Judy was to remain 'at all costs' and, to reassure the public that at least some buildings in the High Street might be saved, Suter's felt obliged to place an advert in the next month's *Petersfield Post*. In fact, one private residence held out against the ever increasing pace of change in the High Street: this was the eighteenth-century house at no. 15 which is still intact today, albeit encompassing a shop (Tiger Rose).

The fierce controversy surrounding Raglan's plans for the town spilt over into the Comment columns of the *Petersfield Post*, where there was a call by Dr Robert Cross of Hylton Road for a town meeting on the new developments which planners should attend. Is the town to become 'a characterless slab of subtopian masonry?' he asked, calling the bulldozing of the old Dolphin (lately the Girls' High School) in order to widen the A3 a senseless act if a bypass were to be built. Raglan was by now seen to be a controlling force in the 'new' Petersfield and the year 1962 had been one of rumour and speculation, with the townsfolk divided on whether they wanted the town to stay as it was, or to expand substantially. There was a growing feeling that the cart was being put before the horse, however, and that the town's first need was for more homes and more job opportunities in light industry. In 1963, for example, there still remained 178 families on the housing list and virtually no employment in the town for school leavers.

SOME CHINKS OF LIGHT

Civic life in the early 1960s was not all dominated by doom and gloom, however. St Peter's Church, which had suffered a terrible and 'mysterious' fire on Palm Sunday in 1962 (probably due to an electrical fault) which had badly damaged the choir vestry, the south aisle roof and the church furniture, since which services had been conducted in the Methodist Church, was again in full use in October 1963 after seventeen months' restoration work.

The official map of the new AONB (Area of Outstanding Natural Beauty) was published in October 1962, illustrating the 151 square miles of designated area around Petersfield which, it was hoped, would allow Hampshire County Council a tighter rein on building and development. It was clear that the early years of the decade were witnessing raised expectations of major growth. The Green Belt around London meant that people were moving away from the capital for a whole range of social reasons: commuting was becoming a norm, job mobility was increasing, the manufacturing base of London was changing and the capital itself was becoming more of a service centre. The Buchanan Report 'Traffic in

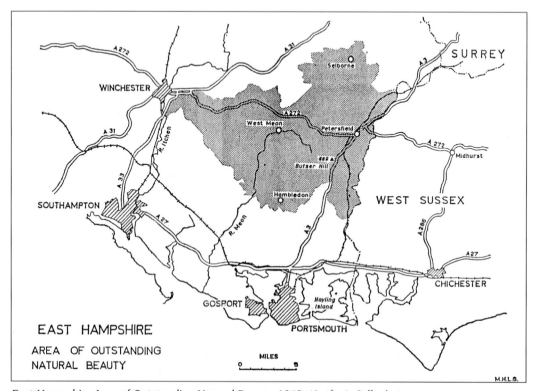

East Hampshire Area of Outstanding Natural Beauty, 1962. (*Author's Collection*)

The open-air swimming pool under construction, 1961. (*Petersfield Museum*)

Towns' and the first real expansion of the motorway network were indications that prosperity and its concomitant ramifications were having a profound effect on social change in general and on the urban v. rural conflict in particular. The new mid-Hampshire Structure Plan of 1968 prepared by the HCC indicated that Petersfield lay in a 'restraint' area (i.e. there was to be no major growth), in part a recognition of its designation as an AONB. In fact, Petersfield is the largest settlement wholly positioned within an AONB anywhere in the country and this has given it some protection from uninhibited urban sprawl.

William III's statue, the ownership of which had passed from the UDC to the HCC in 1962, was repaired and renovated by the latter at a cost of £3,000, although this brought its own controversy, with some residents offering suggestions as to how the money might be better spent in other ways. Experts, however, agreed that the statue was of great artistic and antiquarian value: Sir Leigh Ashton, Director of the Victoria and Albert Museum, wrote:

> This statue has great historical and local interest and rarity. There are few equestrian figures in England that date before 1800, and this 18th century tribute to the memory of the Protestant hero is clearly a monument of considerable importance that merits preservation.

Public amenities were also improving: the new open-air swimming pool (final cost: £13,000) was opened in May 1962 by Sir David Eccles, the Minister of Education; Winton House at last opened full-time as the town library in April 1963 after operating on a part-time basis for fifteen years; thousands of cubic feet of earth and chalk were excavated from Butser Hill to widen the road and improve vision for the increasing number of car drivers; car owners benefited, too, from the extension to the central car park; Weston House, the home for elderly residents in Borough Road, was completed by the UDC in 1964. Finally, there was general agreement on the formation of a Community Association in 1964 which was soon to play an important role as a channel of communication between the public and the town's developers.

After its first five years' existence, Petersfield County Secondary School could boast of eighty-eight pupils who had stayed on after the age of 15 (then the official school leaving age); exam results were improving every year; the curriculum and extra-curricular activities were expanding in range and popularity and the school was generally acknowledged to be one of the finest of its type in Hampshire.

With so much uncertainty surrounding properties in the High Street, business was beginning to stagnate. Lavant Street shops, in the meantime, were thriving and the residential element in the street was slowly being replaced with new shops. Youngsters bought their pop records at Seals (now Petersfield Photographic); cameras were sold at the new Petersfield Camera Centre; the ironmongers, Kyle Ltd, had rebuilt the old-established business of Allsworths (now Rowans Delicatessen); a new DIY shop (D.S. Sole Ltd) had opened; and there were furnishing and fashion shops, a greengrocer's and a garage (Alton Motors) with new showroom and workshops.

John Digby Lovell of Lord's Farm at Sheet, faced with the closure of the Kingsfernsden level crossing which effectively would have cut his farm in two and ruined his agricultural contracting and engineering business, took his case to the House of Lords and won it.

THE *SQUEAKER* CHANGES OWNERSHIP

Ironically, the *Squeaker* itself was also taken over by a giant commercial concern that summer (1962): the *Hants and Sussex News* ceased publication and was incorporated into the *Hampshire Telegraph and Post*, a Portsmouth and Sunderland Newspapers publication. Its new (local edition) title was the *Petersfield Post*, and it carried the sub-heading (*and Hants and Sussex News*), although the inside pages were headed *Hampshire Telegraph and Post*. It was a much larger newspaper than the old *Squeaker*, costing 3d and usually consisting of fourteen pages (but sometimes containing up to twenty-four pages for special editions). The first edition appeared on 6 September 1962 and it covered an area reaching from Bordon in the north to Gosport in the south.

In February 1963, the sub-heading *Hants and Sussex News* was finally dropped and, the following October, the newspaper became simply the *Petersfield Post*. It was probably no coincidence at this juncture that Raglan expressed an interest in 21–3 High Street (then Childs bookshop, now part of Somerfield), which was where the old *Squeaker* had been printed and which was due to close shortly. The *Petersfield Post's* front-page headline 'Childs bookshop to go' in November 1963, and the comment that 're-development mania [was] slowly throttling the charm of Petersfield', provoked an outcry from many, including, once more, Dr Cross, who lamented that it was quite unnecessary to remove the façade or to alter the roofline of the building, especially as there were plans to turn the single shop into three units which could exactly correspond to the tri-partite division of Childs shop front.

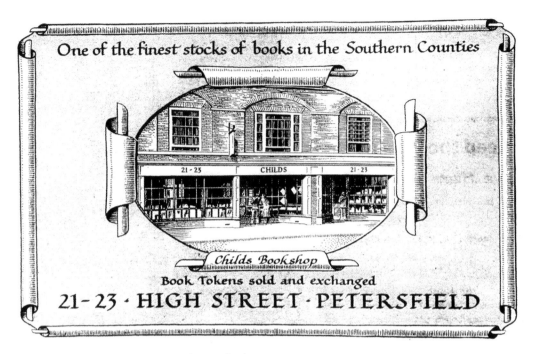

One of the finest stocks of books in the Southern Counties

CHILDS

21-23   CHILDS   21-23

Childs Bookshop

Book Tokens sold and exchanged

21-23 · HIGH STREET · PETERSFIELD

Childs bookshop advert, 1962. (*Author's Collection*)

The demolition of Childs, 1964. (*Petersfield Museum*)

The owner of the premises, Mr A.D. Millard, had been granted outline planning permission to demolish the building and erect three shops and offices on the site; this in itself was described as the 'executioner's axe poised over one of the High Street's most picturesque properties'; however, an ex-employee of Childs did describe the building as 'dirty, decayed and airless', that it had 'several times been flooded and inefficiently dried, [thus] smelling oddly' and that it had 'staff facilities of a most primitive style'.

A Sense of History

Petersfield was, almost unconsciously, undergoing a spiritual as well as a structural transformation at this time. The concurrent and conflicting forces at work within the community were driving unholy wedges through the time-honoured patterns of behaviour and expectations of the townsfolk. As rural gave way to urban, so parochial slid inexorably into civic, and small commerce was abandoned for larger enterprise. At the same time, the architectural backdrop to this dramatic revolution was being whisked up into the flies to be replaced by a descending sheet of gloomy scaffolding.

With the passing of the cattle market in 1963, there had already been a noticeable loss of atmosphere in Petersfield; there were fewer market traders' stalls too, and this meant a large drop in shopkeepers' Wednesday takings throughout the town. Wednesday had for centuries been the day when Petersfield proclaimed its long affinity with the country's largest industry: agriculture. But nostalgia had already given way to sadness, as a photograph of one of the last cattle markets shows: a forlorn Square with near-empty pens, two cows and a handful of calves. After 300 years of existence, the last cattle were sold at the market in May 1963; George Money, a champion of the market for forty years, clanged the bell to call up the farmers, and Alan Hinxman, who had served as auctioneer for forty-four years, invited the last bids. Petersfield had finally rejected the principal facet of a country market town and, with its passing, the rural ethos of the town's existence. Hinxman's lamentation on the market's demise summed up the feeling of many farmers: 'time alone will tell whether Petersfield will gain or lose by its rejection of the farming community'.

What was termed Petersfield's 'housing shame' at this time was not only the size of its housing list, but the large number of flats and houses which were allegedly too old or too expensive to be occupied. Lying on the fringe of the London building 'mushroom', Petersfield had become a target for development companies; however, these had not brought with them the cherished 'homes-for-all' slogan which still echoed through postwar Britain. Rather they brought high prices and high rents, leaving a good sprinkling of properties throughout the town empty for several years, awaiting probable demolition. One consequence of this, of course, was to subtly alter the composition of the town's inhabitants; from being an essentially rural community, with those of average means still able to afford small properties in the centre of town, Petersfield was beginning to witness the signs of wealthier residents establishing themselves and settling in the town. In a letter to the *Petersfield Post* at this time, Fred Kimber wrote:

What we want in Petersfield are more light industries for the young people leaving school. Also cheaper houses for the working class. There are married people with children living in one room in Petersfield and with no hopes of getting a house.

Evidence of this shift in Petersfield's class structure can be seen in the house-building figures: a total of 373 council-financed dwellings against 529 private houses had been built or were in the process of completion in the Urban District Council area over the twenty years since the war ended.

The debate over the future of Childs bookshop represented a typical dilemma facing those who unequivocally called for the retention of High Street properties under threat from Raglan: how to justify the continued existence *in toto* of such properties while simultaneously acknowledging their structural and commercial deficiencies. This problem, arising repeatedly throughout Britain in the 1960s, would be less acute today with our greater concern for preservation, our advanced building renovation techniques and, above all, our more stringent planning regulations which determine not just whether, but also how, a building should be saved. It is to Petersfield's eternal shame that a building as beautiful to the eye and as treasured by its citizens as Childs should have been allowed to perish.

One attractive proposal for the Childs site, later dropped, was for the creation of a precinct situated between the High Street and St Peter's Road on the site of the bookshop; this was to have been in the form of an arcade, housing an intimate pedestrian shopping court, providing premises for sixteen small businesses with accommodation above.

Aware of the potentially devastating human consequences for historic towns such as Petersfield, the Ministry of Housing and Local Government and the Ministry of Transport had jointly published a glossy 21-page planning bulletin in December 1962, entitled 'Town Centres – approach to renewal', in which it pleaded for a display of common sense and cooperation in the necessary work of renewing urban centres. 'Renewal cannot be undertaken without public support and cannot be carried through without private enterprise. Redevelopment should not ignore the qualities of historic buildings. A town's character is an elusive quality and it requires sympathy and resourcefulness to ensure that it is not lost in the process of renewal.' Group Captain Newnham's reply to this was characteristically anodyne:

> There appears to be no valid reason why the various interests should not be integrated provided that the right degree of importance is allowed to each so that the best interests of the community as a whole can be served.

Within his statement in response to the Ministry Bulletin however, there were also some lurking barbs, such as: 'In my opinion, Petersfield deserves better opportunities and prospects than those associated with a sort of sanctuary for elderly people', and 'I believe that by the end of 1963, the town will have improved in looks and attractiveness – there is plenty of room for improvement'.

In fairness to Raglan, there were others who saw the 'opportunities' available for 'development': in February 1963, the long-established grocer's, Forrest Stores, and the tobacconist's, SPQR (now both absorbed into Millets and EWM), were the subject of a development bid by the Bampton Property Group. Forrest Stores, a major grocer's in the town, owned the field at the back of the shop which stretched as far as Station Road. Their delivery vans exited through an archway onto The Square and this site was therefore of particular interest, as it included the right of access to the central car park; almost thirty years later, the whole site became Rams Walk. In March 1963, a proposed design for a row

Proposed design for colonnades of shops and offices on stilts in front of St Peter's Church, 1963.
(*Author's Collection*)

of shops and offices on stilts to be erected in front of St Peter's Church was, thankfully,
rejected. These would have imitated, albeit in a thoroughgoing 1960s style, the old row of
colonnaded buildings which had stood in front of, and therefore partly obscured, St Peter's
Church, creating instead an open atrium leading to a Church 'Close'. Indeed, the true
predecessors of the demolition culprits present in the town at this time had been those
Victorian vandals who, in 1898, had removed the elegant town hall, the offices of the
Hampshire Post, and the former Queen Anne-style Pince's School, later an auctioneer's,
adjacent to the Commercial Hotel (until recently Macdonald, Oates, solicitors) whose plain
flank wall affronts the eye today. The justification for these new buildings was that they
would 'restore balance, bringing accent and character to The Square'.

In November 1963, Flora Twort, in protest against the imminent destruction of a large
proportion of the High Street, produced a pencil drawing of the endangered properties: the
High School, the old Post Office and Clare Cross. The accompanying press article spoke of
Petersfield becoming a 'horrid, ordinary, neon-lighted town'. But the stable door was being
shut too late: just one year later, the Raglan horse had already bolted, carrying off the
seventeenth-century Clare Cross, the eighteenth-century Childs bookshop and the
nineteenth-century old Post Office.

The future of the Girls' High School, originally the Dolphin Inn dating from the eighteenth
century, was deferred by the HCC for another few months, thanks to lobbying by the
recently formed Petersfield Community Association, who had taken the fight to the Minister
of Housing, Sir Keith Joseph, and to local MP Miss Joan Quennell, the Parliamentary Private
Secretary to the Minister of Transport, Mr Ernest Marples. Another conflict of objectives
arose at this point: the HCC had made it clear that it intended to sell the school for (the
then A3) road improvements and widening, but the Ministry denied that it was interested in
such a scheme. Opposition was rapidly becoming a futile enterprise, however: even local

architects were waging a war over the intrinsic merits of the school building and Murray Urquhart, the Chairman of the Petersfield Urban Council (as it was now referred to), thought the building 'an eyesore, and [it] should have been pulled down years ago'. Arthur Gill, the Vice-Chairman of the Petersfield Society, countering the critics of the building's structural soundness, reminded people that the County Council had been satisfied with it when it had been proposed to house the town library there; the Society supported the view that the building should be used again to accommodate community activities.

At the end of 1963, Raglan Chairman, Group Captain Newnham, had declared that he expected Petersfield to grow to 20,000 inhabitants in the following seven to ten years. With hindsight, we might be thankful that, having failed to reach that figure even in twice that amount of time, his enterprise was a signal failure. He claimed that his company's policy was 'to carry through a programme of reasonable development', stating: 'We are not vandals who have come here to destroy everything old. We would like to develop in a style and in a way which is in keeping with the tradition and charm of the town.' The opposition to his plans, he said, 'arose out of sentimentality for the old, and a lack of appreciation of the new'. He likened Petersfield to a large business firm, the heads of which were so cautious

PROTEST BY AN ARTIST

In protest against the rapidly-changing High Street scene, the Petersfield artist, Miss Flora Twort, has produced this graphic pencil drawing of the street as it is now, spotlighting the old High School, doomed to demolition. unless it can be saved at the eleventh hour.

Flora Twort's protest at the imminent demolitions of 1964. (*Author's Collection*)

and careful as to repress the initiative and enterprise needed for the business to expand. Group Captain Newnham cannot have been the only businessman operating in the country at the time who thought he knew what was best for the community, but his lamentable disregard for, and the destruction of, a good part of Petersfield's architectural heritage over this five-year period was tantamount to carnage. His company's blunt elimination of the irreplaceable history to which the townsfolk were deeply attached and which had defined the unique character of the place for centuries was inexcusable and unforgivable.

1964 – THE BATTLE FOR THE SOUL OF PETERSFIELD

The year 1964 was undoubtedly Petersfield's *annus horribilis*. So great and so irreparable was the damage caused to both the fabric of the town and to the feelings of its citizens that it eclipsed all other considerations that year. Indeed, 1964 can be seen as a microcosm of the town's battle for its own soul; the David and Goliath debate over the effect on the town of, primarily, the Raglan Development Company's strategy filled the columns of the *Petersfield Post* with angry and vituperative comments on a weekly basis.

As if the depredations of developers were not enough to bring the town to its knees, there was even a sacrilegious bid by an Andover businessman-farmer to purchase the horse trough in The Square, which had been a gift to the town from Mrs Money-Coutts in 1882. In the *Petersfield Post*, 'Downsman' commented sarcastically that: 'the UDC, which has given up

Sheep Street, pre-1964. (*Petersfield Museum*)

the rest of the town, has said the trough must stay.' Another question of confused priorities. A cartoon in the *Petersfield Post* in the spring of 1964 showed two visitors to a skyscraper-dominated Petersfield, with one puzzled-looking man saying to another: 'Funny – in 1964, this used to be called Petersfield, not Raglansville.'

In February, after many months of rumour and controversy, Raglan bought Childs bookshop premises. This was a building dating from the eighteenth century, but which had been occupied by A.W. Childs' printers and stationers since 1900 and was restored before the Second World War. It also housed the printing works where the *Hants and Sussex News* (the *Squeaker*) was published. After the sale of the shop, Mr Stanley Fairmaner, who had been its manager since 1947, left to open his own bookshop in the High Street.

One month later, the Raglan company bought an old cottage in Sheep Street (now 3–7) owned by Mr Fred Berriman, whose boot and shoe shop it had been for thirty years; the adjoining Spiritualist Church, which boasted forty members with a resident medium, Mr Eric Lewsley, was also included in the deal. Significantly, the HCC had not presented any opposition to Raglan's plans for this part of Sheep Street. The cottage, like the Royal Oak next door, had a timber frame of massive oak and a frontage of some 70ft. After its sale, Raglan now owned virtually all of the west side of Sheep Street, with the exception of the public house. The old cottage revealed a roof beam with the words 'good school', probably dating back to the mid-nineteenth century, although the cottage had at one time also been called 'St Peter's Lodge' and had housed the verger of St Peter's Church.

The *Petersfield Post*, still occasionally the campaigning newspaper it had often been in the past and always bringing reasoned judgement to events, reflected, in April, on the battles now being fought over Petersfield and its heritage:

> It is a sad commentary on our times that those who are concerned to save what they can of the beauties of our towns and countryside are often regarded as eccentrics, or worse. 'Preservationist', in some circles, has come to be regarded as a dirty word: the antithesis of 'progressive'. There was never a time when an informed and organised body of opinion was so much needed to resist the needless despoliation of our old towns and beautiful country.

In June, it became more vociferous:

> A vigorous and militant spirit needs to emerge if Petersfield, already losing many of its unique characteristics, is to be raised above the level of urban uniformity and anonymity.

Fortuitously, the new Community Association was formed that same month and immediately became one of the voices raised against the developments in the town. In particular, it espoused the cause of the old Girls' High School building, which it wanted to save as a community facility.

Meanwhile, the twenty-year-old, 450-strong Petersfield Society was said to be 'unpleasantly shocked' to learn that the local planning authority had given outline consent for Childs bookshop to be demolished, without any prior notice of consultation. It was deeply regrettable that the Petersfield Society was having little influence on events

Students' design for High Street, 1964. (*Author's Collection*)

at this time; once the vociferous watchdog of all aspects of Petersfield's historic heritage, it had been uncharacteristically silent during this period of the town's development. In the days of its campaigning founder secretary, the formidable Miss Mary Ward, who frequently went to Whitehall to fight various preservation causes, its reputation as the guardian of the town's heritage and prestige was second to none. Since Miss Ward's retirement in 1958, it had lost a good deal of its fighting spirit just at a time when the town needed it most.

The HCC, which had followed a policy of negotiating with Raglan over the development of the lower end of the High Street – including the Girls' School, which they owned – unsurprisingly met fierce opposition when they published their next major £500,000 plans in the *Petersfield Post* in July 1964. This scheme not only saw the redevelopment of the lower end of the High Street, but also envisaged building across the end of the street, thereby creating a pedestrian shopping precinct the length of the High Street. The building to replace the old Post Office, Clare Cross, and part of the old Girls' High School was illustrated in the press and provided for six new shops, with flats above, rear access facilities and parking for eighty vehicles. Childs bookshop was also included in the plan, but did not form part of the new main structure.

So important was this scheme that the HCC planning committee – with the consent of the developers – took the unusual step of advertising the application so that members of the public could make written representations. A display was held in the town hall for one week. However, there was really no doubt of the county's firm intentions to sell the Girls' School site and it appointed a property negotiator from the Petersfield firm of Hall, Pain and Foster to negotiate on its behalf with the Raglan Company and the Ministry of Transport.

Dr Robert Cross led the attack on Raglan, claiming that even the younger generation was against the proposals, which flew in the face of any sense of aesthetics or even common sense. The *Petersfield Post*'s comment was that anything Raglan was proposing for the town was 'more nails in the coffin, ready for the burial of Petersfield as a quiet, unspoilt country town'. In its place, it saw a 'hotch-potch of pseudo-architecture and indifferent modern design' and that, although Petersfield should not go too far, too fast (as in Havant), nor be allowed to become a rural backwater (like Midhurst), what the town needed at this point

was a consensus which would reconcile the different views of the modernists and the preservationists. More damningly, it said that 'even among those in responsible positions there are a number content to let the town drift'.

What was perhaps of greater interest and significance for the public in deciding its stance on the future architecture of the town was the exhibition held the same month (July) under the auspices of the Petersfield Society by architectural students from the School of Architecture at the Portsmouth College of Art. For their 'student project', they displayed their own version of the possible development of the High Street: their proposed remodelling of the street retained the old Girls' High School, Clare Cross and Childs bookshop, but allowed for the demolition of the old Post Office. The designs were both more sympathetic and more in tune with what the architect and town planner Max Lock had had in mind for the town. His immediate postwar report on Portsmouth and its environs had stated:

> [Petersfield] has a warm character, the good and bad buildings being jumbled together to form a pleasant whole. There are probably hardly more than a dozen good old buildings in the main part of the town. All the more reason, then, for insisting that any proposed development preserves these wherever possible. We therefore question the merits of development proposals which at one fell swoop would demolish three of these buildings from the High Street. What the Raglan proposals would give is architecture which falls short of acceptable design standards, is over-scaled, lacking in visual continuity, and totally out of sympathy with its environment. We would urge the Raglan Company to reconsider its proposals.

With the almost simultaneous exhibitions of the Raglan plans and those of the Portsmouth architecture students on show in the town, and with a vigorous campaign being mounted by the Community Association for the retention of the Girls' High School as a Community Centre, the Hampshire Planning Committee could have found itself in a moral and political quandary. The Community Association had taken its fight to the Minister for Housing, Sir Keith Joseph, and to Petersfield's MP, Miss Joan Quennell, while Petersfield's new prospective parliamentary Labour candidate, Lady Wilson, a freelance journalist and writer married to Sir Steuart Wilson, a former Head of Music at the BBC, immediately identified herself with the anti-development company movement in the town.

Throughout August and September, the debate intensified considerably: Joan Quennell declared that there was no evidence that the Ministry of Transport had any interest in the Girls' School site, but suggested that the Ministry of Housing and Local Government 'was probably being prodded by the County Council' to acquire part of the land for road widening. Mrs Elisabeth Barnett of Hylton Road, who, with the support of the Petersfield Society, was leading the campaign to save the old Dolphin building, sought a meeting with the Raglan architects to discuss the High Street developments in general terms. The town hall display of Raglan's plans had elicited a great number of representations – urging the retention of the property – from the public.

The 'crisis' meeting convened in Winchester on 27 October between all interested parties included, from the Petersfield Urban Council, Murray Urquhart, Keith Gammon, Alan Ray, George Vince and Mrs A.A. Hayes. Mr Gammon stated that there was an urgent need to widen the pavement in Dragon Street at the side of the High School to allow schoolchildren and mothers with prams to pass safely; Mr Urquhart saw no possible reason for not demolishing the old school and commented 'the town wants tidying up'; Mr Vince said the main thing demolition would bring would be a road improvement. On Friday 30 October, the Hampshire Planning Committee approved in principle the Raglan redevelopment scheme. Two weeks later, demolition contractors moved in to remove the three High Street buildings: Clare Cross, the old Post Office and Childs bookshop.

Major John Bowen, living in the Georgian building 22 High Street opposite the destruction now proceeding in his beloved Petersfield, wrote an epitaph on a black-edged memorial.

A last-minute reprieve for the High School was won after a lengthy debate at the HCC, when a Finance Committee decision to sell the site was deferred until February 1965. At the debate, it was Major General H.T. Tollemache, the County Councillor for Petersfield, who injected some sanity into the proceedings by detailing the events which had let to the impasse between the developers (Raglan) and the conservationists (principally the Community Association). The facts were that, after three years' vacancy, the owners (the HCC) sought to use it as a library, but this was refused by the Ministry of Transport on the grounds that mobile libraries and other vehicles would cause traffic problems at the site. The Ministry were then asked if they wished to purchase the building to improve the A3 and, at the same time, a third of the site was offered to Raglan. Raglan then produced their

---

EPITAPH
For the Georgian houses in Petersfield High Street,
under demolition, November 1964.

We, the mellowed Georgian houses of Petersfield High Street;
Look on perplexed in anger, surprise and dismay,
As our graceful, historic companions suffer defeat,
Are utterly gutted, pulled down and carted away.

Major John Bowen's epitaph for Petersfield's Georgian High Street, 1964. (*Author's Collection*)

plan to develop all three adjacent sites and it was this plan which was accepted in principle by the HCC at the end of October. The desire to acquire the school site was, therefore, never the initiative of the Ministry, said Major General Tollemache, adding that, in essence, the question was whether the Ministry would have required, or still would require, the building's demolition in order to widen the road.

Lady Jaffray, the Bramshott councillor, supported Major General Tollemache in his plea for a postponement, adding that 'Petersfield is at the moment having to fight for every one of its old buildings'.

The second nail in the coffin of the Dolphin building, however, was struck, yet again, by the Chairman of the Petersfield Urban Council, Murray Urquhart, in December. In an angry outburst against those in the town opposing the demolition of the school, he declared: 'They have resorted to gimmicks in an attempt to prevent the orderly development of Petersfield', alleging that the Community Association was none other than the Petersfield Society in disguise!He continued: 'What is disquieting is the amount of support these people have shown they can call up.' Accused later of distorting the reality of the membership of the Community Association and of not allowing the 'ventilation of views [which] is one of the first principles of democracy', he was forced to apologise. Ignorance and prejudice were no less in evidence at the HCC, where Col. A. Murray stated: 'How [the Girls' High School] ever came to be on the statutory list of buildings of special architectural or historic interest beats me.'

And so the breast-beating and heart-searching was to continue into 1965, the aesthetically and socially minded minority as ever pitted against the commercially and profit minded town council, to the general detriment of the town as a whole. As Flora Twort wearily confessed in a letter to the *Petersfield Post* in December: '[This new development] is the ugliest thing I have seen in Petersfield for 40 years and my one consolation is that I'm too old to have to look at it for very long!'

THE TOWN MAP

Throughout the time of Raglan's major dismemberment of the town, much was made in local political circles of a need for a 'Town Map' by the HCC. Ostensibly an excellent idea, it was first mooted in mid-1962 to satisfy those who were demanding a comprehensive development plan for Petersfield, thereby avoiding the piecemeal destruction of the town, but the issue became a farce, with first one delay, then another. By January 1963, the failure to produce the plan had so irritated Raglan that the company decided to proceed regardless with the demolition of properties it owned in the town centre. But, instead of this galvanising the county into producing their blueprint faster, the Town Map was again 'promised' by Christmas that year.

By June 1964, after two years in preparation, 'slow progress' on the Map was reported and, in December, at a planning enquiry, a growing impatience was expressed regarding the Map, whose non-appearance was holding up the sale of George Bailey's Garden Centre (fronting onto Dragon Street) for residential purposes and, more significantly for the town, the reconstruction of the corner site in The Square, where, in 1965, George Money's old shop still stood 'stripped of its roof, a crumbling, decaying mass'. Serious differences between the UDC and the HCC arose over the likely costs and consequences of a

Bailey's Garden Centre, 1985. (*Petersfield Museum*)

pedestrian shopping precinct which was proposed for Petersfield town centre. However, the heinous series of delays and vacillation on the part of the HCC clearly contributed to the opportunism by Raglan, who took advantage of the decision-making void to go ahead with their own plans for the town. Considerable blame can therefore be levelled at the HCC for the disastrous state of affairs which ensued.

COMMERCIAL AND INDUSTRIAL CHANGES

1964, then, had been a year of great change. As the architecture of previous centuries was falling under the developer's hammer, old Petersfield was being torn apart: the High Street was crumbling, demolition boards were up in The Square, and big changes were being wrought in Lavant Street. In a site in Swan Street (now Drum Mead), Calibrated Papers suddenly announced its imminent closure; this company was an offshoot of the paper manufacturers Spicers. It had been two years in the town, in an octagonal-shaped building, set, in the spirit of the new towns developing nationwide, amid shrubs and flower beds, gardens and lily ponds, with a specially designed (hyperbolic parabolic) roof, which provided for a workshop underneath free of supporting columns. Unfortunately, by 1964, it had proved uneconomic to operate in conjunction with its sister factory in Park Royal, London, and it announced its closure. It had employed eighty staff in one of the most up-to-date industrial buildings in the country, and this demise indicated that another white elephant was about to be born. It was suggested that the building could be used as a concert hall, but this idea never materialised. Fortunately, another manufacturer did take over the building: this was UK Plastics Ltd which moved to Petersfield from Kingston, with the lure of 100 new jobs.

In January 1965, industry-starved Petersfield was promised four new factory units in Frenchman's Road on a site originally owned by Raglan, each with an industrial floor area of less than 5,000 sq ft., thereby avoiding the need for an industrial development certificate. The Hampshire Planning Authority did, however, insist that 'no nuisance shall be caused by the emission of noise, vibration, smell, fumes, smoke, soot, ash, dust or grit'. Other conditions stipulated the provision of adequate car parking, landscaping and screening. The result was the 1960s-style 'factory in a garden' complex named Paris House.

At the ITS Rubber factory in Sandringham Road, an £80,000 five-year development and expansion programme was set to quadruple its capacity of rubber products, proof that the industry was responding well to the incursion of plastic products in recent years. Items coming off the production line included rubber seals and car shock absorbers, as well as their traditional output of soles and heels for both domestic and overseas markets. The ITS factory was the largest manufacturer in Petersfield, with a labour force of over 300 employees.

Further development of Bedford Road as a site for light industry was mooted, with the application for an engineering factory covering 4,800 sq ft by Viceroy Developments of London.

Regrettably, jobs were about to be lost at the South Eastern Farmers' Ltd depot (between St Laurence's Church and the level crossing in Station Road) which closed in 1965: for the fifty employees, the news came out of the blue and after a recent pay rise and a reduction in the working week. The government's reorganisation of the Milk Marketing Board for the allocation of milk supplies had hit the depot hard. In recent years, SEF had become part of

South Eastern Farmers' depot, Station Road, 1950s. (*Author's Collection*)

United Dairies and, later, the vast Unigate chain, handling over 45,000 gallons of milk a day from as far afield as Andover and Basingstoke. The milk was pasteurised, cooled and bottled, or sent out in bulk tankers to all parts of southern England. With its demise, another link with Petersfield's rural past had been severed.

Meanwhile, an informal pressure group of local businessmen was discussing the chronic shortage of labour in the area, which was strangling the development of industry in the town; many more houses were required in the lower-income price range, as a good number of local firms employed a large percentage of outside labour and this in turn obliged the firms to arrange and pay for transport to and from the workplace.

A four-day trades exhibition, the fourth of its kind since the war, was held at the town hall in October 1965. About thirty traders took the opportunity to find new business at their own 'miniature Olympia', the visitor numbers enhanced with the presence of thousands of Taro Fair visitors in the town during that same week. Mindful, perhaps, of the town's physical appearance, the four-page special feature in the *Hampshire Telegraph* adopted a note of courageous optimism: 'Parts of the town look empty, tumble-down and neglected, but this is only the chrysalis before the butterfly emerges. The empty demolition sites, the derelict buildings which mar Petersfield today will be transformed into the new shops and houses of tomorrow.'

CIVIC GLOOM

With the death of Winston Churchill in January 1965, the national mood was one of sadness at the passing of bygone glories, and Petersfield undoubtedly exhibited a depressed state of mind for the first half of the year. In January, the UDC reiterated the view that the Girls' High School building should be demolished and, in February, the HCC refused the application by the Community Association to use the school as a Community Centre; instead, it gave its outline planning approval for the site to be developed by Raglan. 'Petersfield Town is falling down' was a typical headline of the time and lurid descriptions of the process, linked to equally lurid photographs, were splattered over the front pages of local newspapers. Three young brothers from a Surrey firm undertook the work; chimneys crashed through roofs, shattered masonry awaited crunching by bulldozers, and Childs and Clare Cross collapsed unsentimentally to the ground. When the demolition gang had finished, they moved on to The Square, where they set about performing the identical rituals with George Money's old second-hand furniture shop on the corner and Mrs Moulder's Little Card Shop next door together with a number of derelict cottages in Sheep Street. No protesters ventured onto the sites to vent their annoyance or disappointment. Rage was mute.

Keith Gammon, Chairman of the UDC, wrote a letter to the *Petersfield Post* explaining that the council had no power to approve or refuse any applications for planning permission, only to make recommendations. However, Elisabeth Barnett, who was shortly to contest Mr Gammon's seat on the UDC, replied: 'If the UDC had weighed in on the side of keeping such landmarks as Childs bookshop and the old High School, some attention must have been paid to its opinion. It was because of the opposition to the retention of the High Street buildings on the part of the UDC that the Ministry of Transport eventually took a firmer attitude on the question of road widening. What a bleak outlook for the town if the UDC is completely at the mercy of chance speculative building!.' The indefatigable Dr Cross also

High Street demolition, 1965. (*Petersfield Museum*)

contested the Gammon letter, adding: 'If the [Girls' High School] building is allowed to go, let it not be said of this town that a large section of its people did not protest to the end.' For its part, the Community Association, representing nearly thirty local organisations, continued its battle to save the building, preparing itself for an appeal to the Minister of Housing and Local Government.

The town presented a dismal aspect: of buildings half knocked down, of new premises half built, and of established shops in sad need of a lick of paint. But, as the *Post* stated, redevelopment of the demolition sites would not cure the town's troubles. Where were the traders, the industries, the houses to stimulate the growth that Petersfield so badly needed at this time? Petersfield's development cart seemed to have got in front of the horse, for there were not the houses, nor the jobs, to satisfy the 8,000-strong population's demands for better living conditions. The unease spilled over into the traders' thoughts too: they were worried about the rumours of closures in the town, became angry at customers' doubts about the future of certain shops, and denials regarding the closing of businesses had to be repeated on a daily basis.

THE GIRLS' HIGH SCHOOL: THE FINAL CHAPTER

To all intents and purposes, the last word on the Girls' High School had been pronounced by the end of 1964, but, despite the death throes it was suffering in the first few months of 1965, more homilies were being preached, to a more or less realistic degree, from a variety of pulpits. Flora Twort confirmed in March that the surveyor for the Society for the

Protection of Ancient Buildings had reported that there was 'no evidence to suggest that it was unsafe' and that it was 'admirably suited for use as a Community Centre both because of its central situation and its variety of large and small rooms. Little alteration would be required to adapt it for this use.' Three months later, the *Petersfield Post* published a last picture of the desolate school with the caption: 'Take a last lingering look at the old Petersfield Girls' High School – the end is in sight.'

One aspect of the whole sorry saga of the 'County High School for Girls' is that the building was almost universally referred to as just that. Such was the prominence given to its (remembered) past as a school, and so great was the demand for an alternative (future) use as a Community Centre, that the original purpose of the building as one of Petersfield's leading coaching inns had practically been forgotten. Where was the sense of history? Who spoke up for its importance in Petersfield's eighteenth-century past? Who cared about Petersfield's heritage as a coaching centre on the London–Portsmouth road?

One interesting by-product of the same saga was the emergence of a contender for Keith Gammon's place on the Petersfield Urban Council in April 1965, the first such election to take place for more than ten years. Keith Gammon, 'father' of the council and three times its Chairman, was opposed by Mrs Elisabeth Barnett, secretary of Petersfield Community Association, who thus placed the High School issue – and the wider issue of Petersfield's future development – at the top of the election agenda. However, out of an electorate of 1086 people in this south-east ward, only 333 voted and the two candidates, both classified as 'Independents', polled 214 (Gammon) and 119 (Barnett) respectively. Mr Gammon's unbroken forty years of service to the town was to continue for another three. As Chairman of the Finance and General Purposes Committee and also of the Urban Development Sub-committee, he remained responsible to the HCC for town planning matters.

Unfortunately, the time for recriminations had now passed. The month of June brought the ignominious dismantling of the High School and, with it, the end of the seven-month battle for its survival. The second half of 1965 brought a lull in events, with everyone awaiting the emergence of the new properties in the town centre. Credit difficulties were holding up a development by the East Hants Property Company which was planning a new private estate of some seventy homes on land adjoining Durford Road which had belonged to the UDC since before the First World War; a mammoth new estate of 550 homes planned for what is now Herne Farm had already been blocked late in 1964 on the grounds that 'development as proposed would be contrary to the provisions of the County Development Plan' (i.e. the infamous 'Town Map'). Meanwhile, the Centre Ring Café (now Keats-Dowlers), operating in Swan Street since 1954, closed, the third café to close in recent years, because its owners – Raglan Developments Ltd – wanted to sell the site; the corrugated-iron (Nissen) huts standing at the rear of the town hall, which had been the home of the British Restaurant during the war years and which now housed various local government offices, were given another five years' life. The UDC had hoped to remove these unsightly buildings, but, as the council itself had said: 'Any new government building should be built in a comprehensive Civic Centre site, instead of being placed haphazardly around the town.' The council yard behind the town hall housed the dustcarts, council lorries, paint shops and workshops and even the mortuary. The uncertainty of the future of local government (the merger of the UDC and the RDC had recently been mooted in March) was having another delaying effect on the town's development.

The Raglan Property Trust, announcing a relatively small increased profit from its year's activities, remarked ruefully: 'There have been delays in acquiring all the sites we considered necessary for a first-class comprehensive development.' It finally managed to sell Swan Court, which had stood empty for four years since its completion, to the Lifeguard Assurance Co. Ltd who was seeking to move out of its London offices. Swan Court had been something of an embarrassment to Raglan who, having built the office block for £100,000, now found itself having to sell it at 'about £120,000'.

The dilemma for Petersfield in 1965 was that, despite the hundreds of thousands of pounds being invested in the town and, with the local building industry at full stretch, there remained a serious housing problem which, in turn, had created a serious shortage of labour. Though the year had been characterised as a 'standstill' year, with apprehension about the outcome of the progress of the demolition taking place, uncertainty about the appearance of the Town Map, a dearth of private houses available, factory development stopping because of a national credit squeeze, the outdoor swimming pool and the town Carnival making huge losses, and snow blizzards which immobilised the town in March, it seemed – to optimists at least – as though things could only get better.

Keith Gammon MBE

Alan Ray.

John Thomas.

THE TIMES STEPS IN

News of Petersfield's plight reached the attention of a columnist of *The Times* on 28 December 1965:

This pleasant town astride the main London–Portsmouth road has the knocked-about look which Londoners came to know so well in late 1940. Buildings are down on two of the main corners, leaving holes which in this small setting have the impact of an old friend just back from the dentist.

All this destructive activity in such an historical setting would, it might be thought, have started off a great preservationist outcry. But there was hardly anybody prepared to man the barricades against the bulldozers. It has been left to outsiders to sound the alarm. An Oxford architect was sufficiently moved by what he saw to write to *The Times*: 'The town had a market square surrounded by shops and buildings of a homely scale. It had wonderful

Kenneth Hick.

half-timbered buildings of conspicuous importance to the vernacular character of this small town. My recent visit has shown not only that the general character has lost much of its charm, but that there are gaps in the frontages where there were once lovely timbered buildings. What are the feelings of all the cultured and sensitive people who are aware of this degradation? Is there no protest?'

This naturally elicited some response in the local press in (tardy) support of the views expressed. Mr W.M. Whiteman deplored the developers' 'random opportunism, showing no visible evidence of any town plan behind the piecemeal replacement, no regard for scale, architectural unity or civic urbanity'. He also condemned the 'aggressive tastelessness' of the replaced buildings. Leslie Sykes regretted the suggestion in *The Times* that local inhabitants had not done enough to protest at the 'horrific happenings' in Petersfield. 'Blame for these', he says, 'is to be attached to an indifferent Urban Council.' Hampshire County Council's planning officer, Mr A.D.G. Smart, promised that Petersfield's 'bombed-out' appearance was only a passing phase, and that the 'new and useful buildings' would blend in with the character of the older buildings. 'I think you can rest assured that the town is in very good hands architecturally.' After attempting to justify the recent demolition of properties in the High Street, he stated that 'there were very few individual buildings in the town of first rate architectural or historical importance' and that 'we knew that if it came to a showdown between ourselves and the developers, we would not have a leg to stand on'. This alleged conflict was referred to as a struggle between 'Beauty and the Beast'!

Departures

If the town was losing its character, so was it also being deprived of its 'characters': it would be futile to try to assess what proportion of the lost soul of Petersfield was owing to its demolished buildings and what owing to the demise of its oldest and best-known personalities, but the combination of the two surely damaged it irretrievably in this period of the mid-1960s. A small town usually breeds known characters and Petersfield was no exception. From the postwar period, older townsfolk still remember 'Nanner' Browning (an old Boer War veteran), Danker Fitt (who owned the monumental mason's yard in Madeline Road), 'Happy' Dench (the rabbit-skin man with his smelly old sack), 'Darky' Parnell (with his huge iron-wheeled barrow), 'Corkie' Corke (who sold ice creams 'as yellow as a buttercup' in his dairy), 'Fishy' Arnett (with generous portions of fish from his stall in the market), Fred Kimber (and his menagerie in Tilmore Road), Mr Aburrow of Dragon Street (the local rat catcher), to mention but a few.

Sam Hardy was another such character. As with several other old Petersfield families, there were many interesting interconnections: Sam Hardy was from a family of brewers in Manchester but, by virtue of the fact that their suppliers of hops since the 1870s had been the Sewards (of Weston Farm and Borough Farm), the two families became great friends. Sam was invited to Petersfield in 1907 to learn about farming (his chosen career) and he lodged at a house in The Spain, which he subsequently bought when the Hylton estate was sold in 1911. Sam also adopted an interest in hunting from Charlie Seward and eventually became the hunt master for ten years between the wars; every Boxing Day, the hunt would meet in The Spain, a great social occasion for the town. Sam would also periodically be seen in the neighbourhood driving his horse-drawn carriage and singing his favourite Harry Lauder songs as he went! He could also be heard summoning his friend Harvey Harrison (who worked in Sheep Street) to breakfast by sounding his hunting horn in the street! When his son was born, Sam held the boy out of a small window, the waiting crowd cheered, a Union Jack was hoisted and their cook and butler brought out the inevitable free beer. This attracted even more people who sang 'God save the King' and a rowdy party followed. That son, Charles, still lives in part of the house today. Sam Hardy died in August 1964, prompting a letter of commiseration to his family from Winston Churchill, whom Sam had known at Harrow, bemoaning the fact that 'Hampshire had lost one of its characters'.

Less than four years after her retirement, through ill health, from her leading role in the Petersfield Society, Miss Mary Ward died in 1962, removing from Petersfield a personality whose forceful presence had been an influence on the town for nearly forty years. Originally trained as a teacher in London, she later studied handloom weaving in Leicester and Haslemere, and then moved to Petersfield after the First World War. She first lived at 19 High Street (now the ASK restaurant), the artists' centre in Petersfield owned by Dr Harry Roberts, with the group of artists which included Flora Twort, where she practised and taught weaving. In the early 1930s, she had built for herself the revolutionary, flat-roofed house at 38 Heath Road East and spent the rest of her life there. Although she worked for many organisations, it was into her role as secretary of the Petersfield Society (she was one of its founder members) that she threw all her energies for thirteen years. Known outside the town as 'Miss Petersfield' for her energetic pursuit of good design and planning within it, her principal and lasting achievements were the listing of buildings of architectural or historic interest in the area and the first Official Guide to Petersfield in 1949, which was subsequently highly praised by the poet John Betjeman.

Plus ça change . . .

'It is time for the Petersfield UDC to take a long look at a potential danger spot in the town: the junction of Dragon Street with Hylton Road, Sussex Road and The Causeway is causing a good deal of public concern.' (March 1962)

'Petersfield and Sheet may part. The idea that Sheet might become a parish separate from Petersfield is being discussed.' (June 1962) (In fact, the parochial church council later rejected this idea.)

'Last week's Petersfield History exhibition (sponsored by the Rotary Club at the County Secondary School) was seen and enjoyed by hundreds of people – and many came away asking the same question: "Is there any reason why Petersfield cannot have its own Museum?"' (May 1964)

'Puma on the run seen near Petersfield.' (October 1964)

CHAPTER FOUR

Modernisation
1966–73

COMMUNITY LIFE

This late 1960s and early 1970s transition period, one of steady social progress rather than of dramatic change, mirrored the national preoccupation with the first stages of a recession after the boom of the early 1960s. In Petersfield, it allowed the townsfolk to recover from the shocks of 1964 while, on the economic front, it was a time for belt-tightening and of anxiety about the future. It must be remembered that, in this period, the whole town closed on a Thursday afternoon and that the traders' 'lunch hour' was precisely that (or longer). The Chamber of Trade was a powerful, if closed, body in the town, unhesitatingly demanding funds from the traders for Christmas lights, while outsiders (such as Derrick and William Ismay who had taken over Bassett's) were slow to be accepted. Despite some economic difficulties, two supermarkets were planning ahead: Fine Fare, which owned the old Forrest Stores site on The Square (now part of Millets and Edinburgh Woollen Mill), were seeking to expand and to occupy the footpath leading from the car park to The Square, but this was later rejected; and a Gateway supermarket opened on the site of the old Childs bookshop. Another new venture, 'Hardy's of Knightsbridge' opened in Lyndum House in the High Street, where Charles Hardy offered 'a West End tailor in Petersfield' – this was Cyril Grimes who came down from London every Saturday to take orders for men's suits.

The mindset of the Chamber of Trade was paralleled by that of the UDC, both organisations being run by people who had been in office for many years and whose tenure seemed to be assured for life. Within the hidebound UDC, the Finance and General Purposes Committee re-elected themselves every year, allocated members to committees, dictated the proceedings and, in emergency, acted as if they were the full council. In essence, it was a sham, with decision-making fixed by the senior members. It was ripe for change.

With its plans to inhabit the old Girls' High School frustrated, the Community Association now sought alternative premises in an abandoned bakery at the back of Chapel Street, on which it took out a ten-year lease. It also launched an appeal to convert the building into a sort of 'town club', capable of holding up to 250 meetings a year for educational courses, exhibitions, functions and other events run by member societies. Sadly, after only a few months, it became evident that an appeal had not generated as much money as expected and the project had to be abandoned.

The Association next turned its attention to using the old Connaught Drill Hall (now The Maltings), previously used by the Territorial Army and army cadets for their training, as a possible alternative premises. However, this move was superseded by the announcement, in 1968, that the former Civil Defence Centre was vacating its premises at the bottom of Ramshill. The building was offered to the Community Association for £10,000 and the committee seized the opportunity to take on the lease of the building, which reopened in September 1968. The Association's status was that of caretaker for the owners, the HCC, until it could raise the money to buy it outright. It achieved this in May 1968 and has been situated there ever since.

Evidence of a more vigorous social, business and community life in the town became apparent in 1969: the clergy and lay members of seven denominations decided to form the Petersfield Council of Churches; a trades fair attracted lively interest; the County Secondary School planned an extension which would allow for a further 300 pupils – an increase of around 50 per cent on its current numbers; 'Operation Splash' was launched to appeal for funds to install heating in the open-air swimming pool and reached its target (of £1,500) in only fourteen months, testifying to the enormous amount of public support the pool had from families because of its safe, attractive and 'fun' environment. Improvements to the A3 passing through Butser were made by eliminating the notorious danger point at Limeworks Bend. Finally, in the same week in July when Prince Charles was invested as Prince of Wales and Apollo 11 set off for the moon, North Sea Gas came to Petersfield.

Subscriber Trunk Dialling (STD) – the automatic telephone service which allowed direct dialling instead of having to pass through an operator at the telephone exchange – arrived in Petersfield in April 1966, although the operators still controlled a manual section of the exchange (in the Post Office) until 1974; international direct dialling became possible in 1978. This new £250,000 facility enabled the number of telephone subscribers and calls to rise rapidly and an expansion of the Charles Street exchange was planned to cope with the demand. The mishaps of old were at once eliminated: local sportsmen, for example, had brought chaos to telephone lines in the pheasant shooting season with direct hits on the overhead cables, and rats, which used to sharpen their teeth on the old cables wrapped in lead, silk and wax, found the more modern plastic coating far less to their taste!

In 1966, the *Petersfield Post* had a new, coloured masthead on its front page. In 1968, its mother paper, the *Hampshire Telegraph*, began to be printed by offset litho, giving full-colour pictures and a clearer text.

RAGLAN CONTINUE TO CALL THE SHOTS

It would by no means be irrational to see the history of Petersfield in the later 1960s in terms of the history of Raglan Developments Ltd. Their physical domination of the town, its Urban Council, its traders and even the conversations of its inhabitants ensured its overwhelming influence on most aspects of local society.

Into the picture at this point came their plans for developing the corner of The Square (where George Money's furniture shop had stood) and that part of Sheep Street between the Royal Oak and the fish and chip shop. What was revolutionary about this £150,000 scheme was that they proposed to create access from Sheep Street through to Swan Street and erect a three-storey block of shops, with flats above, on the 'island' between the two roads. However, Raglan's repeated attempts to develop the corner of The Square met with rejection by the HCC for over ten years, lending the site a 'bombed-out' look.

Proposed Dolphin Court. (*Petersfield Museum*)

It was announced in June 1967, after five years of wrangling, delays and an appeal to the Ministry of Housing and Local Government, that Raglan was to be given the go-ahead for a four-storey block of flats opposite Swan Court (now Garden Court). This was the result of the failure by the local planning authority to make a decision within the statutory period of time. One reason given for the repeated procrastination by the planning department was that it had preferred to see the site as a car park. Petersfield could have found itself with a four-storey car park (holding 400 cars) instead of Garden Court – local residents were probably therefore glad that they had been obliged to accept the lesser of two evils.

By 1968, Raglan owned 2 supermarket sites, 9 shops, 26 flats and 20 lock-up garages in the town. In August that year, the Raglan Trust, which had been formed in 1936 and whose holdings were mainly located in Acton, Chiswick and Wembley, found itself the subject of a takeover bid by Alliance Property Holdings Ltd, of Kingston-on-Thames, which owned 20 per cent of Raglan's capital. The following year, Alliance put forward three members of its own board for election to the Raglan board and the Trust warned its shareholders of this 'back-door' attempt to gain control of the company.

Raglan found itself yet again in the news in 1968: its most significant postwar development in Petersfield, and one which had detonated a storm of controversy at the planning stage (i.e. the razing of the three High Street buildings to make way for Dolphin Court), was now complete and it won a major Civic Trust award in 1968 for the category of 'new buildings, restoration and major alterations in areas of architectural interest or beauty which pay particular respect to the character of their surroundings'. The RIBA assessor stated that the group of shops and flats (now constituting Dolphin Court) 'had succeeded in continuing the general texture of the town'. However, Rodney Hubbuck, a Petersfield architect, described it as looking 'like a seaside marine building on an esplanade', adding

Garden Court under construction, 1973. (The Petersfield Society)

that 'it does not belong to Petersfield with its white-painted weatherboarding, its jagged lead-clad roofscape and a bit of red tiling as a sop to the vernacular'. What seems to characterise the architectural incongruities of this period of postwar Petersfield and condemn Raglan's choice of architects are the harsh, grey, slatey mansard roofs of Dolphin Court and Garden Court, which are totally out of keeping with the warmth of the red Georgian and Victorian brickwork of old.

Speaking of the commercial effect of these developments, the Chairman of the Petersfield Chamber of Commerce. at that time, Mr Robert Fielder, complained that Petersfield was 'out of balance', with too many supermarkets and stores and too few homes. 'Someone was going to get hurt,' he said, 'and that would be the small traders.' There were several shops in Lavant Street now standing empty and also factories which could not get enough workers. The Chamber of Commerce called for an improvement in Petersfield's image as a shopping centre: it wanted to enhance the appearance of shop premises and called for shop windows to be illuminated in the evenings.

INDUSTRIAL DEVELOPMENT

What might have seemed paradoxical only a few years previously – namely, the abandonment of the notion of Petersfield as a quiet, rural market town to be replaced by its new assertive self-promotion as a growth area for light industry – became reality with the publication of a special supplement to the Petersfield Post in 1967. As this newspaper itself put it: 'The town has not been so much led into the light industrial age, as tripped and trodden down by red tape along the way that a few with imagination and willpower have forced it to take.' Maybe, with hindsight, we can now appreciate the advantages of this slow postwar development: Petersfield's steady, even hesitant, growth, not only in terms of its light industrial base, but also in terms of its population, its physical development and its civic progress, must surely be considered to have been an asset compared with, for example, the inordinate industrial growth of Basingstoke or the demographic surge south of Butser.

It could be argued that Petersfield had deliberately fostered the image of a good-class residential area where industrial development was discouraged. Although this view smacks of social engineering on the part of councils and councillors, there is probably an element of truth in it; given the fact that a certain number of councillors had served since pre-war days and that they had often remained practically unopposed at local elections, they more or less controlled the decision-making process for decades, thus providing the core for a conservative style of thinking. Two typical examples of such figures were Keith Gammon and George Bassett. Keith Gammon was surprisingly defeated in an election for the Urban Council in 1968, after. forty-three years of unbroken service. George Bassett was the owner of the ironmonger's in Swan Street (now Between the Lines) and he had been a councillor for forty years. He was Chairman of the Urban Council, an organist and lay preacher at the Congregational Church and a stalwart among the business community in the town. Interestingly, George Bassett's successor was Derrick Ismay, an equally civic-minded businessman who became a UDC Councillor and a JP at Petersfield Magistrates' Court.

What would undeniably have improved the situation for Petersfield would have been a more logical approach to town planning after the war: a lax attitude to planning controls and a lack of foresight produced a random siting of factories where homes should have been developed, and vice versa. The monumental blunder, according to the *Post*, was the decision to allow house building west of the railway, where Buckingham Road and Gloucester Close now stand and which would have been far better suited to industrial premises. The losers from the lack of industrial development in the town have (always) been the school leavers; equally, one might add, the lack of apprenticeships has hindered the proper training of the younger generations so that they might remain in the town to enhance its self-sufficient, 'home-grown' ethos.

Two successful local firms which often passed unnoticed in the ups and downs of commercial life at this time were the Petersfield and Reliance Launderers and Cleaners (P&R) in Rushes Road and the engineering firm DCM in Lavant Street. P&R was founded in 1899 – on its present site and with just twelve customers – as the Petersfield and District Laundry Company, serving the domestic market. In 1958, the business was acquired by the James family and incorporated the Reliance Laundry of Alton, with a customer base of 5,000 extending to Winchester, Aldershot and Haslemere. In the late '60s, the commercial markets of businesses and institutions were added to the clientele, and other types of cleaning services were offered. A subsidiary, Workleen, started later in 1984, dealing with linen and garment rental for hotels, factories and schools.

DCM engineering derived from the old F.W. Tew and Son garage founded in Lavant Street in 1910: the natural progression from car and motorcycle repairs to light engineering began in the 1950s. The company struggled for a decade until Tony Marsh joined the firm in 1968 from Lotus racing cars and the company started to expand until a group of three companies had been formed; the firm moved to larger premises in Lavant Street in 1976.

Light manufacturing industry in Petersfield accounted for about two thousand employees in this period, with an impressive and comprehensive array of skills. The draft Town Map was about to be published and it would show additional sites which would be made available to companies wishing to establish themselves in the area. One good example of this new approach to attract light, skilled industry into Petersfield was the arrival from London, in March 1967, of the organ builders, Henry Willis and Sons Ltd. This old-established firm, founded in 1845, and which had made organs for many cathedrals, including those at Westminster, Canterbury, St Paul's and the Royal Albert Hall, had offices in Southampton and London which it wished to amalgamate; it therefore no doubt seemed logical to set up in Petersfield which, it said, it had chosen for its 'old world charm'. It erected a workshop with offices and stores in Rushes Road, which were demolished in 2004 after the firm relocated to Liverpool.

The major players on the industrial scene in Petersfield at this time were ITS Rubber in Sandringham Road, J.B. Corrie (Flextella) Ltd in Frenchman's Road, HLM Engineering (Clanfield) in Penns Road, Dawlite (Plastics) Ltd in College Street, Industrial and Electrical Rubbers Ltd in Durford Road, F.W. Tew (Engineering) and Son Ltd in Lavant Street, J. Urquhart & Sons Ltd in Bedford Road, Petersfield Timber Co. Ltd in Hylton Road, J. Ellis & Sons Ltd (Sheet Mills) and, a relative newcomer, Edmund White Ltd, lampshade manufacturers in Heath Road (now the premises of The King's Arms).

THE TOWN MAP IS REVEALED

The weary excuse trotted out by the HCC planning authority each time it wanted to block development in the town was to tell applicants that they must wait for the publication of the Town Map, in order not to prejudice the overall planning of the area by piecemeal building schemes. After what seemed like an eternity in preparation, the long-awaited but still non-statutory first draft of the Town Map saw the light of day in October 1966.

In it, the HCC projected for Petersfield a natural and dignified growth rate, the principal development areas being to the south and east of the town, the north and west boundaries being constricted by the route of the proposed bypass (also condemned to be realised rather later than hoped for). One interesting proposal was for the setting up of a local government complex on the site of the town hall, to include a police station, courts and Crown offices. The plan also envisaged a traffic-free town centre; the closure of the Petersfield coal depot (now Focus) and its conversion into a car park for commuters (a relatively new phenomenon); provision for major house building (but virtually only consisting of 'infilling'); three new schools (at The Avenue and Love Lane); increased shopping amenities; and a new library and recreation grounds.

One of the major considerations in these proposals was for a system of traffic control, with a future traffic-free Square, a pedestrianised Chapel Street and one-way circulation through the High Street.

A public meeting to debate the plan, arranged for November 1966, was attended by about two hundred people, whose main concerns revolved around the development of The

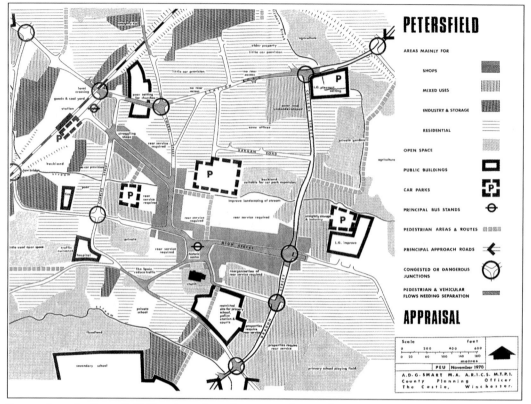

Extract from the Petersfield Planning Policy of 1969. (*Author's Collection*)

Square. Inevitably, the old conflicts between the older residents, wanting to restrict growth, and the modernisers, looking for expansion, came to the fore.

As to the question of pedestrianisation, the HCC and the Urban Council found themselves at loggerheads on the issue: the HCC wanted to eliminate the conflict between vehicles and pedestrians in High Street, Chapel Street and The Square, but the UDC feared that this would result in The Square becoming a bleak expanse of concrete desert, coming to life only on market days.

The UDC wrote a ten-page report of its findings on the Town Map, outlining its opposition to some of the more idealistic (and, in its view, unworkable) plans for the town contained in it. It pressed for a gyratory (one-way) system for traffic at the Old College junction, automatic half-barriers at the Station Road level crossing to minimise delays, the retention for car parking of land behind the north side of the High Street (the HCC had proposed an open space here), and it rejected the HCC idea that the 6 acres of land at Kimber's Field should be used as a recreation ground.

A second draft of the Town Map was published in March 1968 and it was finally adopted and published under the title 'Petersfield Planning Policy' in 1969, with valuable maps added in 1970 giving a (with hindsight) intriguing appraisal of some land uses and an indispensable (but minimal) indication of listed buildings within the townscape.

The Civic Trust Award presented to The Petersfield Society for the removal of overhead cables in The Spain, 1959. (*Author's Collection*)

THE CONSERVATION AREA

Maybe optimism was slowly becoming the order of the day: a plan to enhance 'old' Petersfield by mapping out the Conservation Areas was undertaken by the HCC and followed the lines of the survey developed by The Petersfield Society in the 1950s. Although it acknowledged that many of the town's architectural gems were engulfed in 'a hotch-potch of mediocrity', it did find that The Spain had retained its character unspoiled and that, in The Square on market days, there was a feeling of traditional English rural life.

In 1957, The Petersfield Society had been instrumental in having overhead cables in The Spain removed and was recognised for this improvement by receiving a Civic Trust award. With this map, the county hoped to make a large part of Petersfield the subject of a 'special order' by the Ministry of Housing and Local Government, which would mean that express permission would be needed for even the smallest alterations and additions to houses, gates, fences, walls, and even the colour schemes for the façades of buildings. There would also be special control of advertisements along a section of the A3.

New powers could inject public money into repairs and renovation and both the County and Urban Councils could make grants towards work on properties on the Statutory List. In particular, the Council was concerned about appropriate scale and character, an improvement in shop front design, and provision for the replacement of trees in poor condition.

Two buildings which featured on the Statutory List for preservation but which were tragically demolished, were the seventeenth-century farmhouse named 'Thurston' located in the direct path of the new circulatory system (now Tor Way) and a block of half-timbered houses standing at the junction of Dragon Street and Sussex Road. The latter constituted a serious traffic hazard as they blocked the sightlines for traffic emerging onto the A3 from Sussex Road – and even the preservationists admitted that the junction was so dangerous that demolition was essential. Nevertheless, there had been a terrific battle between the Ministry of Housing and the Ministry of Transport over these cottages. In this particular instance, it was not the developer which had destroyed part of Petersfield's heritage, but the motor car.

ITS RUBBER LTD

This firm celebrated its fiftieth anniversary in 1969. The largest employer in Petersfield at the time, it was now producing over 4,500 different items in rubber. The founder, Mr Arnold Levy, from Sunderland, had gone to Ohio at the turn of the twentieth century to seek his fortune; there, he had learnt a great deal about the rubber and footwear industry and befriended three men whose names were Ingwar, Tufford and Smith (hence ITS) and who were marketing 'concave-convex' rubber heels, a product adopted for the British market (under licence from America) when Mr Levy returned home in 1919. The company expanded to the point where it became a fully independent British firm, with its own electricity and water supply.

During the war, the company, by now renamed the Itshide Rubber Co., created many types of rubber products for the Ministry of Supply, thus fulfilling an important role in the

The Itshide factory, Sandringham Road entrance. (*Petersfield Museum*)

area for 'war-work'. After demobilisation, many men found jobs at the factory. At the request of the War Office, the company began to develop 'Commando'-soled boots for the army, which were an instant success and were widely used in the Korean War and major exploration and climbing expeditions, including the 1953 conquest of Everest.

Moss Levy, Arnold Levy's brother, was chief engineer at ITS. He had nine children and his natural interest in toys led him to ask a local architect, George Gilbert, to design and develop 'Minibrix', a construction toy using self-locking rubber building bricks, thousands of which were exported all over the world. They were a forerunner of Lego, the plastic version of children's building bricks, of the next decade. Another popular line was the 'toys' for dogs – balls and bones, for example, which smelt hideously!

Arnold Levy died in 1955 and, in 1958, Charles Colston Ltd, the washing machine manufacturer, acquired a controlling interest in the firm.

In 1919, when Arnold Levy had first arrived in Petersfield, there was no electricity supply, the company's generators were driven by steam and there were just twelve cars in the town! Fifty years later, ITS Rubber was producing components for Concorde and these were manufactured by injection moulding. In 1973, the company had 370 employees, including many outworkers; however, after a fire at the factory in 1976, which caused £350,000 worth of damage, the company was obliged to buy in ready-mixed rubber in order to continue production.

To mark the company's fiftieth jubilee, it presented the Petersfield Urban Council with a Chairman's chain of office to mark the close ties between ITS and the town. The first person to wear this chain was Ken Oates in September 1969. Ironically, this was the first chain of office for the Chairman of a council which was to have only five more years of life before it was disbanded and the Petersfield Town Council was established. It is the mayoral chain still in use today.

Minibrix. (*Author's Collection*)

Petersfield Town Mayor's badge of office. (*Author's Collection*)

RAGLAN'S SLOW DEMISE

Having put a brave face on the discreet bid by Alliance Property Holdings to gain some control over them in 1968, Raglan found themselves the target of an attempted merger two years later, this time with Greencoat Properties Ltd. The two companies would have combined capital of £2.4 million and assets of over £9 million. The same year, Group Captain Newnham, by now aged 73, was voted out as Chairman of the Trust, a position he had held for twenty years. He and his deputy, Brigadier E.W.C. Flavell, resigned their posts on the board. The new Chairman was James Rowland-Jones, a Poole property tycoon, and his first act was to stave off the merger bid by Greencoat.

Rowland-Jones's appraisal of the situation in Petersfield was that too many sites were lying idle and, after a tour over the town by plane, he came to the conclusion that Raglan had practically turned the centre of the town into a green belt. 'One has to think carefully whether a town wants to be developed before investing in it,' he surmised, 'and from my enquiries so far, Petersfield does not seem to want it.' Inevitably, he was not impressed with the return on the investment Raglan had made in the town, and he continued:

In 1960 when the population of Petersfield was 7,310, it was selected by Group Captain Newnham as a suitable place to inject a large amount of capital. The result in

1970 is that Petersfield and its population of 8,500 has absorbed £750,000 of Raglan's money. I can neither find nor give a financially satisfying reason for what has happened to Raglan in Petersfield, except Group Captain Newnham's woeful lack of knowledge of town planning, building costs and elementary finance.

The merger between Raglan and the Rowland-Jones Construction Co. was agreed at the next shareholders meeting in July 1970, but, by April 1971, they were facing another takeover bid by Alliance and one of the first battles of the new company over the following year was to beat off two further takeover bids by Alliance.

Later that year, the Raglan Property Trust's report for an extraordinary general meeting admitted that Petersfield had been 'a hole in the pocket' for the company. In the meantime, Group Captain Newnham sold his house, 'West Downs', a Queen Anne country residence between Petersfield and Rake, and he departed on holiday to South Africa. He died at his home in Liss in 1974, aged 77.

One outstanding tract of land which Raglan still owned, the site between Swan Street and Sheep Street and including the corner of The Square (now the library), became the subject of debate with the UDC and the Post Office. Raglan was said to be willing to sell, if the price was right. The county was certainly interested in developing the corner site as a public library, but there were doubts about access to the rear of the properties in both streets. In fact, the county took the step of compulsorily purchasing the corner site in 1975 for £60,000 (far less than Raglan was demanding) and spent a further £15,000 to gain rights of access to the rear from Swan Street.

Another site which Raglan had obtained in the early 1960s by demolishing a row of cottages formed part of this area: what became Garden Court was a site bought from Raglan in 1971 by Andersons, a Petworth-based firm of builders, who constructed the block of forty-eight luxury flats we know today. Its outward appearance did not enamour itself to Petersfield residents, who promptly named it 'Colditz'.

The sale of these two sites, then, represented the final chapter in the Raglan story in Petersfield; in the space of barely a decade, the 1960s, the company had remodelled the town as it thought fit. In an almost indiscriminate fashion, Raglan had pursued a policy of piecemeal development, destroying a good proportion of the High Street scene, removing cottages and shops alike, replacing character with potentially profitable, leased premises, many of which subsequently were left empty for want of tenants willing to pay the asking rents. It is no consolation to argue that Petersfield fared better than some other towns in this respect: perhaps it did not bear the scars of the glass-fronted, neon-lit nightmares which befell other towns in the '60s, but the town's heritage had been severely knocked and it would be to future councils, planners and, above all, to local opinion, to ensure that the same sort of degradation did not recur in the remaining decades of the twentieth century. In November 1970, the *Petersfield Post* ran a whole-page article on the town, describing it thus:

Industry is restricted, farming still predominates, the town treads a tightrope between pastoral nonconformity and archaic quaintness. Its rural beauty and agricultural importance may prevent the worst of the 1970s leaving its scar as the true value of open space is realised. Yet, until a new by-pass is built, Petersfield will have great difficulty in deciding how to tackle the problems of the second half of the twentieth century.

The postscript to the Raglan saga was written in 1977, when their Property Trust had to defend a writ against it for unpaid debts. In the previous seven years, it had hived off many of its properties to stave off takeover bids, although it did continue in business despite its fluctuating fortunes (it had incurred losses of £1.5 million in the financial year 1974/5).

HERNE FARM

One distinct advantage of the persisting prevarication over the bypass meant that land for house building was not being released; without an increase in population and a concomitant increase in shopping facilities, the town found itself in a chicken-and-egg situation. At least this may have saved it from another wave of dubious expansion. However, economic growth could not be held back for ever and, once the draft plan had been published and its guidelines followed, there could be new developments in housing. The scene was therefore now set for a population expansion in the early 1970s and hints of it came in 1971 with the first intimations of a massive estate to be built on the Herne Farm site.

The HCC, which had overall authority for planning until 1974 (after which it delegated it to the EHDC), had not yet decided whether to give permission for the development of 78 acres at Herne Farm, which would be Petersfield's largest-ever development. Alan Ray, the UDC Chairman, criticised the apparent inertia in road and school development, slow planning decisions and poor library facilities in the town. The public's views were sought on the Herne Farm scheme, for which the council had received an outline planning application by Glumbo Trading Co. Ltd, a family holding company. This was granted at the beginning of 1972. However, this firm went into liquidation and the land was bought by a new developer, Kebbell Development Ltd; within a year Mr Thomas Kebbell, the head of the family firm, had received planning consent for the whole area, which would eventually contain more than eight hundred houses. Certain conditions attached to the contract drawn up by the HCC, namely that it would be a phased development and governed by strict conditions on, for

Herne Farm estate advertisement, 1970s. (*Author's Collection*)

The first houses on the Herne Farm estate, 1974. (*Petersfield Museum*)

example, landscaping and the incorporation of footpaths into the design. Mr Kebbell subsequently consulted with John Thomas and Frank Ifould (the UDC's surveyor and planning officer respectively) and drew up plans for the first phase of the estate's development programme in Pulens Lane. Initially these were rejected but, after a joint visit to Hertfordshire, the developer, the architects and the councillors all agreed on the style of houses and the overall concept of the estate. Mr Kebbell spoke at a public meeting organised by the Petersfield Society and promised that the first owners would be moving in within nine months. He considered it a privilege to own such a large site where development could take place over a long period of time without pressure; however, in the initial phase, speed of construction was the overriding criterion.

Alongside the housing units, Kebbells envisaged a riverside walk (Tilmore Brook) and recreational facilities. The town's population would eventually be boosted by about 20 per cent on the Herne Farm estate alone. Indeed, the first houses were on sale in the New Year, 1974, and Kebbell expected to complete about 100 houses each year, housing about 2,300 new residents. The major aim of the architects, Meacher, Moyes and Partners, was for a variety of styles of houses and layout at each stage of the building programme, and for mixed designs and rooflines to reproduce a village street atmosphere. The names of the first roads were Butser Walk and Moggs Mead (meaning 'marshy pools' and named after the boggy field which stood there before development).

Unfortunately, the high cost of housing at this time meant that it was virtually impossible for young couples to enter the housing market. In addition, unemployment in the Petersfield area was soaring in the early 1970s and the manager of the employment exchange noted that the growth in population had not been matched by a growth in (industrial) labour. There were vacancies at the ITS and UK Plastics factories, indicating that the most difficult employees to find were unskilled or semi-skilled workers. Prices had also risen with the introduction of decimal coinage in 1971. Despite the generally bleak prospects for young people, there was a 'gold rush' for the new estate by those who could afford the prices, with the result that Petersfield was, not for the first time, becoming a more exclusive (and relatively more elderly) place to live in. With the influx of its new residents, the social balance of the town, hitherto reflecting a sort of Tory-cum-Navy landscape, was slowly to change, simultaneously shifting the political landscape, a factor which was to make itself more evident later in the 1980s.

IN THE SCHOOLS

The 'terrible twins' – the infants' and junior schools in St Peter's Road – were a collection of odd huts and ageing buildings (some more than 130 years old) with outside toilets and cold classrooms which were too small. The proximity of the gasworks to the huts in Hylton Road were an added olfactory distraction. Boys and girls had had separate entrances and playgrounds at the junior-cum-senior school. While secondary education was proceeding apace, the primaries suffered from cash starvation. There were up to 300 children in the infants' school in 1971.

After more than twenty years, the County Secondary School and the junior school both lost their Headteachers, Mr E.C. Young and Miss E.B. Hayes retiring in 1971. Mr Young, who had effected the transition from the old St Peter's Road School to Cranford Road as Head, was a high-profile, charismatic character who exerted a strict sense of discipline over his pupils, who were in awe of him. His school was quite progressive for the era, providing an education in practical subjects such as woodwork and metalwork, cookery, gardening and rural studies, as well as academic subjects, thus matching the different needs of its wide intake. Children who had passed the 11-plus examination went either to Churcher's (boys) or Havant Grammar School (girls) at this time, but those who hadn't been successful, and who often considered themselves to be second-class citizens, were reassured under the good guidance and sense of purpose during Mr Young's tenure.

Miss Hayes had first come to Petersfield County primary school (the present infants' school building) in 1951 when there were 360 pupils and had seen this figure grow to 500 by 1958 when the schools split and the seniors went to Cranford Road, thus relieving the pressure on space in the St Peter's Road premises. A new junior school for Petersfield, to be situated in Love Lane and to accommodate 320 pupils, was planned to be completed by 1974.

Churcher's celebrated the 250th anniversary of its foundation in 1972. After falling into financial difficulties in the 1930s, it had given up its independent status during the Second World War and was now offered assistance by the HCC to become a Voluntary Aided school, the only one under the Hampshire Education Authority. It continued to offer boarding facilities and even had a footbridge built across the main road by the Royal Engineers from Longmoor so that the boarders could reach Mount House (by the entrance to Hoggarth Close) in greater safety. The bridge was named Wilkins Way after their Bursar, Mr A.J. Wilkins, and remained there for almost thirty years. The same year (1972), an appeal for £9,500 for a new multi-purpose teaching block for the expanding school was achieved in nine months.

After much anxiety and deliberation, and just as it was announced in 1972 that the national school leaving age would be raised to 16, Hampshire Education Authority mapped out its plans for the reorganisation of secondary education along comprehensive lines for the Petersfield area: as with the secondary schools in Bordon and Horndean, Petersfield's County Secondary would become an 11–16 non-selective mixed comprehensive school from 1974. In fact, a year later, the Petersfield scheme was revised to an 11–18 comprehensive system based on the County Secondary School. Churcher's, which had run smoothly since the war under the voluntary-aided system of school governance, would be allowed to continue to operate a selective system, but with considerably fewer pupils from the Petersfield area itself. This was eventually to become the main sticking point in deciding its future.

At the early stage of the negotiations, Churcher's College was destined to become a mixed sixth form college as, it was stated, 'there was no real workable alternative'. Churcher's responded that it was unable to accept this decision and the Chairman of Governors, Keith Gammon, stated quite clearly that they wished the school to retain its grammar school status. Cold animosity reigned between the Governors and the county authorities as political principles and historical status came into conflict. As a result of these evidently irreconcilable differences, the county decided to proceed with turning comprehensive without taking account of the wishes of Churcher's. In 1973, another Churcher's governor, Alan Ray, who was also Chairman of the UDC, felt that to remain as a selective boys' school would be against the wishes of the majority of people in the area, and yet there were also genuine doubts about the wisdom of taking on the mantle of a sixth form college for Petersfield, thereby totally changing the ethos of the school. This was to be the beginning of a protracted period of soul-searching by Churcher's, whose natural instinct was probably to go independent (although a minority of governors and staff did express their opposition to this option), but the threat of losing their considerable financial support from the County caused a reconsideration of all the options available. Sadly, it was just at this period that the Headmaster, Mr David Goodfield, died unexpectedly after seven years at the school and it fell to his deputy, Mr Donald Brooks, to take on the battles with the County and eventually steer the College towards independence – which it obtained six years later.

THE 1972 LOCAL GOVERNMENT ACT

For some time, there had been a debate over how the UDC and the RDC might merge, although the local (Conservative) MP Joan Quennell, newly elected with an increased majority at the 1970 election, felt that the resulting area of local political responsibility would be too large. The 1972 Local Government Act brought an end to the speculation with the announcement that there would be a two-tier system of local government from 1974. The new HCC would have ninety-seven members, an average of just less than 1,000 electors per member.

More hot air was expended in the Petersfield area, however, on a mini-conflict over the name and the representational strength of the new District Council which would be set up to cover the Alton and Petersfield areas. The name East Hampshire seemed too unimaginative, while Alton and Petersfield (vying with Petersfield and Alton as the preferred alternative by Petersfield Council!) seemed too long-winded: it was an uneasy marriage. To preserve local pride and the peace, East Hampshire had to be accepted by both parties to the dispute. Unfortunately, there arose a further problem of where to site the new council.

On a basis of one councillor to represent between 1,000 and 1,500 electors, the new council would have forty-two councillors and, to ensure that each councillor would be nearer to his or her electorate, the Home Secretary was requested to grant the retention of the old ward system for dividing the district.

Petersfield UDC wanted the rural and urban districts to have an equal representation with Alton, even though the Alton population was 2,000 higher than that of Petersfield, but this demand was later dropped as a conciliatory gesture. The first Chairman of the new council would be Lt Col Michael Digby, elected in preparation for the changeover in 1974; the majority on the first new council was held by Independents, with twenty seats.

THE COTTAGE HOSPITAL

Petersfield Cottage Hospital celebrated its centenary in 1971. Originally a single-storey twelve-bed hospital built by public subscription, it had expanded to a two-storey building in 1911, thanks mainly to the generosity of Sir Heath and Lady Harrison, relatives of Leonard Cheshire, the founder of Le Court and other Cheshire homes. The hospital had had many additions since its foundation, but still relied greatly on voluntary contributions for its survival.

With the increase in the town's population, it was planned to build a compact new health centre adjacent to the Cottage Hospital which would combine various branches of the health service, including doctors' surgeries and welfare and health clinics (then housed in Love

The old Petersfield Hospital. (*Petersfield Museum*)

Lane). Plans for a new local hospital drawn up in the early 1960s had been shelved on cost grounds but were later revived, and a strip of land was bought from the Church Commissioners which formed part of the vicarage garden (now part of Swan Surgery) with the intention of creating a much larger hospital site in the Charles Street–Swan Street area, which would include The Forge corner. The Revd Canon Ronald Granger said he had known of the plans when he moved to Petersfield thirteen years previously, but believed that the seventy-year-old, three-storey vicarage would probably be retained as an administrative block.

Meanwhile, a consortium of local GPs had recently moved into their new surgery next to the town hall in Heath Road (now the Citizens' Advice Bureau), a practice which they bought into privately. The last remaining member of a long-standing doctor's family in Petersfield, that of Dr Robert Cross, retired from his practice in town. He was the last of three generations of doctors named Dr Robert Cross and it was his grandfather who had lived at Shackleford House in Dragon Street (now Worcester House), the original home of the Worlidge family in the seventeenth century.

PHYSICAL AND SOCIAL CHANGES WITHIN THE TOWN

In 1970, 'the case of the farcical facades' took place, when Barclays Bank in The Square was rebuilt and its neighbour, Forrest Stores, was redeveloped as a supermarket and shopping arcade. What some considered farcical was that the planners insisted that the existing Georgian façades of the stores should be retained, so the first floor of the building was propped up while the ground floor was reconstructed as the supermarket. On the west side of The Square, Southdown buses closed their office 'for reasons of economy' after fifty years in Petersfield.

Barclays Bank (demolished) and Forrest Stores, 1969. (The Petersfield Society)

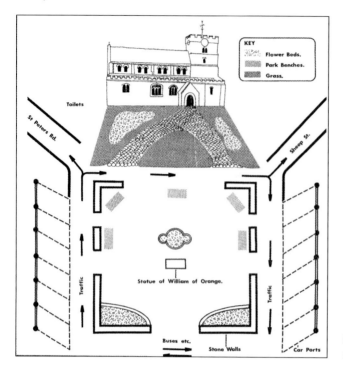

Plan for a redesigned Square, 1970s.
(*Author's Collection*)

The most significant townscape development in the early 1970s was the creation of a
gyratory system of roads to alleviate the A3 traffic bottleneck at the bottom of Ramshill. To
achieve this, part of the old railway embankment close to Love Lane entrance had to be
removed, as had the former Luker's brewery building in College Street, which had stood
derelict since the fire which destroyed it in 1934, and its near neighbour, the Second World
War services' 'Home from Home' canteen, which had also stood empty for many years after
its use as an annexe to the County High School for Girls. The accompanying demolition of a
hundred-year-old house, The Pines, and the farmhouse, Thurston, was probably inevitable.
Tor Way was opened in July 1975. In 1967, College Street had already witnessed the
demolition of the early Victorian British School – the first 'penny school' in Petersfield, when
children paid for their Sunday school lessons – which later became a public hall attached to
the Congregational Church (now The United Reformed Church).

In the past, proposals to change any Petersfield shopping area previously open to traffic
into a pedestrian precinct had led to objections from shopkeepers, claiming they would
suffer loss of trade. However, the experience of pedestrianising Portsmouth's shopping
streets led to the opposite effect; it might therefore be seen as a lack of political boldness
and will on the part of the town council which has prevented such an experiment in
Petersfield. Over the years, various plans for alleviating the traffic problem in the town have
been put forward, not least those schemes which suggest the creation of one-way traffic in
St Peter's Road and Sheep Street, as this 1973 map demonstrated:

The bypass saga continued to exercise the minds and frustrate the patience of many
members of committees and councils. Major General Sir Humphrey Tollemache of Sheet, a
county alderman, complained that he had been pressing for this scheme for about ten years or

Jenny Sandys' sketch for a proposed refurbishment of The Square, 1973. (*Jenny Sandys*)

more. It is worth noting here that the new M3 motorway had been operating since early 1971 and this, together with the modifications carried out in recent years to the A3 both at, and south of, Butser, could well have affected the decision-making by the Ministry of Transport.

A new sports hall was built at the County Secondary School in 1971 and a third storey to the telephone exchange in Charles Street was added in 1972, although part of the old operator service was still functioning from the Post Office in The Square.

The Heath Pond was slowly evolving. From being the marshland of 1741, when the people of Sheet, angered by the drowning of their animals grazing there, threw up a bank around the marsh and created a pond watered by natural springs, it had become the jewel in the crown of Petersfield, providing a natural leisure spot for residents and visitors, and the small island in it was now a regular roosting place for ducks and geese. Sporadically, the Pond would become polluted and, in 1974 for example, dozens of fish died and swans and Canada geese were found to be diseased and deformed. In September 1976, the Pond practically dried up after a long period of drought; the water level had dropped 18 inches since the previous winter to expose a wide expanse of sand, mud and litter, and at the deepest point there was only about 3 feet of water. A major dredging operation had become a necessity but, as with all major political decisions, there was an associated financial commitment and it took another decade before the operation could be afforded.

The Congregational Church celebrated its 250th anniversary in 1972. It had been Petersfield's original Free Church, an Independent Meeting House built by Protestant non-conformists in 1722. Under the auspices of the Petersfield Council of Churches, a housing association was formed to combat the town's growing housing problem. A survey published in the *Petersfield Post* called for a new look for The Square: for traffic to be removed and trees to be planted, for the entrance to St Peter's to be enhanced and for benches to be provided. Readers felt that William's statue and the market should remain, however.

The social and cultural scene faced some setbacks as well as successes. The Drama Festival, founded by John Dowler in 1948 and which had attracted up to about fifteen entries each year, found that it was unable to support itself and was put into cold storage for lack of new talent and a waning interest from the public. A similar degree of apathy attached itself to the relatively new creation of the Petersfield Sports Council and it was disbanded in 1972. The annual carnival attracted as many as forty floats in 1970 and the old trade fair turned itself into a Homes and Hobbies Fair in 1971.

The Petersfield Area Historical Society, which had its beginnings in the WEA local history classes and was created thanks to the enthusiasm of Dorothy and Edward Grainger in 1973, has thrived since its very first meeting. It is a prime example of the valuable contribution made by the town's residents to their own cultural history and which gives Petersfield its particular intellectual substance.

DEPARTURES

The year 1969 marked both the death of Jim Seward (at the age of 91) and the selling off of the last three of the Seward family's steam traction engines from their Victorian workshops in Chapel Street (now Park Road), which were subsequently demolished. The engineering and haulage firm had been founded by Jim's father, Walter Seward, in 1886 and the firm's engines were extensively used for agricultural needs, road building and general transportation. The advent of petrol-engined lorries in the 1920s put paid to the firm which did not adapt to changing times, although Seward engines were still being used for threshing duties on Petersfield farms at that time. Many people remember the four remaining traction engines in the workshop in the 1950s, lovingly polished, oiled and greased by their owner in what was, effectively, a museum of the steam traction age.

The death of newspaper-seller Fred Kimber in March 1970, at the age of 85, brought sadness to the people of the town, some of whom had known him for nearly seventy years as the little man with the big voice. In his peaked cap and greatcoat, winter and summer, he was a real part of old Petersfield and his disappearance from his patch beside The Square Brewery left people thinking that that corner would never be the same again. As a young man he had been Petersfield United's centre forward, but was known in the postwar years mainly as the ubiquitous newspaperman, employing young boys for paper deliveries until the Headmaster of Petersfield School upheld the law which forbade young people under 18 being employed as street traders.

He was a real Petersfield institution, causing more than a touch of apoplexy in local authority bodies with his Tilmore Road scrap merchant's yard and menagerie, where the occasional roar of a lion might greet a passer-by at the dead of night. There were some people who could recount the time when five monkeys escaped from the menagerie, one of which was caught in St Laurence's Church! Fred was the first man in the country to hold a licence for keeping, selling and training performing animals; he used to import them, train them and sell them to road shows or zoos. But it was in The Square that he felt most at home, thriving on the cold weather, his shoulders hunched, tugging at his

The old cricket club pavilion,
destroyed by fire in 1973.
(Author's Collection)

muffler and banging together his mittened hands. Part of old Petersfield died with him that winter.

In 1972, Kathleen Merritt, the conductor of the Musical Festival, stood down after a career lasting fifty years. She continued to involve herself in the musical world of Petersfield by conducting her own 'Kathleen Merritt orchestra'. She was awarded the MBE in the Queen's Birthday Honours in 1952 in recognition of her services to music.

Plus ça change . . .

'Torrential rain in Petersfield put the subway at the station under 2 feet of water.' (October 1966)

'Thousands of dead perch found floating in the Heath Pond. The perch are victims of a killer fish disease which wiped out the Pond's carp population in 1967.' (May 1970)

'There is no reason why Petersfield's long-awaited by-pass cannot go ahead.' (Hampshire Roads and Bridges Committee, 1972)

CHAPTER FIVE

Reorganisation
1974–8

LOCAL GOVERNMENT REORGANISATION

The Petersfield Urban and Rural District Councils met for the last time in March 1974 and four men, with a total of 138 years of service between them, retired: Mr C.F. Underwood, Mr F.E. Ifould, Mr W.A. Voice and Mr N.P. Scott. The Clerk to the RDC, Mr G.H. Walker, also retired and Mr George Bassett resigned two months later, at the age of 78, having served on the UDC since 1953.

The EHDC (East Hampshire District Council) and the PTC (Petersfield Town Council) which replaced the four councils (the UDCs and RDCs of Alton and Petersfield) did not break entirely with the past, because several previous council members and their staffs simply took up positions with the new bodies. In Petersfield, the old UDC and new town council had run in parallel for a while and Alan Ray and Kenneth Hick served on both bodies. Kenneth Hick, who became the first town mayor of the new town council, was in fact Petersfield's first town mayor since 1885, when the town had lost its borough status (and therefore its right to have a mayor) for the first time since 1150. The *Petersfield Post* described the new situation as 'a topsy-turvy world that strips Petersfield of virtually all its independent local government power, and yet gives it back the dignity of mayoralty'. Acknowledging that the new town council was little more than a parish council and that the title of town mayor would have been more appropriate when the more prestigious Urban Council was in power, it hoped that the new role would encompass a good deal of civic ceremonial work as well as the task of chairing the council meetings. The title of town mayor was conferred on the new leader of the town council in honour of the burgesses of Petersfield who had stood up to the Jolliffes (the dominant family in Petersfield politics for two centuries) in the early nineteenth century.

The new EHDC had more spending power, more overall influence and more means of sustaining it than did any of its predecessors. For example, it took on local planning work (hitherto dealt with by the HCC), and had to start conservation work from scratch. The major drawback for electors was that the new body was more impersonal and more remote from them than the old UDC, and it therefore enjoyed less trust than before.

Lt Col Michael Digby became the first Chairman of the new East Hampshire District Council. In fact, he remained an EHDC councillor for nearly twenty-five years and was also an HCC councillor for nine years. The good relations that existed between the town and the new EHDC bore fruit: the town council kept control of the Heath (as the Heath was registered as common land, it belonged to the parish); the first year's activity by the new councils saw them integrating effectively; the EHDC, with responsibility as the new Local

Last meeting of the Urban District Council, 1974, Chairman Alan Ray is in the centre. Committee members: rear table, left to right: J.A. Sedgwick, W.G. Voice (Treasurer), J. Thomas (Engineer and Surveyor), F.E. Ifould (Clerk), G.J. Bassett, A.J. Ray (Chairman), K.A. Hick (Vice-Chairman), R. Stokes; front table, left to right: M.G. Neale, D.J. Ismay, Miss E.M. Whapham, K.A. Oates, Mrs E.V. Bulmer, Major E.R. Durston, Mrs M.J. Nicholas, C.R. Basche. (The Petersfield Society)

Planning Authority, began to increase the public housing stock, despite a difficult prevailing economic climate; finally, local government reorganisation brought with it a new openness – the long overdue reform of the end to council secrecy and the right of admission for press and the public to all council committee meetings. For its part, the town council, although deprived of a good deal of its erstwhile powers, now found itself in the role of a pressure group fighting for local interests and acting as spokesperson for those interests. The first annual Town Meeting took place in 1975, allowing the public to participate in the democratic process; about forty people were present.

In 1976, the election of the first woman town mayor of Petersfield, Elsa Bulmer, set a new precedent; her deputy was Joy Nicholas, completing what the Post described as 'petticoat rule' at the town council. Mrs Bulmer had been Chairman of the new EHDC Housing Committee for the past two years, was a founder member of the Petersfield Housing Association and Citizens' Advice Bureau, sat as a local magistrate and she led the appeal for a minibus for the over-sixties.

It soon became clear that Petersfield's central position in the new district should permit it to suggest the construction of a purpose-built site for the new EHDC and its officers. The old UDC had given up its meeting chamber (the 'Small Hall' on the first floor of the town hall, now the premises of Perkins Slade Ltd) to the EHDC to accommodate its finance department. However, an ambitious plan to build a new Civic Centre on the existing town hall site at a cost of £2 million, which would have replaced the swimming pool and doctors' surgery, was rejected as too expensive. Thus began a battle between Petersfield and Alton to stake their respective claims as the administrative centre for East Hampshire. Temporarily, the EHDC was being housed at the old RDC offices in the Old College building in College Street. Chance played its part here and the problem was suddenly resolved when the EHDC managed to buy the office complex owned by the Lifeguard Assurance Group at Penns Place, to which the company had moved after eleven years in Swan Court.

The Lifeguard offices, including a £500,000 wing which had only been erected for the company a year before and never used, represented a bargain for the new council. Lifeguard had grown rapidly to become one of Petersfield's major employers but were currently going through a difficult financial period; they had closed eleven of their branches in the UK and about two hundred staff were to be made redundant nationwide over a two-year period. The 200 staff employed in the Petersfield headquarters were dispersed between Swan Court and Penns Place, where they owned two two-storey office blocks and a new extension which served as a large clubroom for 300 people. It was this latter room which eventually became the new EHDC Council Chamber when the council moved into their new premises in 1976; the old Lifeguard boardroom became the new committee room. In addition, the EHDC benefited from the luxury touches enjoyed by their predecessors: double-glazing, air-conditioning and carpets. Lifeguard thus found a ready buyer, the EHDC saved itself a good deal of money, and Petersfield beat the competition to become the civic 'capital' of East Hampshire. Although all the EHDC personnel were not able to be accommodated in the new buildings – the housing and health departments and other supervisory staff remained at the Old College site – there was room for about two hundred staff at Penns Place.

One bone of bitter contention, which lasted for half of 1976, was the proposal by the EHDC to sell the town hall back to the PTC, which it had taken over during the local government reorganisation two years previously, for £50,000. The town council already owned the concert hall (now Festival Hall) but not the whole building and, swallowing their pride and bowing to *force majeure*, they attempted to negotiate a deal which permitted them to develop the whole site, including some adjacent land, in the future. This was rejected by the EHDC, however. The following year, the town council took out a loan to purchase the Hall on the EHDC's terms.

NATIONAL POLITICS

There was increased local interest in the parliamentary election of February 1974 when Tim Slack, who had been Headmaster of Bedales for the past eleven years, resigned to pursue a political career as a prospective Liberal candidate. Having won the nomination, he went on to poll over 21,000 votes, 35 per cent of the total votes cast, the best result for the Liberals since before the Second World War and slashing Joan Quennell's majority from over 20,000 to just over 9,000.

Concurrent with the changes in local government, Petersfield's MP, Joan Quennell, resigned later in 1974 after fighting five general elections. Her mother had died shortly before the February elections and she inherited the family's Dangstein estate near Rogate;

she subsequently sold her house in her Hampshire constituency in order to manage it. The Conservative party selected Michael Mates, a forty-year-old Lieutenant Colonel in the Queen's Dragoon Guards, as their parliamentary candidate for that year; in October, there was almost a repeat of the February general election when Mates headed the poll with a majority of nearly 9,000 votes. Tim Slack, again the Liberal candidate, lost a good deal of his erstwhile support and left politics to become Director of Studies at the Wilton Park European Discussion Centre in Sussex.

Michael Mates thus became only the third MP for Petersfield since the war and only the sixth in the twentieth century, all of whom had been Conservatives. At the 1974 general election, the boundaries of the constituency reached as far as Winchester, Eastleigh and the Meon Valley; however, over the more than thirty years of his tenure as MP, Mr Mates' constituency slowly shrank in size geographically as Petersfield and nearby towns increased demographically. The later removal of Portsmouth and Southampton as unitary authorities added to this change in his political base.

As to the future planning of Petersfield – which was subject to central government and even European Union controls – the town came under the policy covered by the Mid-Hants Structure Plan written in the 1970s and eventually published as the Hampshire Structure Plan of the early 1980s. It was fortunate for Petersfield that its development was seen as one of 'restricted growth' at this time, and only three areas were allocated for housing expansion: at Herne Farm and at the Causeway and Ramshill sites, the last two being dependent on the construction of a bypass. Paradoxically, while the continued delay in building the bypass frustrated the vast majority of residents in Petersfield, its absence can, with hindsight, be seen as a positive factor in delaying population growth. As for the Herne Farm estate, the EHDC ensured that its expansion proceeded at a slow rate in order adequately to meet proper infrastructure requirements.

THE PETERSFIELD POST

From being an offshoot of the Hampshire Telegraph, the Petersfield Post was reborn in 1974 as a separate and independent newspaper, thus giving Petersfield its own local paper again. It consisted of sixteen pages, cost 3p, and was published on Thursdays. It had been part of the Hampshire Telegraph series since 1962 and had moved in 1968 to The News Centre in Hilsea where its mother company, Portsmouth and Sunderland Newspapers Ltd, had established its headquarters. The new Post struck a chord with older readers, who saw it as the reincarnation of their favourite Squeaker. By 1976, however, the Post had been completely redesigned and had been transformed from a 16-page broadsheet into a 32-page tabloid, renamed the East Hampshire Post, perhaps envisaging some competition from the Petersfield Herald, part of the Farnham Castle Newspapers group, which started life the same year.

EDUCATIONAL INDECISION

While the majority of parents apparently rejected the establishment of an 11–18 comprehensive school in the Petersfield area, preferring a central sixth-form college to serve both Alton and Petersfield, the new Minister of Education in the Labour government approved the Hampshire comprehensive plans under which Petersfield County Secondary would become an 11–18 school for about 1,000 pupils. Ironically, this scheme had been approved by the previous Conservative Education Minister, Margaret Thatcher.

Meanwhile, Churcher's was still struggling with the obligation forced upon it by the HCC to adhere to a quota system for pupils recruited from a wider area than hitherto. It had to accept just five boys from each of its feeder schools, including Petersfield's own new Herne Junior School, with the majority of its pupils coming from Havant, Waterlooville and Hayling Island. The main regret, of course, was that Churcher's could no longer be considered a 'local' school and this seemingly inequitable (but politically correct) quota system created bad feeling with many Petersfield parents.

By 1977, Churcher's were told that they had only six months left to decide whether to join Hampshire's comprehensive education plans or to become an independent school. There were currently 446 pupils at the school, including 117 boarders. Emanuel School in Wandsworth, which had been evacuated to Churcher's in the war and which was, like Churcher's, a voluntary-aided school, went independent that year, as had most of the direct-grant schools in the country.

Herne Junior School opened its doors in February 1975. Most of its 400 pupils and staff simply transferred from their old school in St Peter's Road, but the new surroundings gave a feeling of space, an educational island with playing fields on one side and Love Lane sports pitches on the other. Originally, the infants' school was to have shared their campus, but the land was sold for housing and access to it through Love Lane was blocked. Inside the new building, the arrangement of classrooms was semi-open plan, with tables and chairs in informal groups, and there were now learning facilities for cooking, craftwork, first aid and music. Keith Williams, its first Headmaster, who was to remain at the school for fifteen years, was quite a visionary and enjoyed a good deal of autonomy. He introduced diagnostic testing, predicting where children would go and providing appropriate work for them to meet their potential; he also began to offer residential school visits (rare at the time). In many ways, Herne Junior was a showcase school for Hampshire, benefiting enormously from its pleasant situation in the middle of a growing housing estate which provided its (relatively affluent) intake.

FACILITIES FOR SPORT

With its increased population, but dearth of sports pitches, Petersfield desperately needed to find space to enlarge its sports and recreational facilities. At Love Lane, the town's only sports ground until the early 1970s, there were only two football pitches, a rugby and a hockey pitch, with nearly a dozen teams wanting to use them. The council had already looked at using part of the school playing fields (then situated at The Avenue) for a bowling green and at developing the Bell Hill recreation ground.

It was at this juncture (in 1974) that the new PTC made one of its most important decisions, one which was to have far-reaching consequences. It was offered a 26-acre site on land forming part of Penns Farm and, thanks to the foresight of Alan Ray, the last Chairman of the old UDC, the PTC was persuaded to buy Penns Farm to use as playing fields for future generations of Petersfield sportsmen. At the same time, the planning authority (HCC) insisted that the PTC also purchase the additional (Heathfield/Barnfield) section of the site which the county had earmarked for a school. When, later, the HCC decided instead to put their new school (Bohunt) in Liphook, this extra land was superfluous and its subsequent sale, in piecemeal plots, became the major source of income for the PTC for years to come.

Town councillors were so encouraged by the potential of the new site at Penns Farm that, with the help of Scouts and Guides, they set about removing stones from the ground themselves in preparation for its use as playing fields. The disadvantages of the site were that it was situated on a flood plain, had poor vehicular access and limited availability of services, which would inevitably lead to high development costs. Despite these, the town council believed it to be an excellent site, especially if an enlargement could be negotiated.

In order to fund the development of this Penns Place site and to build a new sports complex there, the town council planned to sell half of the Love Lane sports ground to Kebbell for housing development. There was an urgency attached to this scheme, because the government's new Community Land Bill would slash the income from the sale by £120,000 in three months' time. After an acrimonious battle with local residents, however, the Love Lane sale plan was dropped. The Penns Place site had originally been designated in the 1969 Petersfield Planning Policy as a site for a new secondary school, but it was now unlikely to be necessary under the educational reorganisation proposals.

Two misfortunes befell the sportsmen of the town in the 1970s: in 1973, the charming old thatched cricket club pavilion on the Heath, which had served the players since 1881, was destroyed by a fire and, in 1976, the Love Lane sports pavilion was lost in a similar fashion. Golfers, however, saw their fortunes rise: they bought extra land from the landowner across Sussex Road to create an extra nine holes for their course. Their membership at this time (1976) was around four hundred, with an active ladies' section.

Perhaps with a view to recouping the expenses involved in the purchase of the town hall itself, the town council decided in 1977 to make a second attempt (the first had been a dismal failure in 1965) to promote professional wrestling events.

Petersfield United Football Club had its most successful season in its history in 1978 when it became Hampshire League Division IV champions; success clearly bred success and the team became Division II champions two seasons later.

Petersfield Rugby Club celebrated its fiftieth anniversary in 1977. It was as a direct result of Churcher's College making rugby its prime winter game that the club was formed (at the College) in 1927. Their first games were played at Bell Hill, with changing facilities at the Volunteer Arms (now on the site of Meon Close). After closure during the Second World War, when players joined the services, the club started up again in 1948 and moved its matches to Love Lane. Their best seasons came in the early 1960s and it was in the 1970s that earnest efforts were started to buy and build a clubhouse of their own at the Penns Place sports grounds. This was realised in 1979 with the opening ceremony of the £15,000 building, conducted by founder member Frank Guy, the first secretary of the club in 1927. In 1958, Jim Hetherington, an ex-Churcher's pupil, became full back for the Cambridge and England rugby teams, an international honour equalled by Tim Rodber, also an Old Churcherian, who won forty-four caps for England between 1992 and 1999.

The *East Hampshire Post* announced the inauguration of a 5-mile cross-country hill run, the 'Great Butser Run', in November 1978. Their sponsorship of the race aimed to encourage physical fitness, promote interest in the new Queen Elizabeth Country Park (opened by the Queen in 1976), and to raise money for the Petersfield Arts Council – which went towards the remodelling of the town hall the following year. In that first year, there were 270 competitors who, despite the pouring rain throughout the event, raised over £1,000. In its second year, the event attracted over 600 runners.

What sealed the destiny of sports teams in Petersfield was the approval of the EHDC, in 1977, for a town council scheme to develop 40 acres of land at Penns Farm adjacent to the EHDC offices as a 'mini' sports centre. It was especially likely to please squash players, whose club was disbanded in 1975 because of a lack of facilities in the town. Thanks to the existence of the highly successful open-air swimming pool in the town, the suggestion that an indoor pool be built at Penns Place received less support. Nevertheless, the combined encouragement of the two councils represented a welcome fillip for the town's sportsmen.

Angling, a sport which suffered from a low profile in the local press, nevertheless catered for a sizeable number of adherents in the 1970s and, after some conflict with officialdom in 1974, the Petersfield Angling Club finally won a 21-year licence from the town council in 1979 to fish the Pond. The need to control angling was evident (until 1979, anyone could come to the Heath Pond to fish) and proper controls were established that year to ensure the Pond was kept in good order; rubbish was cleared away, erosion of the banks was monitored (railway sleepers had been placed around the edge in 1964) and bailiffs were appointed to keep an eye on the general environment of the Pond. It is now recognised by everyone that, without these environmental safeguards, the Pond would die. The Heath, including the Pond, is owned by a Heath charity set up in the 1850s by the Bonham Carter family, for which the town councillors act as trustees.

CELEBRATIONS

The Petersfield Carnival, as with carnivals in other rural towns, had its origins in the agricultural events which marked the passing of the seasons or special days of national celebration; farm carts and wagons laden with produce and accompanied by agricultural workers would slowly wind their way around the town. Photographs of the procession through Petersfield on the occasion of Queen Victoria's Diamond Jubilee in 1897 and moving film of the Horse Show at the Causeway in 1912 still exist, for example.

However, the Petersfield Carnival proper as we know (or knew) it was not born until 1923, when the local Guide troop was the governing body, assisted by several local retailers. Each business took part, following the theme of the year for its float, and there were various competitions held in front of the town hall. The high point for Petersfield's postwar carnivals had been the 1950s, when real enthusiasm and a conscious desire to cast off the wartime deprivations held sway; the 1960s carnivals tended to be fundraising events (for the swimming pool, for example) but enthusiasm got the better of financial wisdom and in 1965 the loss incurred by the carnival committee took several years to pay off and the next carnival did not take place until 1970.

Since 1958, the Petersfield tradition of Carnival had always been upheld by the efforts of the Standing Joint Committee, consisting of volunteers from the Round Table, the Rotary

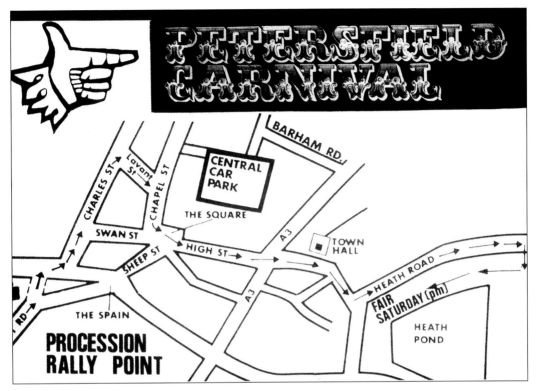

Petersfield Carnival route. (*Author's Collection*)

Club and the Chamber of Trade. After 1974, they were joined by the Lions, the SEB Social Club and the Community Association. The most laudable achievement of this group had been the construction of the open-air swimming pool in 1962 and their joint efforts led to a new pride in the town. The carnival had usually lasted for anything up to a week in the past, but it was reduced to two days in 1975, despite there having been fifty floats taking part the previous year.

In 1977, celebrations to mark the Queen's Silver Jubilee replaced the carnival: after thanksgiving services on the Sunday, there were arts events throughout the following week, financed by local concerns, and an ox-roast in The Square attended by about seven hundred people. The theme chosen for Petersfield by the town mayor, Elsa Bulmer, to encourage home-town pride in the jubilee, was 'Clean for the Queen'; this was aimed at improving the appearance of the town generally and a plaque was awarded for the best-maintained street in Petersfield, won by Madeline Road.

The most ambitious project during the jubilee year was the proposal to carve a giant white horse on the chalk slopes of Butser Hill. Originally suggested by Prince Michael of Kent, the horse (measuring 358 feet from nose to tail) received the backing of naturalists and preservationists and it would not cost the ratepayers a penny; however, after a survey in the press revealed strong public opposition to it on the grounds that it was in an area of special scientific interest, i.e. the Queen Elizabeth Country Park, no planning application was made for the proposal and the idea was dropped.

The human cannonball at the carnival, 1960s. (*Author's Collection*)

Whitman Laboratories. (*Author's Collection*)

ESTÉE LAUDER

This company came to Petersfield in 1970 and moved, with nearly 400 staff, into Frenchman's Road in 1972. In 1977, they sought to enlarge their operation by submitting proposals to replace their premises with a large new plant nearby. Whitman Laboratories Ltd, part of the Estée Lauder International group, wanted to consolidate and expand the multi-million-pound export trade of Petersfield's biggest commercial employer by building on 14 acres of farmland to the west of Princes Road. This would provide 100 more jobs in the general field of cosmetics manufacturing – perfume, make-ups and treatments. The dilemma for the EHDC was that the site lay outside the area of the Town Plan and, if they were to insist on following the Plan's precepts, then job opportunities would be lost. Both the EHDC and the HCC approved the plan.

RETAIL OUTLETS

Not for the first time, nor the last, there was a fear in the early 1970s of the shopping centre of Petersfield being eroded by the trend towards non-retail outlets such as estate agents' and building societies' offices, banks and restaurants. The Chamber of Trade took the matter up with the town council, who in turn referred it to the district council, with the aim of producing a fixed policy concerning the use of shop premises in the town. The counter-argument was that the town had many more shops than twenty years previously and, in any case, with the growth in tourism and holidays in Britain, Petersfield stood to gain from its situation and its guest facilities. Thus, for the first time, people were asking questions about this change of role for Petersfield: should there be a municipally funded caravan and camping site in the area, or a publicity officer appointed in the town, or perhaps a visitor information bureau? These kinds of questions revealed a shift of emphasis in the thinking of the town towards its visitors and of its function as a tourist centre, serving a new type of clientele.

One particular retail transformation during this period is worthy of mention: that of the Folly Market. The name Folly is centuries old and probably refers to a building situated in the present lane, which formed part of the old London–Portsmouth road through the yard of the old White Hart Inn (now Winton House). The Folly Market building was built at the beginning of the twentieth century by Mr Victor Britnell, a solicitor, who had a yearning to run his own bicycle business. His wife considered 'trade' to be beneath her dignity, so he opened the cycle shop while she was away on holiday! From being a shop, the building became Petersfield's first garage – his own two cars were the first in Petersfield – and the old showrooms and workshops are today's new Folly Market, which opened for business after its conversion in 1978. Mr Britnell opened a second garage in Station Road and continued in business until the end of the Second World War; that site is now occupied by Britnell House. Mr Britnell's first garage was sold to Wadham Stringer as a car showroom.

The June 1978 opening of the Folly Market was a great success: with its complex of twenty-six new shops, it represented the most important commercial development in the town for many years. That same summer, work began on creating the Folly Wine Bar on the first floor of the building fronting onto Dragon Street.

PUBLIC AND PRIVATE HOUSING

Several housing schemes were started in this period in both the public and private sectors: 36 new detached houses were being offered for sale (from £19,950) at Kimbers; 100 new council houses and flats, the first to be built in Petersfield for several years, were constructed at Rival Moor Road; 50 private-sector, low-cost houses were constructed between Durford Road and Rival Moor Road; 46 houses were built in Stoneham Park in 1978; and 80 new houses were built south of Cranford Road.

For the elderly, Siward House was opened in 1976; work started on another home for the elderly (Silverlands) at Ramshill, half of which would be allocated to a disabled children's centre; and a further development for the elderly was completed by the Hampshire Voluntary Housing Society in 1978 with its two-storey 24-flat block named Burgesmede, built in the garden of Winton House, probably on the site of a bowling green once used by Samuel Pepys in the seventeenth century.

The Petersfield Housing Association (PHA) was formed in 1973 at the instigation of the Petersfield and District Council of Churches, who felt that young married couples without children, who stood no chance of being housed by the local authority, had a particular need for housing in the Petersfield area. However, the adoption of Provident Society rules meant that the PHA had to serve all those in need of accommodation and many elderly people were thus also able to take advantage of the scheme. For its first ten years, the PHA was run by a group of volunteers but later, in the complex world of housing development and management, it took on a professional team of part- and full-time workers. By the mid-1990s, their stock had grown to over one hundred dwellings. Fundraising went hand in hand with property purchase and development: between 1976 and 1978, for example, the PHA made several flats available in Station Road and, in the summer of 1978, Elsa Bulmer, a PHA founder member, raised over £1,000 by swimming the Solent from Ryde to Southsea! It was a dramatic event for, in the icy waters (even for August), she was in danger of losing consciousness and had to be pulled out with just 100 yards separating her from the shore.

Because of uncertainties in the housing market, Raglan found itself having to make drastic reductions in its development programme; nevertheless, it still held onto the corner site in The Square which it proposed to develop with a 3½ storey block in red brick, with mansard roofs and an arcade at ground-floor level. This was a plan of which the EHDC approved, as it did of a terrace of seven houses in Sheep Street which Raglan had planned. This site had lain derelict for seventeen years and, with two new construction sites on its doorstep, the Royal Oak closed. In fact, it remained closed for eighteen months; interestingly, workmen refurbishing it for the new owner uncovered part of the old front façade advertising 'Amey's Petersfield Ales, Stout and Porter'. Before the pub was taken over by Whitbread's, the Royal Oak had been an outlet for beers from Amey's 'Borough Brewery' (at the junction of Frenchman's Road and Swan Street) and the postwar owner had been Brakspeare's Brewery, Mr Brakspeare being a nephew of Miss Amey. It was taken over by Bob Scholes, vice-president of the Petersfield Rugby Club, as a free house and trade more than doubled in the three years he owned it. Subsequently, it was sold to ex-Fleet Street journalist Charles Govey and his wife.

The second phase of Kebbell's development of the Herne Farm estate began in 1977, with the construction of forty-four more homes (flats and houses), the social centre, and the planting of 100 trees between Moggs Mead and Herne Junior School. What is interesting here is that the EHDC planners were invited by Mr Kebbell to visit his development at Carpenders Park in Hertfordshire – his first development to include a social centre – and it was this which decided their choice of buildings for Petersfield. They subsequently drew up a diagrammatic brief for him, showing the position of the old Midhurst branch line, the access points for the estate, the places where trees should be retained, the rough outline of roads and emphasising the need to provide rear parking for the residents of Moggs Mead. For his part, Mr Kebbell took trouble over the construction of decent brick walls, landscaping, footpaths and the creation of occasional cul-de-sacs for safety and privacy. The social centre provided a shop and a meeting hall available to the general public and a swimming pool and squash courts exclusive to Herne Farm residents, for which they paid an annual management charge. Inevitably, architectural styles and public tastes developed over the course of construction of the Herne Farm estate and individual buyers demanded different criteria; this in turn led to clear differences between the houses of the early 1970s (at the Pulens Lane end of Moggs Mead) and the 1980s and 1990s (towards Tor Way), where greater density has also been a consideration. In walking the length of Moggs Mead, one can witness the development of thirty years of such changes.

DEPARTURES

Solly and Horace Filer, who had inherited the Savoy cinema in Swan Street from their father, sold it to Spedeworth International in 1978. Solly had also been a UDC councillor for many years and was its Chairman from 1947 until 1950. In this role, he had been the town's representative who presented food gifts from the New Zealand government to the elderly residents of Petersfield in 1949. The brothers left Petersfield after the cinema sale, but retained some of their business and property interests in the town.

Lady Mary Thistleton-Smith, the longest serving JP at Petersfield Magistrates' Court, sat on the bench for the last time in 1975, after thirty years of service. She had also been for ten years Chairman of Petersfield Juvenile Court, the aspect of her work which she described as the most important.

One of Petersfield's best-known and most respected citizens, Keith Gammon, died in 1976. He had served for forty-three years on the old UDC, had been a governor of Churcher's College since 1935, and was awarded the MBE in 1955. The Gammon family has lived in Petersfield for more than three hundred years; Keith Gammon managed Herne Farm after the First World War, subsequently ran a builders' merchants at Haslemere, then became the ARP controller for the UDC and RDC and was Chairman of the Food Committee during the Second World War, as well as being a Hampshire county councillor. He was also a founder member of the town's rugby club and fought strongly for thirty years for a swimming pool to be built in the town. Among the tributes paid to him, it was his public service which was uppermost in people's memories and Elsa Bulmer said of him: 'His distinguished record of service on the council is unequalled in living memory and surely is unlikely ever to be repeated.'

Another of Petersfield's most notable figures, Colonel Sir Reginald Dorman-Smith, the town's former MP and a Governor of Burma, died in March 1977. After an early career in the Indian Army, he returned to farm at Frensham, became a magistrate and was first elected to parliament in 1935. He was knighted for his services to agriculture, was Minister of Agriculture in the Chamberlain government, then rejoined the army for a while before returning to Hampshire as High Sheriff of the county.

In January 1978, Alan Hinxman, who had been well known in farming circles in the Petersfield area for the past fifty years, died at the age of 81. He was associated with the Portsmouth firm of Hall, Pain and Foster for many years, a business which he acquired in 1969 and ran until his retirement in 1975. He was an expert in agricultural valuations, but was best known as an auctioneer at the annual Heath Fair and the cattle market in The Square.

Plus ça change . . .

'Petersfield's chronic shortage of rented accommodation at the cheap end of the market is a major problem for young singles and couples who cannot afford to buy their own home.' (January 1974)

'There is only one answer to the difficulties facing the open-air swimming pool at Petersfield – put a roof on it.' (August 1974)

'It is now more than 20 months since the reorganisation of local government took place, yet many people are still in the dark so far as which council does what.' (December 1975)

CHAPTER SIX

Consolidation
1979–84

CONTROLLING GROWTH

Already in 1977, the EHDC had taken their battle to stop the overdevelopment of land – 226 houses on the 17-acre 'Josephi' site to the south of Durford Road – to the High Court. They were challenging the 1976 decision by the Secretary of State for the Environment to allow the scheme, and claiming that the development constituted interference in the natural beauty of the area and that the overall population forecast for the area was wrong. The case judge quashed the previous decision and sent it back to the Department of the Environment.

The tenth anniversary of the publication of the Town Map in 1969, the realisation that the population of the town had reached approximately ten thousand, and a certain, inevitable end-of-decade consciousness spurred the Petersfield Society into calling a public meeting 'to help formulate guidelines for controlling the area's development in the 1980s'. It was an attempt to promote awareness of, and to contribute to, the forthcoming Mid-Hampshire Structure Plan which was due to be published in April 1979. Expressions of concern were raised over the growth rate of Petersfield, which was 'faster than was practicable'. Commercially, there was a desire to see some growth to ensure the vitality of the town, but not to yield to domination by any individual company; an appeal was made for the enhancement of the visual appearance of the town by minimising street 'clutter' such as the number of lamp posts, signs and cables; finally, there was a move to fight the trend away from small, local schools which gave villages life, in favour of larger, more impersonal establishments.

Petersfield town councillors, in the meantime, were maintaining their opinion that they did not want to see more non-retail businesses in the town centre; they reiterated a policy established in 1974 which precluded retail premises being changed to non-retail premises in Lavant Street and Chapel Street and the north-west of The Square.

The council's contribution to the debate over a new District Plan showed that they were adamant that the town population should not increase to beyond 14,000 by the mid-1990s; that all non-conforming industrial sites should be moved to the outskirts of the town; that offices should be sited only at first-floor levels and above in the town centre; that superstores should be kept outside a 15- to 20-mile radius; and that housing priority must be given to houses for first-time buyers and for the elderly.

Contrary to the national scene, where strikes were rife at the end of the 1970s, the Petersfield area was experiencing flourishing growth in commerce and industry, notably with the thriving new Folly Market and the recent expansion of Whitman Laboratories. Nevertheless, the EHDC still maintained a close control of such developments: it did not, for example, offer the kinds of positive financial resources to new firms wishing to come into the area that 'development areas' or new towns could provide, nor did it have available a ready supply of industrial sites, nor again did it employ an industrial development officer. Since most of the sites earmarked for residential development in Petersfield belonged to the EHDC, it behoved the council to make the correct decisions at the correct times: the onus was on them to ensure the proper, reasonable and sensitive development of the town. It still is.

The evidence from such reports and public meetings is that, by the start of the new decade, Petersfield was beginning to control its own destiny. More open debate, a greater breadth of thinking and more comprehensive planning policies were being determined which were to eliminate the haphazard nature of development that had too frequently prevailed hitherto. The developments of the 1970s had reflected some confidence on the part of the town, rather than the depression provoked by those of the 1960s: most of the building which had taken place had been an economic process of filling in – the 800 homes of Herne Farm, for example, lying between two prongs of established built-up areas, or the Penns Place offices of the EHDC and the adjacent sports grounds slotted between Heath Road East and the River Rother on the eastern edge of the town. Roads, too, featured in this phase of the town's development: new dual carriageways on the A3 (shortening the travelling time between Petersfield and Portsmouth), the Tor Way one-way system, and the Moggs Mead spine road linking Pulens Lane to the town centre. Petersfield was changing

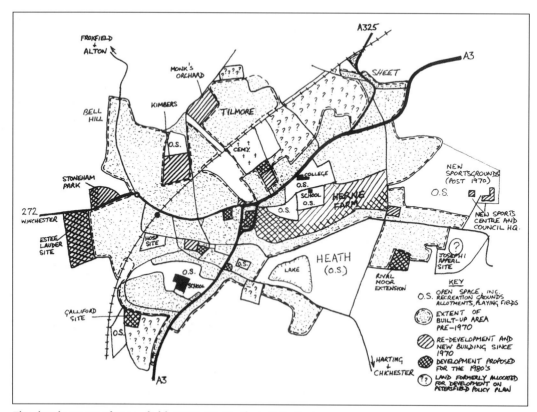

The development of Petersfield, 1960–90. (*Author's Collection*)

surely, but slowly, and much of the development was producing a tidier appearance and better use of the land available. A rough map showing the development of the town since 1970 was published in the press in November 1979.

THE BYPASS ROUTES REVEALED

Many years of waiting came to an end when finally, in 1979, the draft proposed routes for the bypass were published by the Department of Transport: the four route options (temporarily named the red, green, blue and orange routes) for the A3 upgrade from the south of Petersfield to the north of Liphook were outlined in brochures that were delivered to 10,000 households in the area. As far as Petersfield was concerned, three of the routes would pass to the north of the town and only one (orange) to the south.

Since the debate over the respective merits and the ensuing controversies of each of the routes had only just begun, it would be premature to comment on the plans at this stage. Frustration, however, was at its peak and town mayor, Nickey Edwards, had already hit out at the forty-five years of indecision over the bypass which was resulting in poor planning of the future growth of the town. Suffice it to say that, with hindsight, it was still to take more than a decade for all such problems to be resolved and for the bypass to be constructed. In 1979, no one foresaw this degree of difficulty – and that was perhaps just as well, although Petersfield was undoubtedly suffering from a phantom planning blight affecting hundreds of properties.

A meeting organised by The Petersfield Society brought over four hundred people to the town hall; a 'No Bypass' group was formed; all the four routes were opposed by local farmers, despite the compensation which would be offered to them; the town council preferred the red route, with modifications; and Bedales found itself within a hundred yards of three of the routes (in response, they performed an original musical satire 'Bypass the parcel' in the summer of 1980). To add to the colour confusion, an alternative 'brown' route (the orange route with modifications) was proposed by an active pressure group representing the interests of Steep residents and there was even talk of a tunnel to link Dragon Street to the Causeway to provide a rapid exit from the town to the new motorway.

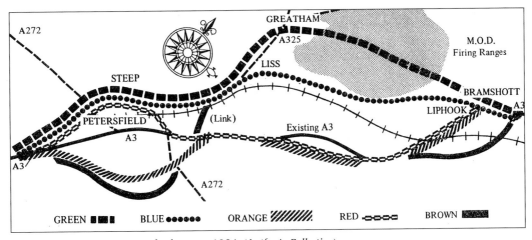

Proposed alternative routes for bypass, 1984. (*Author's Collection*)

Michael Mates asked for a meeting with the Minister of Transport, stating: 'I wish to assure myself that there is no undue delay in the process leading up to the announcement of the proposed route. I am conscious that the dragging out of this matter is causing concern.'

INDEPENDENCE FOR CHURCHER'S COLLEGE

Another political hot potato was rescued from the educational oven in 1979: after six years of debate and dispute, the wind of change brought by outside politics had had the predictable effect of driving Churcher's College out of the state system. In fact, Churcher's had always been independent of the state, its existence being the result of the endowment of Richard Churcher from 1730 until 1877 when it was housed at the Old College, then from 1881 until 1896, thanks to the bequest of land at Ramshill left by William Nicholson, MP. In 1896 it received its first grant from Hampshire County Council. Under the 1944 Education Act, it became a voluntary-aided school (although not until 1951) until the 1976 Education Act made it impossible for the College to survive within the comprehensive system, and it opted for independence once again.

Events justified the new policy: applications for entry to the school exceeded the places available, an Independence Appeal succeeded in raising £150,000 in less than ten weeks for bursaries to fund boys from poorer backgrounds and to expand the school's facilities, and the appeal acted as a catalyst, increasing the size of the Old Churcherians Club to some 500 past pupils. The Headmaster, Donald Brooks, said that the school's size would remain at about 450 boys, but that the governors might consider a scheme to allow entry to girls in the sixth form. This in fact occurred in September 1980, when five girls entered the school. Boarding education at the school would continue. The following year, Churcher's celebrated its 250th anniversary. Its new-found independence had ended many years of wrangling with, among others, the parents of Petersfield children who now knew where they stood; regrettably, the decision had also driven a wedge between the richer and the poorer of those parents.

Shortly after going independent, Churcher's purchased the Blue Anchor pub (which stood on a site now occupied by the entrance to Hoggarth Close) from its owners, Ind Coope brewery, for school and residential purposes.

THE TOWN HALL AND FESTIVAL HALL

The town hall was originally the brainchild of the Petersfield Musical Festival organisers, Dr Harry Roberts and Mr A.J.C. Mackarness, who, in the mid-1930s, sought new premises for future festivals, the early festivals having taken place at the old Drill Hall (now The Maltings) in Dragon Street. On 6 October 1935, Taro Fair day, Lord Mottistone, then Lord Lieutenant of Hampshire, opened the building which immediately became the principal arts centre of Petersfield. Built very swiftly by local labour from 1934 to 1935, to a design by the architects Seely and Paget, it was planned to incorporate both the concert hall and new offices for the UDC as an integral unit. It had been intended simply as a utility hall and no one envisaged the enormous number of uses to which it was subsequently put.

A £30,000 scheme for redeveloping the town hall in five phases to better satisfy the needs of local arts groups was first proposed in 1976 by the Petersfield Arts Council and designed by local architect Kenneth Claxton. The plan was generally considered as imaginative as it was bold, simple and inexpensive. It consisted of linking the present three halls, i.e. the 'large town hall', the old 'small hall' and a recently built hall on the east side of the building to replace the small hall (which had become EHDC finance department offices); creating a new front entrance foyer and also a new rear entrance to the building; installing new, retractable tiered seating for easier storage; fitting a suspended ceiling to improve the acoustics; creating better bar and catering facilities and improving the stage, technical and dressing room areas. A public appeal subsequently launched by the Petersfield Arts Council brought in donations, covenants and financial support from both local and outside arts and educational groups. The extensive works were financed jointly by the HCC, the EHDC and the PTC as well as by the multifarious efforts of the Petersfield Arts Council.

By 1979, the remodelled building was completed and the redesigned section was renamed the Festival Hall. Some of the original character of the old building was preserved by fitting 1930s-style lights.

THE COUNCIL'S PLANS THWARTED

Another large, and particularly contentious, building project which was planned in 1979 was an extension to the Penns Place (EHDC council) offices. Michael Mates said he had had more correspondence about it than on any other matter since his election five years before; the town council also opposed the spending of an alleged £1 million on the extension, and the defunct Ratepayers' Association was reconstituted with the specific intention of blocking it. One of the aims of the scheme was to centralise the Old College departments at Penns Place. In September, the council's own planners rejected the plan on the grounds of poor road access at Durford Road; however, the council performed a volte-face in November and, by one vote, reversed their decision to allow the extension to proceed. This, however, might have put plans for completing a new sports centre at Penns Place in jeopardy. One year later, all four plans for the extension to Penns Place were rejected, but not before £61,000 of ratepayers' money had been spent on a preliminary study for the project. The construction of the second phase of the sports complex at Penns Place (the sports hall and social area) began in December 1980.

It was at about this time that confidential discussions were taking place between the EHDC and 'two or three' developers regarding the building of a supermarket on council-owned land in the town centre. Ron Moores, the Chief Executive, revealed to a puzzled Policy and Resources Committee that the potential clients wished to remain anonymous. Shortly afterwards, £6,000 was spent by the EHDC on commissioning a survey of shopping habits in the town, part of the preparation for the new District Plan (published in 1982).

The beleaguered EHDC, intent on pursuing a favourable press coverage, seized the opportunity to display its new coat of arms, granted by the College of Arms that year (1979): the 'Armorial Bearings of the East Hampshire District Council' bore, among other symbols, a natterjack toad, in reference to the animal's breeding ground in the district.

DEVELOPERS AND RESTORERS

The Petersfield Society inaugurated a new annual award in 1980, aimed at rewarding those who contributed most to improving the environment of the town: this was The President's

The Petersfield Society's President's Owl award.
(*Author's Collection*)

Owl, a wooden sculpture by George Taylor of the Edward Barnsley Workshop. The Society had principally concerned itself with the preservation of established architectural heritage, but it now sought publicly to recognise anyone who had improved or restored the environment with carefully balanced development, be this in the field of design (such as Burgesmede) or refurbishment (such as the Folly Market) or a general tidying-up campaign (such as the area in front of St Peter's). The Society continued to remain constantly vigilant over any development within the town and, although it did not always succeed in persuading councils to rethink their policies on what it felt to be heritage sites, it often provoked sufficient public concern to save a building. An example of failure was 35 Lavant Street, where, despite objections from the PTC and The Petersfield Society (who claimed the three-storey building would visually overpower the neighbouring Victorian buildings), the EHDC agreed to the demolition of one of the last private houses in the street to make way for offices for a firm of accountants. An example of success was 35 College Street, where a campaign gained the support of two local societies and two former town mayors of Petersfield. This is a part Tudor and part seventeenth-century building which was owned by Wadham Stringer, the car dealers, who wanted to replace it with a car showroom and offices. To the campaigners' and the town's relief, the company failed in its bid. Wadham Stringer had already demolished another old building in College Street in the 1950s – a mid-nineteenth-century building used as a grain store during the Crimean War, which subsequently became a cheese factory, then a corn and seed store.

Six years after the construction of the Herne Farm estate had started, there was a common assumption that it had become a rather elitist development, with house prices high and the residents almost exclusively owner-occupiers from well-paid professions. Two hundred homes (houses, bungalows and flats) had been completed on the estate in the first six years of its existence and Kebbell planned about a further five hundred in the next six years. However, one aspect of life on the estate which made it unique in Petersfield was its resident-operated management company, which was responsible for the running of the estate's social and leisure activities. It was this that sometimes gave rise to the impression that Herne was operating as a community within a community, although its influence was widely disputed by those who chose to find their friends, entertainments and interests in the town as a whole.

THE PAKISTAN–PETERSFIELD CONNECTION

A remarkable story turned up in the press in November 1980 about one of Britain's most ambitious cannabis smuggling rings which, totally undetected, had been bringing drugs into the country from Pakistan and using Petersfield as its UK headquarters!

Two container lorries with cannabis worth at least £6 million had been transported into the old bakery building in Station Road (on the site of Gloucester Court) from where the drugs had been distributed across Britain. The police investigating the case discovered that the bakery had been leased from the Co-op in 1977, whereupon the new tenant began bricking up the windows and making a good deal of noise – cutting up the containers, it later transpired. The gang working on this were filling bins with chunks of heavy metal which were then transported to a scrapyard at Bordon.

Further investigation showed that the container parts, recovered by chance from the scrap dealer – who had saved them to repair old containers – had imprints on them which indicated that many oblong alloy boxes had been transported in them. Back at Petersfield rubbish tip, some of these boxes were found and information from the Drugs Squad proved that the cannabis on the Pakistan route came wrapped in tinfoil, was packed in alloy boxes and then hidden in containers.

The final link in the chain was found when a tiny sliver of golden tinfoil used to wrap the cannabis was discovered inside the Petersfield bakery's oven. By that time the lease of the bakery had expired, the building been vacated, and the gang had moved on to new premises in Fareham.

PLANNING FOR THE 1980S

If 1979 had been a controversial year – with the publication of the A3 bypass routes, the row over the Penns Place extension and the secretive hint at a new supermarket in the town centre – 1980, 1981 and 1982 were to be no less contentious, with the continuing debate over supermarket plans, the development of the Fairley Court site (now Grenehurst Way), the demolition of the Amey architectural folly in Swan Street and its replacement by new industrial units, and the publication of the Petersfield Area Local Plan.

The four-acre site in the middle of the new circulatory traffic system between Tor Way and College Street had been derelict for about ten years since the demolition there of Fairley Court, a large house used as a café in its final years. Owned by the district council and earmarked for housing, the ground next to the George Bailey Garden Centre was to become the subject of a public inquiry because of Department of Transport concerns about access to this major development (more than eighty houses and flats were proposed) alongside the A3. Part of the land was also owned by the United Reformed Church and a private home named Grenehurst.

The Swan Street folly, one of the first buildings ever constructed using poured concrete, was an eight-bedroom mansion constructed in 1896 by brewery owner Mr Thomas Amey, who, since experiencing a fire at his farm in Stroud, had such an obsessive fear of fire that he insisted on a totally non-inflammable home. The walls, floor and roof were all of concrete, but this in itself was sufficient to create incurable problems of condensation and, as the roof cracked, water had penetrated into the

Amey's Brewery labels. (*Author's Collection*)

interior. Mr Amey's daughter Elizabeth had remained in the house, which stood opposite the family brewery adjacent to the railway line, until just before the war. In its heyday, the Amey's 'Borough Brewery' owned a chain of public houses throughout the south, including one next to Waterloo station. After the war, the business was run as a limited company until it was taken over by Whitbread's in 1952. After its eventual closure, the building served as a store and depot for the Petersfield Rural Council and then the EHDC until 1981 when it was demolished. The brewery building itself still stands (now Littlejohn Bathrooms).

The refurbishment of Winton House as Petersfield Voluntary Centre culminated in 1980 after a campaign lasting three years, led by the Chairman of their committee, Joyce Perry. It ceased its activity as the town library in 1981 and the new library in The Square opened in June that year. In its twentieth-century history, Winton House, originally the home of a YWCA (Young Women's Christian Association) centre for arts and social events for young women, had been a temporary home for many other organisations: a doctor's surgery, a hostel for servicewomen and Land Army girls, a canteen for firewatchers and ARP wardens in WWII, a preparatory school, a rehearsal centre for the Winton Players (hence their name) and, for the past thirty-three years, the library. Now it was to become the permanent home for the Voluntary Centre, with nine flats and bedsits upstairs for the Petersfield Housing Association, the smaller of the two housing associations in Petersfield and catering for needy individuals or groups of local people. The larger association, Drum Housing, with about four thousand property units at its disposal, is the body to which all the district housing was transferred.

Part of the site of the new library building in The Square had also had an interesting history: originally part of the George Inn, it was converted into two private houses in the early nineteenth century when trade declined; later, these two premises became a Temperance Coffee Tavern and, on the corner, George Money's second-hand furniture and hardware shop. Finally, before Raglan demolished both premises in 1971, they had served as the Southdown bus office and a card shop. The 14,000 volumes housed in the former Winton House Library were shifted by the staff to the new building, where a further 19,000 volumes awaited them. The new library was a stunning building of clear architectural merit and the architects, Nick Bourne and Mike Morris, were presented with The President's Owl by The Petersfield Society.

The new library, 1986. (*Petersfield Library*)

'PETERSFIELD – THE FUTURE'

By far the most comprehensive and detailed document concerning the next decade was the review published by the Petersfield Society in May 1981 entitled 'Petersfield – the Future'. This 28-page document, coordinated and drafted by Christopher Napier, had taken three years of study and consultation to produce: it covered sections on planning, strategy, housing, industry, commerce, employment, the local countryside and villages. Recognising that 'Our town is at a critical point in its development, having moved beyond being merely a self-contained market town, serving an agricultural area, into a more urban stage', it was a vision of Petersfield as its residents wanted it to be; its publication was timed to appear before the EHDC issued its Draft Plan for Petersfield early in 1982. It supported the Government-approved strategy for the area, which was summed up as 'restraint', and believed that Petersfield people wanted to keep the town relatively small, with housing growth restricted to local needs and large-scale industry and commerce to be limited.

It proposed a one-way traffic system for the town, but rejected wide-scale pedestrianisation. It saw The Square as an important social centre, with an 'apron' area linked with the church entrance, and public houses and cafés keeping the town centre alive in the evenings. The review called for all developments to be assessed on 'visual amenity' guidelines, saying that the Heath should be kept relatively natural and that new buildings should rescue what it termed 'areas of outrage' – such as the telephone exchange in Charles Street. It called on housing associations to provide more houses for letting and more community facilities in the town hall area of town. It supported the brown route for the bypass.

The review was intended to help the public brief the planners and, encouraging the fullest participation from Petersfield people in putting their views across, it urged everyone to seize the moment to look at the future of the town – at a time when its character was rapidly changing from a small market town to that of a larger conurbation. As a review aimed at stimulating public debate, and therefore participation in the planning process, it was probably the best such document ever produced concerning Petersfield: Mr A.S. Postle, the Chairman of the EHDC Planning Committee, called it a 'superb document' and the Chief Planning Officer, Alan Billenness, complimented the Society on the presentation of the review, as it had avoided a conflict in the public mind over what was comment and what was plan or policy.

THE HANBURY CHARTER

A 1599 Latin manuscript on vellum, the Royal Letters Patent granting Thomas Hanbury of Buriton the rights of the 'lord of the manor' over the 'borough of Petersfeilde' (sic) and signed by Elizabeth I, was bought at Sotheby's in 1981 for £993 by the Petersfield Area Historical Society after a race against time. The society's initiative in buying the letters – after hearing about the auction less than two weeks before the sale through David Allen, the subeditor of the *East Hampshire Post* – won praise from Town Mayor David Lancaster. Donations from over a hundred individuals and many local societies covered the cost of the

PETERSFIELD
THE FUTURE

A REVIEW BY
THE PETERSFIELD SOCIETY

'Petersfield – the future', the Petersfield Society's 1981 document. (*Author's Collection*)

manuscript, which was officially presented to the town by Mary Ray, Chairman of the Historical Society. The scroll was cleaned and restored by Roger Powell, and an oak casket carved to house it by Oscar Dawson, both of the Edward Barnsley Workshop in Froxfield. It was then deposited at the Hampshire Record Office in Winchester.

THE PETERSFIELD AREA LOCAL PLAN (1982)

The changing face of Petersfield and its surrounding villages over the next ten years was the subject of this plan, covering aspects of construction, employment, housing, shopping, health, transport and open spaces.

Its most controversial suggestion for the town was allowing the rebuilding of the southern side of The Square, in front of St Peter's Church. It also declared Petersfield to be the main centre for jobs and proposed about 10 acres of land for warehousing and factories north of the Bedford Road industrial estate, to be served by a new link road.

The plan stated that housing growth should be slowed to 1,750 new homes to meet local needs and it proposed the release of land in Buckingham Road and Cranford Road. It suggested an overnight lorry park at Moggs Mead (a compulsory purchase order on this site was later rescinded) and a new car park at the Station Road coal depot.

All in all, the plan sought to protect the countryside, prevent unnecessary development and resist losing agricultural land; this naturally elicited some favourable comments from the Petersfield Society, who welcomed its general policy of restraint and its emphasis on conservation, with the involvement of voluntary organisations in this field. In comparison with The Petersfield Society's review of the previous year, however, the earlier document was far better presented and much more thoughtful. One critic categorically stated: 'Petersfield must not let its future be settled by officials from the backwoods – the Petersfield Plan is the business of Petersfield people. Why can't the district council let well alone?'

At the public inquiry into the Plan held one year later, which lasted a whole week and heard 118 representations on 30 contentious issues, the district council were accused of acting out of profit motives rather than for planning reasons. Among others, there were objections to the suggestions in the plan on parking, to the siting of the Whitman Laboratories, and to a proposed roundabout next to the Jolly Sailor public house (to slow traffic passing near to the new Galliford's Maple Down estate). Public opinion won a victory to save The Avenue playing fields as a recreation ground: once earmarked for a new infants' school, the site was now found to be surplus to requirements (Herne Junior School having opened in 1975, releasing part of the St Peter's Road site) and the HCC withdrew its demands on the space. It was a prime example of several organisations in the town working together, pressurising the town and district councils and seeking redress for what was deemed to be inappropriate and ignorant planning by higher authorities. Lessons in democratic power and public accountability had been learnt.

THE PETERSFIELD HERITAGE TRUST

A cursory glance at the local press in the early 1980s reveals the extent of the changes afflicting Petersfield at that time: from a vague statement by the owner of the Savoy cinema that its future 'depended on its audiences', via references to the closure of four hospitals in

East Hampshire (including two in Petersfield), to the imminent sale by auction of the 70-acre Causeway Farm site, all exemplified the changing face of the town and countryside around. But something subtle had changed in the outlook of Petersfield's inhabitants: fully aware of the devastation of the 1960s and mindful of the need to preserve the historic environment of the town and countryside, coupled with the recent successes of pressure groups in rejecting proposals emanating from outside bodies, people's awareness of their power over change was increasing. The *Petersfield Post* spoke of 'a more positive attitude [developing] in the past decade which attempts to save buildings of note by taking the more enlightened and flexible approach commercially for their refurbishment and re-use'.

To these ends, a Petersfield Heritage Trust was being established along the lines of other Civic Trusts – the political and financial climate now being more favourable towards such trusts. Within Hampshire, for instance, the most successful local trust had occurred at Romsey, where a considerable number of buildings, mainly cottages, had been refurbished since its formation in 1974. A trust could act in conjunction with a local authority to acquire grants for environmental improvements to individual buildings, some of which may be problematic because of their location, and some simply more humble buildings, such as cottages forming part of the general environmental backcloth, in need of attention. Two

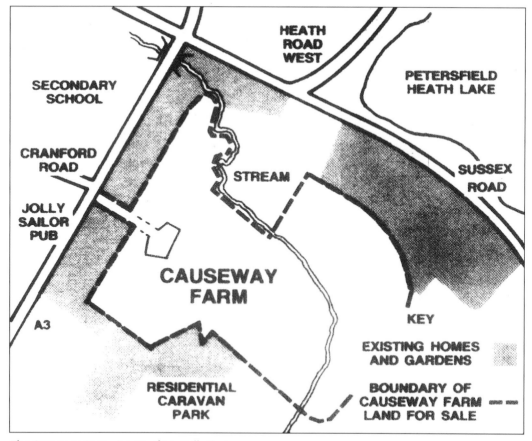

The Causeway Farm site. (*Author's Collection*)

buildings came under the first of these categories: The Grange, which was the last remaining part of the Jolliffe family's Petersfield House (now The Grange surgery) and the Council School in St Peter's Road; in the second category was 36 College Street and a row of cottages in Sussex Road (the Golden Ball cottages there had already been demolished).

The sale of Causeway Farm in 1983 following the death of farmer Mr E.G. Coombes started a new controversy: although the land was not included in the current Petersfield District Plan, its situation on the outskirts of the town led the agents to believe that 'there was a considerable amount of hope that it would fall ripe for residential or industrial development' in the future.

The proposed new community hospital in Petersfield, to replace the Petersfield Cottage Hospital (essentially for minor injuries) and Heathside (geriatric) Hospital, the Grange maternity hospital at Liss and the King George VI geriatric hospital at Liphook, would cost about £5 million and provide about 130 beds (a figure later amended).

POPULAR PASTIMES

Two events probably stand out in the local collective memory. In June 1981 Prince Charles married Lady Diana Spencer, on the occasion of which a beacon was lit on top of Butser Hill and hundreds of people gathered in Petersfield Square to celebrate.

The second, the following January, eliciting less awe, perhaps, but no less visual admiration, had been the streak by Erica Roe, a 24-year-old employee of Frank Westwood's Petersfield Bookshop, who performed her topless act at Twickenham rugby ground after asking her employer for the day off 'because of an eye infection'. For the deception, Mr Westwood was inclined to sack Erica, but he gallantly relented later after his shop was besieged by the press and TV crews who swarmed around Petersfield the following Monday morning. Despite the instant fame that this brought her – interviews, offers of work, contracts from girlie magazines, (fully clothed) photoshoots at a fashion studio and the like – the novelty wore off after a year. She had been known in Petersfield since her arrival four years previously, working at the Folly Bar and The Harrow, at Steep, but her job in the picture-framing department at Petersfield Bookshop was overtaken by the sickening pursuit of the media, the business world, and not a few encounters with some grotesque types whose unwelcome overtures drove her back to her work in a Petersfield shop. With her younger sister, Jennie, she opened a clothes boutique, 'Erica's', in the Folly Market in 1983 (once frequented by Princess Caroline of Monaco, it was rumoured), but this did not bring financial success and she planned to make another move into promoting sportswear.

THE LOCAL ECONOMY

The government's optimistic noises regarding the economy in this period were not entirely shared by Petersfield's traders, though Petersfield had not suffered the harshness of the recent recession which had blighted the business world in the later 1970s. Less dependency on industry meant fewer redundancies – an advantage for the predominantly small-scale firms which operated in Petersfield. The town's own Job Centre opened in 1979 and the Tourist Information Centre in 1983.

The town, in common with East Hampshire generally, was still shifting away from its old agricultural focus towards an industrial one, and the EHDC estimated that, since the mid-1970s, the amount of land in the district dedicated to industry had virtually doubled. In Petersfield, examples of such growth were to be found in the Bedford Road estate, the former Amey brewery site (providing seven new units) and the new Whitman Laboratories plant. The new District Plan would, if implemented, add a further 10 acres to this latter area on the edge of the town. At the other side of town, HLM Engineering, established in 1967 on a site opposite Churcher's College, was booming; it produced tools for injection moulding components for the motor industry.

The Chamber of Trade and its 100 members, under the chairmanship of Michael Pickett, had a certain influence through their participation on the Standing Joint Committee which represented various charitable organisations in the town (the Lions, Rotary and Round Table). Jointly, they organised the carnival and, in 1982, provided the funds for six 'Welcome to Petersfield' signs on all the main entrances to the town.

By contrast, Lavant Street was undergoing one of its periodic downturns: four shops were closing and London House (now Petersfield Photographic) remained unused, because the owners had been refused planning consent to open as a betting shop. The licensee of the 100-year-old Railway Hotel public house (on the site of Lavant Court) was given a month's warning of a change of tenancy; Whitbread's, the owners, denied that the site was earmarked for redevelopment following closure. Four months later, it closed and was demolished in 1985. The antique shop at the corner of Charles Street and Station Road became the 'One Stop' convenience store (now Tesco Express) in 1984. Even Chapel Street was not immune from the poor economic climate and there were a few empty and boarded-up shops there too.

Three Petersfield pubs underwent changes in the early 1980s: the Bell Inn (now Foggy's) in St Peter's Road stood empty for a year before being bought and transformed into a row of four shops. The Good Intent was passing through difficult times. It had had three changes of owner in the past two years and was in the hands of the receivers; however, it did continue to trade throughout this time. After nearly three hundred years of history, the Red Lion closed as a hotel in 1983 and was refurbished by Whitbread Beefeater as a restaurant and bar only: this became an instant success. The old tap bars in Heath Road ('The Tap'), once an alehouse in its own right with its own cellar, where Taro Fair horse dealers used to clinch their deals (and get drunk and brawl), became the new kitchens. During the war, the larger bars at the front used to be full of Canadian and American soldiers, while upstairs in the first-floor ballroom, youngsters would hold dances and private parties.

POLITICAL CHANGES

In May 1981, Major Hugh Rose, a Conservative, who had been a county councillor representing Petersfield since 1968 and was Chairman of the County Planning and Transportation Committee, was surprisingly defeated by the Liberal, Ken Bulmer, who gained one of the seven Liberal seats on the new county council in only his second election contest. It was a considerable achievement for Ken, whose wife Elsa was a district councillor and a former town mayor of Petersfield. He was to remain on the HCC for twelve years and was made an honorary alderman when he retired.

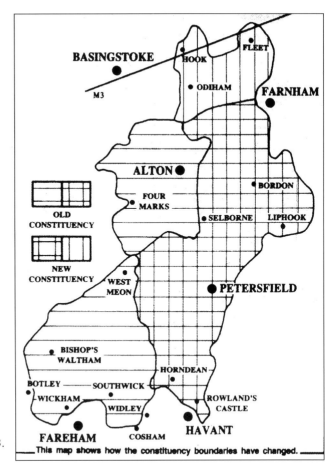

Constituency boundary changes, 1983.
(*Author's Collection*)

Changes were afoot, too, in the general elections two years later, when the Petersfield constituency saw its boundary change for the first time in 400 years. It would also be appropriate here to mention the old Borough of Petersfield, which, in the Representation of the People Reform Bill of 1832, was seen as one of the worst 'rotten boroughs', where the seat could simply be bought by the highest bidder. In living memory, the constituency had always been considered one of the safest Tory seats in the country; indeed, in 150 years, there had been only three Liberal MPs (1832–7; 1866–74; and 1880–5) and the last of these had crossed the floor of the House to join the Tory benches.

Michael Mates's majority increased dramatically to over 22,000 votes in the 1979 elections (which brought Margaret Thatcher to power as Prime Minister). Now, however, the electorate in the new 'East Hampshire' constituency was to be vastly different, with 30,000 voters in the Fleet to Odiham belt replacing those in the Alton, Meon Valley and Bishop's Waltham areas. In size, the new area had an electorate of approximately 80,000 – considerably above the national average electoral quota – over an area 25 per cent larger than the Isle of Wight. In the ensuing general election, Michael Mates had a majority of more than 18,000, confirming the domination of the Conservative party in this largely prosperous, professional, house- and car-owning, low-unemployment constituency.

YOUTH ISSUES

Neil Slatter grew up in Petersfield in the 1960s and 1970s and, after a motorcycle accident had put him in a wheelchair as a teenager, he began to devote his time to improving the lot of the town's teenage population. When, at the age of 25, he heard the story of three Petersfield teenagers trying to commit suicide for a variety of reasons, he decided he wanted to represent the views of their generation. He organised monthly meetings for the 14 to 19 age group at the Voluntary Centre, visited all the secondary schools to promote his idea, called for a café for young people and set up a youth forum for the exchange of ideas. Meanwhile, Petersfield Youth Club was running discos which were attended by about one hundred young people from Petersfield Secondary school alone, and organising outings and visits, but, at the same time, was being denied any form of support from the community such as that afforded to the elderly: voluntary help, finance and organisational management.

A £14,000 youth wing at the Petersfield School (now the site of The Studio @ TPS) was said to be underused because teenagers did not like returning to their school in the evenings.

This *cri de coeur* was clearly heard in some quarters and the town council decided to give the town's newly formed BMX club some land at Love Lane to build a track. Although resented by Petersfield Football Club, who lost some of their practice pitch in the process, they eventually had to agree to give up the land for a one-year trial period. Kebbell Development were also opposed, on the grounds that the presence of the BMX track would deter prospective buyers of houses on the Herne Farm estate. Despite these objections, the PTC gave its permission for the land to be used for five years and the track was opened by the town mayor, Beryl Jones, in 1984.

There had not been any call for job opportunities at this time, merely for recreational facilities; indeed, the area managers of the government's Youth Training Scheme claimed that there were plenty of jobs available for nearly every school leaver in East Hampshire. In fact, in Petersfield specifically, there had recently been a drop in the number of school leavers.

FACELIFTS

A plan to landscape the Heath, which involved felling some trees, removing scrub, culling the Canada geese and dredging the Pond, was proposed in the mid-1980s. In addition, a safety surface was laid around the children's play area, banks were reinforced, paths were resurfaced with hoggin (a combination of gravel and sand) and the Pond was shored up with railway sleepers.

In the town during the same period, all the main roads in the centre of the town were resurfaced and pavements and kerbstones renewed, the favoured material for the work being mellow York stone aggregate, with reconstituted stone (resembling granite) for the kerbs. The cost of repaving The Square was to be £60,000 and represented the EHDC's main contribution to the 1984 Festival: the place was to use 'mock cobbles' and limit the parking of vehicles to short-term stays only.

Petersfield courthouse also underwent a facelift, with an improved, but smaller courtroom, a new waiting room, a holding room for prisoners and better facilities for interviewing. After many years lying derelict, the old 1930s gasholder in Hylton Road (on the site of the present FitzRoy Centre) was demolished, removing a considerable eyesore on the Petersfield townscape.

A call for the market to be rid of its 'tattiness' was made by the Chairman of the Petersfield Chamber of Trade, Adrian Organ. He suggested that the market be run by a management company, that, if necessary, it should be held on only one day in the week to raise the quality, and that traders' vans and cars be moved from The Square to make more room for stalls. He also called for the pedestrianisation of streets in the central area on market days. Sir Hugh Casson, President of the Royal Society, became the patron of a new trust which hoped, by public subscription, to revitalise The Square. The trust was a by-product of the preparations for the town's 1984 Festival, instigated by The Petersfield Society, which planned to celebrate various anniversaries that year, principally that of the town itself (i.e. the 800th anniversary of the oldest record of the Charter recognising the foundation of Petersfield in 1184), but also those of the Scouts (75 years), and the EHDC and PTC (10 years each).

In 1980–1, the Community Centre completed a considerable expansion of its Ramshill site: it added a new exhibition hall, kitchen, entrance hall and general office and enlarged its reception area and committee room. It was, and still is, an ideal centre for its work: centrally placed, sufficiently large for its needs, and with space for car parking off the main road. For over forty years this Centre has represented a microcosm of Petersfield society, reflecting what the town traditionally stands for: an enormous voluntary effort by teams of people dedicated to providing facilities for the numerous clubs and societies of the town. The Community Centre, a registered charity, is financially self-supporting and has continually been able to improve and expand its facilities.

THE SCOUT AND GUIDE MOVEMENTS

The 1st Petersfield Scouts, one of the oldest troops in the country, had flourished under Charles Dickins's direction and many people still remember the waste paper collections during and after the war, the regular camps held in north Wales, the firing range at the back of the (Heath Road) Scout hut, the mulberry tree in the garden of Mr Dickins's house, Clare Cross in the High Street (now part of Dolphin Court), and even scrubbing Mr Dickins's front doorstep!

Like the Scouts, the Petersfield Cub Scout history goes back to the earliest days of the national movement in 1914, and 'Charlie' Dickins served as Cubmaster from its inception until his death in 1962.

There were two companies of Guides and two of Brownies in Petersfield, who met in St Peter's Hall and the Infants' School Hall respectively. Scouts and Guides – which, together with Sunday School, had played a much larger part in children's lives in the earlier postwar years – have a long and interesting history in Petersfield. In pre-war days, the Guides met in their hut in the garden of Winton House, where Burgesmede now stands; it was Alan Ray, Chairman of the UDC at the time, who oversaw the planning of the new Guide hut in 1976, for which the enormous sum of £33,000 was raised, behind Weston House in Borough Road.

DEPARTURES

Within the space of two years, Petersfield lost three of its outstanding musical talents: Thomas Warden Lane, Alan Lunt and Kathleen Merritt.

Thomas Warden Lane, who died in 1983, had been senior history master at Churcher's College and had played a leading role in the musical life of Petersfield for some fifty years. He was the organist and choirmaster at St Peter's Church for more than thirty years, the conductor of the Petersfield Choral Society and Petersfield Operatic Society, and was closely associated with the Petersfield Musical Festival as conductor and committee member, becoming its President when Sir Adrian Boult died. It was thanks to the close integration of schoolteacher-musicians like Warden Lane into the life of the local community in general that the Musical Festival has been such a unifying factor in Petersfield society. Churcher's contribution to music in the 1950s had been particularly strong, with the Headmaster, Mr G.T. Schofield, directing Gilbert and Sullivan operettas and the Deputy Head, Mr Cottle, and his wife also participating in orchestral concerts.

Alan Lunt died in 1984: he had also played a major role in Petersfield's musical history. By profession a solicitor, he had also been an organ scholar at Oxford and a Major in the Territorial Army. As Chairman of the Petersfield Musical Festival, he developed it from being a competitive event involving small local choirs into the wider week-long celebration we know today. Competitions between ladies' choirs did continue after those for mixed choirs had ceased, but in general choral singing has become less popular at the Festival over the years.

Music, Petersfield and Kathleen Merritt were also synonymous. A local Old Bedalian and a graduate of the Royal College of Music, Miss Merritt first attended the Musical Festival in 1908 at the age of 7 and became its President in 1984. She founded her own orchestra just before the war and played in the Orchestral Hour concerts on the BBC. After the war, she formed the Southern String Orchestra (she herself was a violinist) which became the Southern Orchestra Concert Society, one of the largest promoters of first-class music in the south of England. She was also instrumental in supporting the building of the town (now Festival) hall and was awarded the MBE for her services to music in 1972. She died in 1985.

Petersfield lost its Elim Pentecostal church in 1985; formed in the 1930s, it had become part of the nationwide evangelical movement, offering a centre for Bible study, Sunday school and prayer meetings in a room above Arnold's the opticians in the High Street. Vic Walker had been its founder in Petersfield and its honorary Pastor after the war. The church moved to new premises in Hylton Road in 1964. However, building maintenance proved to be too costly and the church was closed and the property sold in 1985.

Plus ça change . . .

'Grin and bear it – that was the philosophical approach from some Petersfield commuters to British Rail's mammoth 20% New Year fares increase.' (November 1979)

'The banks of the stream running through the central car park are covered with small litter.' (March 1980)

'A new 50-room hotel may be built in Petersfield.' (November 1988)

CHAPTER SEVEN

Reinvigoration
1985–9

A NEW ERA

There is no doubt as to the importance of 1985 in the recent history of Petersfield: the closure of the Savoy cinema, the transformation of the somewhat Dickensian Itshide factory site into a housing estate; the intense debate over the arrival of a super-market in the Central car park; the opening of the bypass public enquiry, the deaths of Flora Twort and Kathleen Merritt; the imminent demolition of the Railway Hotel; the green light for the new community hospital and the new-look Square all captured the attention and the imagination of residents as they watched the town develop on all fronts, industrial and commercial on the one hand, social and cultural on the other.

The late 1980s was therefore a period of intense development within the town: it also witnessed the redesigning of the Festival Hall entrance, the dredging of the Heath Pond, the provision of a BMX track, the new youth centre in Hylton Road, the launch of a 'Pride in Petersfield' campaign, the opening of the new Avenue pavilion and Churcher's College becoming co-educational.

Reporting all these changes was a new-style *Petersfield Post*: in 1987, it exchanged its *East Hampshire Post* masthead for the simpler *Petersfield Post*, which separated from the *Bordon Post* later that year. Its weekly circulation figures of 27,000 represented a 10 per cent increase on those of 1986.

THE SAVOY CLOSES

Silent films had first been shown in the town at the Electric Theatre (now the site of the Nationwide Building Society) before the 1920s; then, in 1921, local businessman Hyman Filer, originally a tailor, accepted the building as payment by a customer for a cloth debt. Fourteen years after acquiring it, he partly demolished the premises and then extended it along Swan Street, where it became the Savoy, built around the structure of the old 395-seat Electric Theatre. Hyman Filer's sons, Solly (or Sol) and Horace became associated with the business of running the Filer cinema circuit (the South Downs Cinema Co.), which included cinemas in Bordon and Littlehampton.

Before the war, people flocked from miles around by horse or bicycle, especially on market days, to go to the cinema, and local buses waited until the end of the shows to take people home. The films were often planned to finish by 9.55 p.m., to allow cinema-goers to get to the pubs before closing time! George Bailey's fruit shop opposite the cinema (now Lunn Poly) sold peanuts and bananas to the children to eat during the films. During the war,

The Savoy cinema, 2006. (*Author's Collection*)

the Savoy helped in the war effort, boosting morale by showing uplifting films of heroic Allied troops and their Hollywood counterparts. In fact, the cinema was only shut in the first fortnight of the war, when cinemas were ordered to be closed for fear of bombing raids. American soldiers from the area would frequent the cinema, and Brenda Heath remembers them throwing chocolate down to the 'one-and-nines' in the stalls!

In the postwar period, the cinema was very popular, with its stalls and circle seating, three changes of programmes every week, and Saturday morning pictures for children, for 3*d*. But the atmosphere was often thick with cigarette smoke and the auditorium was becoming seedier as the 1960s and 1970s progressed. Gradually, Petersfield people began to prefer to go to the larger cinemas in Guildford or Portsmouth.

The warning signs over the future of the Savoy were probably there in 1984, when, in April of that year, plans were announced for the 700-seat Savoy cinema (now Vertigo nightclub) to present live shows the following autumn: the town's potentially biggest live entertainment centre aimed to provide bingo (which it was already offering once a week), pop groups, cabaret and media stars in addition to its customary programme of films, in an attempt to reverse the dwindling number of patrons it was experiencing.

The Savoy was due to celebrate its fiftieth anniversary as a cinema the following year. Unfortunately, the plans never materialised and the cinema had to close in January 1985 after the manager's announcement that audience figures had dropped unexpectedly fast the previous year. In fact the Savoy's owners, Spedeworth International (renowned for their stock car interests), had already closed East Hampshire's only other cinemas at Bordon and Alton. The new video age was blamed for the decline in cinema-going just as television had hit the film industry in the 1950s. Two cinema workers who found themselves redundant were the cashier, Jo Collis, who had worked at the cinema since it opened in 1935, and the projectionist, Peter King, who had been there since early in the war.

Perhaps the saddest aspect of the closure was the sale of items from the Savoy: the lots included rare period photographs of Marilyn Monroe, Betty Grable, Audrey Hepburn, Lauren Bacall, Rosemary Clooney, George Cole, together with a commissionaire's uniform, gold velvet curtains and the technical equipment and interior furniture of the cinema. Many of the relics went to the new 'Victorian Inn' opening in Portsmouth.

As the lights went down for the last time at the cinema, it was perhaps appropriately optimistic that the final film was *Ghostbusters*. The television age heralded the demise of cinemas throughout the country, although the art of cinema continued to thrive, as does all fashion in art, in waves.

The Savoy was sold for more than £250,000, making it Petersfield's most expensive redevelopment site, working out at £2½ million per acre. The identity of the buyer remained a mystery, but it was clear that a property developer saw in the building's central position the possibility of its conversion into shops. However, these plans, including the suggestion that the new supermarket could be housed there, were thwarted by the EHDC, and the Savoy remained shut for two years until another developer bought it, with the intention of converting it into a cinema and leisure complex. In fact, it was to remain closed for a further six years, when it was bought by yet another development company, the Portsmouth-based Tanfern Ltd, whose laudable aim was to retain the building for community use as a separate cinema on a newly constructed first floor and a social-cum-entertainment centre on the ground floor, perhaps housing a youth club, snooker hall, gymnasium or social club. Again, this project was never to be realised.

THE ITSHIDE FACTORY

As with the Savoy, so with ITS: the writing was on the wall in 1984, when, after several lean years of business and with the buildings becoming ever tattier, plans for converting the whole – or even half – of the factory area into housing were announced. Naturally, the outcry to save the 600 jobs at stake was heard above that of the profits tumbling into the firm's accounts, with the proposed construction of up to 127 houses on the 6-acre site. To assuage the irate workforce, promises were made about shifting the factory to the Bedford Road estate and, by January 1985, Colstons had sold the whole Sandringham Road site to a developer.

Plans for the new Bedford Road site were suddenly scrapped that August, however, as the costs were said to be too high; meanwhile, the discussion over the new homes on the old site found the developer, Dominion Homes, embroiled in the wider planning implications of Petersfield losing a lucrative industrial site. A government inspector was finally brought in to resolve the issue, but ITS Rubber then announced that, after failing to find satisfactory new premises in the town, it was pulling out of Petersfield altogether and moving to Corsham in Wiltshire.

THE ENHANCEMENT OF THE SQUARE AND TOWN CENTRE

The whole debate on the possible enhancement of The Square went back a long time – the Petersfield Society had first proposed improvements in 1974 – but the issue of car parking (and the dilemma of whether to build a central multi-storey car park) had all too frequently dominated the discussions and led to stalemate between the interested parties. The latest proposals, which included a reduction in the number of car parking spaces from 74 to just 14 was opposed by the PTC, the Chamber of Trade, the Petersfield Society and the Parochial Church Council, with the result that the PTC attempted a takeover bid for The Square in 1985. It was a similar situation to that of the town hall offices, where what was properly the town's domain should revert to town council jurisdiction. Not only that, but it was the town, and not the district, which had been granted the market charter 800 years previously, as former town mayor, David Lancaster, pointed out.

The approval of plans for re-paving The Square with sandy-coloured, radiating cobbles in the centre, included such details as a dark herringbone tile pattern on the surrounding roads, new lamp standards incorporating floodlights for the statue, and bollards and trees deliberately positioned to create a boundary and obviate the necessity for enclosing the area. After decades of wrangling over the presence of cars on The Square, vehicles were finally banned when the refurbishing works were begun in March 1986 and completed that summer.

Foresight and expectation ran concurrently with the imminent arrival of the bypass and various aspects of this phenomenon made themselves felt around 1990. Apart from the improvements to The Square, various other enhancements to the town centre were proposed or effected during this period to capitalise on the expected reduction in town centre traffic, Petersfield's permanent *bête noire*. The possibility was raised of the pedestrianisation of the town centre; a major new survey listed Petersfield with five other towns in England which would be 'rehabilitated' following the completion of a bypass; and a £150,000 development project for St Peter's Church envisaged repairs to the roof, the purchase of a new organ and changes to the altar and chancel. Transport Minister Malcolm Rifkind said of bypasses that they could achieve great environmental benefit for towns: opportunities could include the introduction of traffic calming measures, improved provision for pedestrians and cyclists, and landscaping and environmental enhancements.

THE BYPASS (continued)

The public inquiry – held in both Petersfield Festival Hall and in Rake Village Hall – into the new 12-mile A3 bypass for Petersfield and Liphook, which was to last nearly four months, ended half a century of waiting.

The idea of a bypass had first been mooted in about 1936: the Headmistress of the Girls' High School had pronounced in a school assembly that year that she didn't think anything would happen immediately, but that it might occur by the time the second form were grandmothers – and how right she was! The area around Petersfield was classified as a 'reserved route' in 1955; in the late seventies coordinated pressure began to build up on the Ministry of Transport when a former local government officer (Bill Voice) and a local councillor (Col. Michael Digby) initiated a thirty-strong non-political pressure group with a petition signed by more than 2,300 people, about half of the adult population of Petersfield. Other pressure groups were formed in the villages affected by the routes, many linking together under the umbrella of a Joint Action Committee which put forward its own 'brown' route. Supporters and detractors had prepared their attacks as well as their defences, with one group's advantages triggering threats to another group's, and a No Bypass Society contesting everybody. The alternative – tunnelling under Petersfield instead of building the bypass! – would cost £97 million, it was estimated. One thing was certain: the inquiry would be a marathon.

By 1986, the rumour was that the 'green' route was to be chosen, but a last-minute delay occurred when the Ministry of Defence insisted that the firing range at Longmoor be resited. The final focus was on two of the proposed routes but it was the brown route which had probably always been likely to be the main contender and, after a relatively fair and friendly inquiry, with excellent contributions to the debate by local representatives (the Ministry of Transport dismissing their own consultants as superfluous as a result!), the final go-ahead was awaited.

THE SUPERMARKET CONFLICT

The debate over the bypass had evidently generated a rare passion for public affairs and, when the next public meeting was called in November 1985, this time to discuss the proposed supermarket on the Central car park site, about three hundred people arrived to hear the proceedings in the small Petersfield Town Council Chamber, thus causing an uproar, and police were called to keep order. The meeting was postponed and took place in the Festival Hall a fortnight later, when more than four hundred people attended. A town councillor, complaining that the issue was being discussed as a confidential item by the EHDC Policy and Resources Committee, called for a referendum on the subject.

Rumours of a new supermarket on the Central car park had resurfaced at the end of 1984: the EHDC had set up a working party to discuss the idea, following many approaches for such a scheme from prospective supermarket chains and more secret sessions followed the leak that 'a national chain might be preferred by the council'. Indeed, up to a dozen firms were said to be interested in developing the site, but their identities were being kept strictly confidential.

It was the parking issue which first dominated the thinking of those who saw any encroachment onto the Central car park as a loss of space for this amenity; however, these fears were overcome by promises not only that no parking spaces would be lost, but that a link with The Square and Chapel Street could be effected in order to boost ancillary trade.

Town traders feared an increasing trend of shoppers driving to out-of-town superstores and hypermarkets in Havant, Waterlooville or Chichester and this was felt to be a good reason for accepting a new supermarket in the centre of town, whose presence should act as a magnet, stimulating a general uplift in their own fortunes and revitalising Petersfield as a shopping town, despite the associated fear that some of their trade would be plundered by a new store.

By a large majority at the first full council meeting to discuss the proposals, EHDC councillors supported the idea that a 20,000 sq ft 'upmarket' store, about a third of the size of a hypermarket, would benefit the town 'as long as the Central car park survives'. The council's deliberations over the whole issue appear to have been, at best, ambivalent and muddled and, at worst, obstructive and backward-looking. Their suggestion that the new shop should have a High Street and Chapel Street frontage would have destroyed a whole range of the smaller, independent shops for which Petersfield was (and still is) particularly known.

The Chamber of Trade strongly supported the provision of a first-class food market in the town centre as it would increase business for everybody. With an increasing population and many people choosing to shop outside the town, it was imperative to make a decision without delay. Petersfield Chamber of Trade, originally formed in the 1920s and currently with a membership of around one hundred firms, represented the complete spectrum of local businesses and commercial life. It made its voice heard in discussions over such issues as car parking, street cleaning, bus services, conservation and the Petersfield Plan.

A study ordered by the EHDC from the London-based consultants Hillier Parker warned that traders and shoppers could desert Petersfield if a new supermarket were not built in the town. The Central car park would be the ideal place for it, according to this study, as 'existing supermarkets fall a long way short of ideal and are too small by modern standards'. The report claimed that there would be room for a store of 35,000 sq ft and still leave space for adequate car parking. A new presentation of the consultants' plans, to include the authority's requirements on design and cost, would be made to the public later in 1986. However the EHDC bowed to public pressure and rejected the Hillier Parker scheme strongly recommending store and decked parking on the Central car park site, although the same consultants were brought back to design a large store which would integrate with the existing shops in the High Street and Chapel Street, as residents had demanded.

By 1987, the supermarket saga was still rumbling on like an out-of-control shopping trolley; there were four contenders remaining in the race for the contract: Presto (who were situated in the old E.J. Baker butcher's shop), the Gateway and Fine Fare Group, Prudential Assurance, and Waitrose. In January 1988, Waitrose doubled its bid for the contract, and a public meeting was organised in the town hall to display the four sets of plans. The next month, the EHDC recommended the bid by Waitrose, whose store would be double the size of the then Gateway store in the High Street (now Somerfield). The Waitrose plan, backed by Prudential, would create 100 new jobs and retain the current car parking spaces. It was approved in March and work was due to start in January 1989. Last-minute hitches included the takeover of the Fine Fare company resulting in the sale of its premises (now the entrance to Rams Walk), and a short debate over the choice of (yellow) bricks for the new construction. Since the National Westminster Bank at the other end of what was to become Rams Walk was also constructed of yellow brick, this was not considered incongruous. As to the final selection of a town centre store, the construction of which was deemed by independent consultants to be indispensable for the commercial expansion of the town, the planning policy committee visited four different companies' sites in the south of England. The Waitrose development at Witney in Oxfordshire, with its spacious, beautifully landscaped store, enhanced by a central shopping mall, influenced the team decisively.

SHELTERED (AND OTHER) HOMES

The old Railway Hotel and the former infants' school site were both replaced by housing for the elderly in the mid-1980s, the Hotel (where Lavant Court now stands) by forty-two flats in a warden-supervised scheme, and the school by thirty-one flats to be called St Peter's Court. In view of the tremendous surge of interest in these properties and the clear local need for accommodation, the Chief Planning Officer, Alan Billenness, called for the inclusion of a local occupancy clause in the planning consents (although this was difficult to enforce). According to the developer, Dominion Homes, however, about 80 per cent of the new flats were going to local people anyway. Elsa Bulmer, for thirty years Age Concern's champion in the town and their representative on the EHDC Housing Committee, voiced the concern that many of these sheltered homes were too expensive for local folk. It was clear to Dominion that most of the new flats were being bought by the wealthier residents of the town, precisely the market they were catering for.

Dominion were also responsible for the development of the ITS factory site where, in 1987, an inspector from the Department of the Environment overturned a decision by the EHDC to refuse the construction of eighty new homes.

Not for the first time in its recent history, Petersfield heard the plea that it was becoming an old people's town. The town mayor, John Sinclair Willis (the son of Henry Willis, the organ builder), reiterated the fear that there was too much sheltered housing and also too many expensive properties that the young could not afford. In fact, house building in this period was particularly buoyant: Laing Homes built Drum Mead on the old UK Plastics site in Swan Street in a mere 16 weeks and the 66 houses were snapped up rapidly; 16 flats and garages were built by Unit Construction in College Street; Reema Construction built 49 low-cost houses in Rival Moor Road destined for young families; 56 starter homes were planned on the old Welcome Inn site (now Meon Close) in Station Road; Wimpey Homes built 111 houses at Meadow Court off Durford Road; 27 new flats were added to the Heath Lodge site in Sussex Road when the Lodge itself was converted into four flats; 5 new town houses were completed in King George Avenue; finally, planning permission was granted for the first phase of starter homes on the old ITS site in Sandringham Road. A sympathetic conversion of the old malthouse in Dragon Street resulted in the creation of 14 flats and 4 houses on the site (now the Maltings).

What had in fact occurred was that there had been a general economic boom in the mid-1980s and this had sent house prices soaring everywhere and builders scrambling for land to develop. The fact also that Petersfield was within easy commuting distance from London was another factor in its development: as London house prices soared, Petersfield began to see more and more commuters leaving the capital to settle in the town in (for them) relatively easily affordable houses.

With the new Right to Buy legislation of 1980, the number of people applying to buy their council houses increased dramatically and, in 1988, there were 2,500 such applications in the East Hampshire district. The town council thus enjoyed a considerable land sale bonanza. However, the Local Government Act of 1988 enforced dramatic changes on local authorities, effectively putting an end to the use of money from council house sales to build more homes. The new laws shifted the focus of the district councils from providing housing to working with other groups such as housing associations. The EHDC, therefore, no longer needed to shoulder the whole financial burden of house building; in addition, developers were now forced to add a certain percentage of low-cost housing into their schemes.

Meanwhile, by 1985, Kebbell's had reached the halfway point in their development of the Herne Farm estate and were given approval for a further 49 houses south of Moggs Mead. They had completed more than 400 houses in their first decade in Petersfield and were planning to construct a similar number over the next ten years.

DEATH OF FLORA TWORT

Flora Twort died in 1985 at the age of 92. Petersfield's most successful professional artist had moved to the town from Hampstead in 1918, shortly after completing her formal training as an artist. She had been attracted to the town when, on her first visit, there had been no cars in sight and she had been able to tie her horse to the railings in The Square

Flora Twort.

Mary Ward.

Mary Ray.

Katie Pitt.

while she went shopping. Shortly after her arrival, and with the help of Dr Harry Roberts, she opened a bookshop and craft workshops at nos 1 and 2 The Square (now Lunn Poly, The Kitchen, ORYX and Spice Lounge restaurant) where she and two friends, Hester Wagstaff, who made jewellery, and Marie Brahms, Harry Roberts's secretary, livened up the town with their Bohemian lifestyle.

Much of the life of Petersfield before the advent of cars became the subject of her early watercolours, but she excelled particularly in portraiture. She continued to paint until she was in her eighties. She gave several of her paintings to the then Urban District Council (the PTC now owns them) and, after selling the bookshop in 1949, she moved into a studio in Church Path (now the Flora Twort Gallery) where she remained until her death.

'PRIDE IN PETERSFIELD'

This campaign, the aims of which were to reinvigorate the town's economy, to inject some optimism into traders' outlook on the future and to raise the profile of Petersfield within and outside the town, was instigated by the new town mayor, Kenneth Hick, in 1987. 'Pride in Petersfield' campaigned for a better shopping environment generally, with a greater number of free short-term parking spaces in the town, a reduction in vandalism and litter, an enhanced Square (more seating and 'shrubs in tubs'), and more late-night shopping evenings during the Christmas season. 'Pride in Petersfield' (its motto was 'Petersfield: a place to visit, a place to shop') later spawned the 'Petersfield in Bloom' campaign and its winter manifestation, 'Petersfield Christmas Lights', both of which have outlived their origins.

With the economy of the country on the upturn, it was imperative that not only the supermarket problem be resolved, but that the rest of the town's shops should be seen to be profiting from the boom. 'Pride in Petersfield' was a bold and positive initiative made at a time when the fortunes of the town seemed to be declining. One of the first challenges it confronted was to persuade all shops to open all day on Thursdays. Since time immemorial, there had been a half-day closing that afternoon and the more commercially minded and go-ahead traders wanted to drag the town out of its 'sleepy market town' torpor. There had been a period of commercial uncertainty – mainly owing to the indecision over the new supermarket – and several well-known establishments had closed or were in the process of changing hands.

With the bypass route now virtually certain, the proposal to create a new business park at the southern end of Bedford Road, filling a 13-acre greenfield site between the Whitman Laboratories and the new A3 was particularly welcome. This eventually became Vision Park.

Regrettably for many people, the Punch and Judy, a restaurant and tea shop since pre-war days, had shut in 1987, shortly before Petersfield magistrates were due to hear a case against it for breaching the hygiene regulations. Later it reopened as a bakery, but the enterprise was short-lived. Unfortunately, only two years after the Punch and Judy's closure, the Donkey Cart restaurant and bakery at 1 and 2 The Square also closed for the same reasons.

Another long-established firm, Moulds, the builders, who had been in the town for 100 years, announced that their offices in Dragon Street were the subject of an application for the conversion of their yard into flats and offices. In Chapel Street, several shops had changed hands the previous year, including Bowyer and Mendel (furnishings), Freeman's (hairdressing), Dewhurst's (butcher's) and the International Stores, the grocers which had ceased trading in 1985 after nearly a century in Petersfield.

One attempt at attracting custom into The Square which met with official – and officious – resistance, was made by the Market Inn, whose licensee put out three tables for customers on the pavement in front of the pub, to be met by the police who threatened him with prosecution. It was another decade before the so-called café culture began to make its presence felt in Petersfield.

If the town was to benefit from the tourists it was seeking to encourage, then the hotel and B & B situation had to be radically overhauled and expanded. The district council's apathetic attitude to tourism, its lack of a policy on the subject, the lack of a town brochure to promote tourism and stimulate cash flow through the town, and the lack of facilities for visitors to the town all militated against success in this important area of the British economy as a whole, and of East Hampshire in particular. For its part, the Southern Tourist Board had had little success in persuading the EHDC to interest itself in the 'problem'. As for hotel and private accommodation, there were only thirty-five beds in Petersfield and Liphook together to cater for the many hundreds of passing tourists arriving through Portsmouth and heading for London in the summer months. The Concorde Hotel (in Weston Road) was still functioning, but the old Drayton Hotel (in Station Road), the Railway Hotel (in Lavant Street) and the Red Lion (in College Street) no longer took guests.

THE TEENAGE YEARS

Although the youth club based at Petersfield School was already successfully in operation with several hundred members, it did not open in the school holidays. There was also a social centre for young people variously known as 'The Barn' or 'The Gravediggers' (after the old town mortuary which had been on the site!) which had been established behind the Heath surgery in Heath Road in 1985 and was open on Saturday evenings and one day in the week. It was in 1987, however, that more sustained efforts were made to provide premises and activities specifically for teenagers in the town. The *Petersfield Post* conducted a survey of teenage opinion involving all 700 pupils of Petersfield School, youth organisations, leisure centres and cafés to determine what facilities were available for them and what they still lacked. The same year, 300 competitors attended the British BMX championships held at the Love Lane track and a campaign for a new indoor swimming pool was launched, although PTC councillors recognised that its running costs might be a burden on the rates in future years.

In 1988, the PTC purchased the disused Elim church in Hylton Road (now the site of Port House) for conversion into a youth centre. It seemed entirely consistent for the youngsters, previously delighting in their association with the mortuary, now to move in as neighbours of the abattoir! Having sought a property close to the town centre, but sufficiently far away from a residential area where they could make as much noise as they liked, the old church seemed ideal. The combined efforts of councillor Elsa Bulmer and youth worker Neil Slatter, with the strong support of town mayor Nickey Edwards and the Chairman of the Finance Committee, Beryl Jones, ensured that at least a temporary solution had been found for young people, while hoping that larger premises might become available in the future. The Elim church site was, incidentally, seen as a good property investment for the town council for the future. Unfortunately, owing to the uncertainties of costs for the HCC youth budget

The new Festival Hall entrance and additions, 1987. (*Author's Collection*)

in 1990, the county withdrew from the management of the Hylton Road centre. However, when 'The Shack' opened its doors in April 1992, it was announced that £1,200 had been awarded to the project by the High Meadow Trust, a fund created by the Townsend family for the Petersfield community at the end of the war.

In fact, the lease on 'The Shack' ran out after two years. So in 1994 the youth club found itself homeless for 6 years – apart from a brief sojourn at Winton House – until it finally moved, this time to the old, long since derelict, lampshade factory beside the town hall, in the summer of 2000. It was renamed 'The King's Arms' and, adjacent to the CAB (Citizens' Advice Bureau) and Scout hut, seemingly appropriately situated. It now caters for differing age groups of teenagers on six days a week who use it as an after-school drop-in centre, where they can gather to chat, play pool, use the Internet, and eat and drink (non-alcoholic) in the bar. It also acts as a centre for a nursery school, the HCC Youth Service, the Petersfield Youth Agencies Forum and the Youth Alpha Initiative.

AN IMPROVED FESTIVAL HALL

The biggest capital project ever undertaken by the PTC was the £650,000 extension to the Festival Hall in 1987. The driving force behind the improvement was the Chairman of the Public Halls Committee, Kenneth Hick, and the money was raised from the sale of land to the east of Barnfield and Heathfield Roads – land that the PTC had been forced to buy in 1975 when it bought the adjoining playing fields, but which became a gold mine for the council thanks to soaring land prices. Among the projects this income funded were the Festival Hall extension, Sheet Village Hall improvements, a new pavilion in The Avenue and new play equipment for the town's recreation grounds.

The Festival Hall had become inadequate over the past few years and the PTC took advice from the Arts Council on possible improvements. The results were admirable: they included adding a motorised stage extension; installing an audio system in the auditorium; adding a Green Room and new dressing rooms for performers; building an orchestra pit; constructing a scenery dock and lifts for the easier handling of stage furniture; and creating the Rose Room for receptions. The architect of the new extension was, again, Kenneth Claxton who had designed the first alterations almost ten years earlier.

THE HOSPITAL HICCUP

Although the site for the new community hospital in Petersfield had been earmarked and purchased in 1985 ('to keep its priority status'), there remained one blockage to the whole site being developed quickly: the vicarage. Despite the purchase in the early 1960s of a strip of land on which the vicarage stood, negotiations with the Church Commissioners over the rehousing of the vicar, Canon Ronald Granger, were unresolved. This caused a double postponement of the starting date for the construction of the hospital, as a new, suitable home was sought in the Petersfield area. However, the delay did allow the last fête to take place in the vicarage garden in 1986.

Finally, a new vicarage was found in 1987 – Shackleford House in Dragon Street – and construction of the new hospital was begun the following year, costing £4.5 million. It was to be a 62-bed, multi-purpose centre which would bring together the health services hitherto scattered throughout Petersfield and Liss, the first such community hospital in the Portsmouth and South East District Health Authority. As yet, the future of the old hospital was uncertain.

THE CARNIVAL

The old Petersfield carnival had abandoned its tradition of an annual street procession in the 1970s and, by the 1980s, had become a much more intermittent affair: the 1980 carnival itself had been the first to be held in the town since the Queen's Silver Jubilee celebrations of 1977. At the next, in 1984, the theme was the 800th anniversary of the granting of the town's foundation Charter; the next carnival was due to take place in 1986, but had to be scrapped ten weeks before it was due to happen because of 'management and organisational problems'. Although it did take place – with great success – the following year, the organisers acknowledged that their main objective was that of fundraising for civic improvements, thus transforming future carnivals from civic pride events into pure charity-collection opportunities, perhaps a reflection of the times. In 1989, for example, the beneficiary of the street collections was the new hospital.

DREDGING THE HEATH POND

A plan to carry out the dredging of the Heath Pond was formulated in 1987 and the work begun in 1988; over the previous sixty years, about 50,000 cubic metres of silt had built up on the bed of the Pond and this had been partly responsible for the death of an increasing number of fish as the resulting growth of algae sucked the oxygen from the water. The last such operation had been carried out in the 1920s when the Pond was drained and cleared out.

The plan was not without its problems: first, the work was delayed in order to allow the Taro Fair to take place as usual that October, but the Wall family, the Fair operators since before the war, were warned that the Taro might have to find an alternative venue for the following year (the first time since 1820 that the Heath could not be used); secondly, the following spring was a particularly dry one and water levels in the Pond dropped considerably; this in turn caused the dredger to become marooned in the middle of the Pond and it was obliged to wait until the water level had risen again to continue its work; thirdly, the resulting 'bunds' (mounds of excavated silt and mud) left around the edge of the Pond were considered to be a danger to children playing on them; finally, a (reduced) Taro Fair had to be held at Penns Place in 1988, although a small Fair did take place on the Heath again in 1989, with an additional, free firework display to attract visitors. Although the work finally took two and a half years (and cost £150,000) to complete, it had been a successful operation; the bunds were dispersed, the area was re-landscaped (by the HCC) and the Pond filled up naturally again – from a combination of water from the small brook crossing the golf course and natural drainage. The Petersfield Society planted trees on the Pond island in 1990.

THE EAST HAMPSHIRE DISTRICT LOCAL PLAN

The draft of this plan which first saw the light of day in 1982 reached its next stage in 1989. The responses from the parish and town councils, the development companies and individuals had been generally favourable towards it, indicating that it had been handled with a degree of sensitivity and local awareness rarely seen in the past. Petersfield Town Council welcomed the report: it accepted the areas allocated for further – especially low-density – development and the resistance to large-scale out-of-town shopping facilities, and it praised the view that there should be no development between the boundaries of Petersfield and Sheet or Steep.

The EHDC, however, looking at the wider picture, had some reservations: Nickey Edwards, the Chairman of its development policy committee, shared the shock of that committee when it read that the (Conservative) government was expecting the district to find an extra 1,000 homes in the next decade, over and above the 3,100 already planned for in the report. Most of this would be in Bordon and Whitehill. Between 1977 and 1989, permission was granted for 1,900 houses to be built in Petersfield, but the new demands threatened the AONB and, according to Mrs Edwards, would not solve local needs, but merely increase the number of commuters coming into the area and thus overwhelm the infrastructure in place.

This clear statement perhaps marks the moment when Petersfield found itself under siege, not just from development *per se*, but from the effects of high land prices bringing high house prices and the confirmed entry of Petersfield into the London commuter belt. Mid-Hampshire had always been regarded by planners as a low-growth area for houses (compared with north-east Hampshire, for example), but the government's new demands were asking it to provide more homes than it needed for its own anticipated population growth. Petersfield's infrastructure, particularly water drainage, traffic movement and parking was at breaking point.

PRESENT AND FUTURE OPTIMISM

Within the town, 1989 saw some significant developments on existing sites: the Methodist Church opened its new hall; the Old College (bought by the HCC in 1987) reopened after extensive renovation work; and the Physic Garden was inaugurated behind 16 High Street. This last acquisition, a real historic gem for the town, was the result of a generous benefaction by Major John Bowen, who lived at no. 22, the last privately owned house in the High Street (now Ingoldsby House). The half-acre walled garden at no. 16, also owned by Major Bowen, was one of the last identifiable medieval gardens on a burgage plot in Petersfield High Street. The garden gift was developed by Mary Ray and a team from the Petersfield Historical Society into a seventeenth-century medicinal herb (or 'physic') garden, incorporating a topiary walk, herb garden, knot garden, rose bower and a small orchard. It became Petersfield's newest contribution to the recognition of its seventeenth-century heritage, the period when John Goodyer and John Worlidge, influential in their respective fields of botany and agriculture, were resident in the town.

The early 1990s promised to be as progressive and productive as the later 1980s: in 1989, the EHDC approved in principle the endorsement of a site for a new swimming pool at

The Physic Garden. (*Tony Struthers*)

Sculpture of Major John Bowen by Carole Ackworth, 2006. (*Author's Collection*)

Penns Place; Churcher's College sold its Love Lane and Ramshill land (the former boarding house, Mount House) to build a new £1-million classroom block (New College) and sports hall; the bypass was said by Michael Mates to be on schedule and the start and completion dates (1990 and 1992) were at last revealed; the ceremonial turf cutting for the new £12-million community hospital took place; the blueprint for the new Prudential-managed supermarket and associated development went to the planners; plans were unveiled for a new £500,000 surgery next to the hospital in Swan Street; and St Peter's Church launched an appeal for a new roof and organ.

This was a remarkable turnaround in the fortunes of the town after so many years of frustration and waiting, and town mayor Nickey Edwards was distinctly upbeat about the immediate prospects for the 1990s in her New Year message: 'This is a town which has really blossomed in these past years. It is a time for hope and a real time for feeling that Petersfield is doing a good job.' The town's finances were also on a good footing, thanks to land sales paying for capital spending.

DEPARTURES

Eric Hampton, known widely in Petersfield as 'Buster', retired from his post as Head of Science at Petersfield School in 1985 after thirty-six years' service both at the old Senior School in St Peter's Road and at the new Cranford Road site. A Petersfielder by birth, Buster was (and is) well known for his work within the community, principally for his work as the town's Group Scout Leader since 1962 and for his membership of the Swimming Pool Committee. His first equipment as the school's only science teacher when he started his career in 1949 was rather rudimentary: it consisted of an aquarium and two beakers, supplemented shortly afterwards by a second-hand Bunsen burner. Half of the pupils who bade him farewell on his retirement claimed that he had also taught their parents. In 1989, Buster was awarded the Silver Wolf badge, the highest award in Scouting.

Another Petersfield resident who retired in 1986 was John Freeman, whose hairdressing business in Lavant Street was the last such shop owned by his family; his grandfather had started a hairdresser's in College Street over a century before.

One remarkable Petersfield resident, whose family is known for its longevity, died in 1986. At the age of 103, Mrs Emily Bennetts was the town's oldest inhabitant, whose mental faculties never deserted her: she regularly read the local and national newspapers, wrote to friends and relations around the world and still kept a daily diary, written in immaculate copperplate script, until beyond the age of 100. She first settled in Petersfield in 1911, when horses' hooves and nightingales were the only sounds – apart from the occasional train on the old Midhurst line – to be heard from her family home at the foot of Ramshill. She had been the Headteacher of Sheet Junior School since 1919, and, in 1940 had seen part of her bedroom ceiling collapse when Petersfield's only Second World War bomb hit the Love Lane Workhouse opposite the family house.

Plus ça change . . .

'Petersfield needs more tourists.' (January 1985)

'"Are we making enough of our new-look Square?" The *Petersfield Post* raises the possibility of using The Square more fully for entertainment and social events.' (January 1987)

'EHDC give permission for scheme to demolish the Savoy [cinema] and build 17 sheltered homes for the elderly.' (May 1988)

'Plans to use former cinema for sheltered housing rejected by EHDC.' (April 1989)

CHAPTER EIGHT

Acceleration
1990–5

DEVELOPMENTAL SURGE

The remarkable start to the 1990s, involving the multi-million-pound schemes for the four outstanding major projects (the hospital, the bypass, the indoor swimming pool and the Rams Walk shopping centre), represented a huge surge in Petersfield's development, the like of which had never before been witnessed in such a brief period of its history. Within the space of four years, the last-minute modifications to all these schemes were effected, the objections all circumvented and all four projects were realised by the end of 1993. Given the nationwide recession during this period, Petersfield can consider itself to have been lucky with its timing and its finances.

The hospital site was the subject of some controversy even as the work began on it in December 1989: the suggestion that Steve Pibworth's forge should be resited was categorically rejected by him, saying that he had no intention of moving his workplace from where he had operated for more than forty years. In any case, the health authority had made no moves to buy his land and, as he stated, 'craft workshops are part of our heritage – the centre of towns used to be where things went on. You can't start to neaten things up by moving them to industrial estates where the rents and rates are high.'

As for the old Cottage Hospital building, a bid to save it for the community was launched: Petersfield Housing Association were interested in buying it and converting it into rented flats, while both The Petersfield Society and town councillor Katie Pitt aimed to save the building, as it had originally been built by public subscription and financially supported until, and even after, the NHS took it over in 1947. However, the Portsmouth and South-East Hampshire Health Authority were obliged to sell the site to the highest bidder and plough the money back into district health care; only by selling the maximum amount of land, it was argued, would it be possible to raise sufficient money to fund the construction of the new hospital.

The community hospital was completed in 1991 after eighteen months' work, four months ahead of schedule, and the first patients were admitted in the autumn of 1991. It provided 62 beds, of which 20 were on a GP ward, 24 on a ward for the elderly, 10 places in a day ward, and 8 beds in The Grange maternity unit. There were also beds and places for mental health patients, outpatients and community health departments, units for physiotherapy, X-ray, ultrasound, speech therapy, chiropody, dental surgery and a minor injuries unit. The one regret expressed by those who had known the old hospital was that the new building had been erected too low down on the site, with the result that there are no longer enjoyable views across to the Downs – a source of life, hope and healing – for patients in the wards. When the adjoining Swan surgery opened in 1992, the Citizens' Advice Bureau moved into their old premises by the town hall.

The official date for the start of work on the bypass was 5 December 1990, but even before that date there were doubts as to the type of surfacing prescribed for the new road. Concrete had been chosen for its lower cost, but the construction company, Tarmac Construction Ltd, was said to be using a new-specification concrete, in order to reduce noise levels, which had been considerably revised since the A27, traffic noise from which had caused such a furore from local residents had been built at Emsworth. An asphalt surfacing would have cost £500,000 more. However, after a vociferous public anti-concrete campaign and some quiet diplomacy by Michael Mates, it was announced that the Ministry of Transport had made 'a mistake in the contract document' and that the bypass would get its tarmac.

Apart from the report of a spree at Sheet, when joyriders took a giant dumper truck for a spin, work proceeded rapidly and, after only ten months, half of the twenty-five new bridges to be constructed had been completed. The £37-million, 12-mile bypass was finished two months ahead of schedule in July 1992 and the Roads Minister, Kenneth Carlisle, performed the opening ceremony.

The indoor swimming pool, first mooted in 1987, had received approval both from the PTC, who wanted to ensure that it would be sited in Petersfield and not elsewhere in East Hampshire, and from the EHDC, who granted it planning permission in 1991, although it was only passed by two votes because of doubts about its eventual running costs. The £3-million pool was to be attached to the existing leisure centre at Penns Place, where land had been offered by the PTC (on the town mayor's casting vote!) 'with no strings attached'. In fact, the argument in favour of building the pool was that it was the one facility which would almost certainly bring the leisure centre out of debt. It was opened in 1992 and, in

The Taro Centre swimming pool, opened in 1992. (*Author's Collection*)

conjunction with the leisure centre, was renamed the Taro Centre. Since then, the predictions about its profitability have been proved correct.

The whole supermarket affair had been a long and occasionally bitter saga: accusations of secrecy and betrayal were bandied about before, during and after the public inquiry in 1985. However, the EHDC finally chose the Prudential scheme in 1988, and this was given planning permission the following year. The objections by Gateway and other traders (standing on the sites now occupied by Milletts, Edinburgh Woollen Mill and New Look) to the compulsory purchase orders for the new complex caused a year's delay and forced another public inquiry in 1990, but this stumbling block was removed when Gateway closed its store and so the part demolition of a Southern Electricity shop, Page One (bookshop) and Occasions (a family-run fancy-goods business) went ahead in 1991. The first floors of these premises were kept intact to retain the Georgian look of the north side of The Square, but a gap created by the demolition allowed for the entrance of what was to become Rams Walk. The original planned name of Tilmore Walk was found to be erroneous, as it is not the Tilmore Brook but the Drum River which passes through the town at this point, where there had once been a 'Ramsbridge'. What was also satisfying for historians and architectural preservationists was the discovery, on the former Forrest Stores site, of a building which had been damaged when the shop was created, and that some of the old timbers of the

Andrew Cheese's sculpture *The Downsman*, installed in Rams Walk in 1999. (*Sara Sadler*)

Rams Walk, 2006. (*Author's Collection*)

original large Tudor merchant's house there were still intact. They can be seen today inside the Edinburgh Woollen Mill shop.

The shopping mall with its twenty-two units was designed by the same firm of Winchester architects who had designed the modifications to the infants' school in St Peter's Road. The work was completed within eighteen months, in the spring of 1993, and Waitrose and some of the smaller shops opened that autumn. At first, the effect of the completion of the bypass on Rams Walk was a negative one and people seemed to be travelling out of town to other supermarkets, but this was reversed once Waitrose was opened. Indeed, the Petersfield branch of the store became one of the most successful in the country and, far from alienating Petersfield shoppers, it acted as a magnet to draw people into the town. Andrew Cheese's sculpture *The Downsman*, based on a representation of his grandfather, was placed in Rams Walk in 1999, adding a further sympathetic dimension to this pedestrian-friendly zone.

At the same time, modifications to existing car parks were planned for the expected inrush of shoppers: 75 more spaces were created at the Swan Street car park and the 51-space park at Castle Yard was built opposite. A new car park at the British Rail station was also envisaged. Petersfield's determination to ensure a high parking capacity for incoming shoppers was now fixed for years to come.

As the *Petersfield Post* remarked in 1990, with these four projects underway: 'We must not worry that Petersfield will change beyond recognition because, after all, it is the people who give a town spirit – not the buildings.' This is too blasé for comfort, and not an entirely accurate analysis of 'spirit', but nevertheless it does reveal that, after much soul-searching and many a conflict, it had finally come to terms with the inevitable. It would be up to future generations to ensure that the 'spirit' of the town was retained as far as possible against a recognisable background. Perhaps humour is a sign of confidence: in the spring of 1992, readers of the *Petersfield Post* were disheartened to read the following notice on the front page:

April Fools'
Day press
report, 1992.
(*Petersfield Post*)

> **A GIANT orange tarpaulin this morning covered Petersfield's famous statue of King William, as workers prepared to begin construction on a giant chrome and glass palace covering the Square. The statue will be moved tomorrow, to make way for the last phase of the town centre development. Plans for the structure, which has been given royal approval, were kept under wraps until last night. *ALISTER HENBLOW* reports.**

What the following week's protesting correspondents had failed to notice was the date at the top of the newspaper: 1 April!

GATHERING MOMENTUM

Alongside the surge in development in and around the town, there were other signs of a sustained momentum in civic growth in the first half of the new decade: educational, international, cultural and commercial.

The appointment of Mrs Kathy Bell to the headship of Petersfield School in January 1990 brought a new dynamism to the school. Her enthusiasm for what she described as 'a very happy, friendly, supportive school with enormous potential' translated into a desire to improve pupils' discipline and development, enhance the school's reputation in the town and pursue an active involvement in the community. Kathy Bell brought in a new school uniform, introduced the name 'The Petersfield School', set up a £25,000 resource centre, opened a crèche partly staffed by childcare pupils, introduced a code of conduct to encourage good behaviour, and developed an extended sixth form (there were 100 sixth formers in 1992) with a greater range of subjects offered to students. It seemed to some like a return to the old days of discipline, strict uniform codes, a house system and competitiveness. But it worked, bringing lower class sizes, giving the pupils a new pride in their school, producing higher achievement in the academic and sporting fields, a larger intake from Herne Junior and local village schools, greater numbers staying on in the sixth form and a period of great excitement for Mrs Bell who, in four short years, had managed to turn the school around from its semi-comatose state. When, in 1994, the school gained grant-maintained status, there was access to building money, the school expanded its science, maths and humanities blocks and created new courses for sixth formers.

Kathy Bell and Alison Willcocks, who was appointed Head of Bedales in 1995, had much in common: both the first female Heads of their respective schools, both history graduates and in their forties, they formed a strong relationship and cooperated academically to their pupils' mutual benefit. Unfortunately, The Petersfield School seemed to have peaked academically by 2002 and it became necessary to abandon its financially extravagant sixth form in 2001, a year after Mrs Bell herself had decided to leave the school.

Meanwhile, at Churcher's College, the new Headmaster, Geoffrey Buttle, was also going for growth. He oversaw the first entry of seventeen 11-year-old girls to the school in 1988, the year he arrived, although the decision on this had already been taken by his predecessor.

Geoffrey Buttle and the first Churcher's girls intake, 1988. (*Churcher's College*)

Girls were accepted at Churcher's for the first time mainly for financial reasons, although there had also been some pressure on the governors to accept the sisters of boys already at the school. Pupil numbers had been declining and the new Head embarked on a massive building programme to provide the facilities which had already become the norm in other public schools in the 1980s. The twenty-one extra classrooms in New College, a sports hall, a new library, a dedicated science building and the transformation of the old boarding house of Ramshill into a sixth form centre all followed, financed partly by the sale of land on the school site, and partly by an appeal to Old Churcherians. As facilities improved, so did pupil numbers and, from around four hundred and eighty pupils in 1990, the school moved to about five hundred and sixty in the year 2000. Boarding was phased out in the same period through lack of demand. Churcher's participation in the town's activities has always been substantial: as at The Petersfield School it was music which brought schools and the community together, and the two teachers responsible, David Groves and Anne Claxton respectively, have played a large part in this integration. Churcher's have also played their part in promoting Petersfield's town twinning, Rotary and Scout movements, contributed widely to the town's sports teams, and opened its doors to the town's societies for various sporting, intellectual and gastronomic functions.

The first efforts at twinning Petersfield with a town in France had faltered in the 1980s, but the combined efforts of three successive town mayors (Beverley-Anne Silk, Eric Goffe and Liz Mullenger) came to fruition when the official charter between the towns of

Petersfield and Barentin (close to Rouen in Normandy) was signed in October 1992. The Mayor of Barentin, Michel Bentot, came over with a group of thirty Barentinois for the ceremony against a backdrop of a decorated Town Square, a French week at the library, a marching band and morris dancing. Among the guests was a delegation from Warendorf, Barentin's twin town in Germany, with whom they had been twinned for twenty-five years. The next logical step, in the later 1990s, was for the Twinning Association to complete the triangle by linking Petersfield to Warendorf; after some, mainly political, hesitation, this was achieved by the official signing of a second twinning charter in 2006. Barentin Way, part of the Ramshill estate, was named in 2004.

One unfortunate and unforeseen consequence of the first twinning contact was the visit by a group from Petersfield to Barentin in 1993, when Petersfield's new town flag flew into trouble over its design. The crest, adopted earlier that year to replace the 'King Billie' image, consisted of a heraldic emblem associated with the town for 300 years: an amulet surrounded by three spherical 'pellets' within the Hampshire rose. The problem arose when the flag caught the attention of some French humorists who referred to the design as 'le clown'. The problem was solved when it was pointed out that the flag should have depicted four pellets in the first place. The dignity and honour of Petersfield were retrieved by the time of the next visit.

Nostalgia has always drawn the crowds in Petersfield, whether it has been through exhibitions of the town's past, lectures or film shows on 'Old Petersfield', or articles in the

Petersfield Museum Trust (Mary Ray, Liz Mullenger, Teresa Jamieson, Wilf Burnham), 1993. (*Liz Mullenger*)

Petersfield Post on people and events from days of yore. Perhaps this satisfies a yearning for Petersfield's past glories or its former small rural community values; perhaps it merely represents the common denominator among that section of the town's population for whom reminiscence is a cosy and satisfying pastime.

Whatever the reason, if reason there needs to be ('*le coeur a ses raisons*'), the call for a museum in the town had been heard periodically for at least forty years and, in the mid-1990s, a group of enthusiasts from the Petersfield Area Historical Society actively began the search for a potential site from which to promote the town's heritage. The abundance of local museums only served to highlight Petersfield's lack in this respect: Wilf Burnham, who had founded the Liss Historical Society before coming to live in Petersfield, had the support of the Petersfield Society, Teresa Jamieson the town mayor, and The Petersfield School's Kathy Bell in trying to find both finance and an appropriate location to house all the artefacts which the Historical Society had already amassed. A Museum Trust was eventually set up for this purpose and, fortuitously, with the Magistrates' Court closing in 1995, this building was transformed within a short space of time into the ideally situated and historically important site for the new Petersfield Museum.

Commercially, Petersfield was bucking the trend of a national recession in the early 1990s: thanks to the new bypass and the imminent opening of the Rams Walk shopping mall, property companies were targeting the town with three schemes for a total of nearly three hundred new homes and a new office block; a new EHDC Local Plan was submitted for approval and led to another public inquiry; three stores in the town (Woolworth's, Curry's and Superdrug) defied a threat of prosecution by opening on the Sunday before Christmas in 1990; developers unveiled plans for a new housing estate behind the Causeway and the old Savoy cinema was under the new ownership of Tanfern Ltd, who were planning to reopen it as an entertainment centre. However, they abandoned this project a year later and the building was sold to Newblock Ltd who opened Oscar's nightclub there in 1993.

Sporadic efforts have been made in Petersfield to bring retail and business together, with the aim of promoting the town through such bodies as the Chamber of Trade, the Retailers' Association, Petersfield Marketing Limited, Petersfield First! and the Association of Petersfield Enterprises. The Chamber of Trade, a long-established body but only intermittently effective, and the Retailers' Association, begun in 1990, existed alongside each other, performing a large amount of charity work and aiming to enhance the town's image. There was, however, a certain amount of conflict generated between the two groups and this problem was addressed by successive town mayors in the early 1990s. A marketing panel, sponsored by Prudential (the holding company managing Rams Walk) was set up to promote the town, assisted by the newly created Town Forum, which consisted of representatives from the HCC, EHDC, PTC, the Retailers' Association, the Police, the Chamber of Trade and the press. Its role was to discuss matters of common concern and, primarily, to ensure that Petersfield's unique selling point – its small businesses – were protected so that they would remain viable. The Town Forum was comprehensive in structure, innovative in strategy and an admirable example of the efficacy of collaborative enterprise. Unfortunately, it was perceived by the town council as too powerful a body, undermining the democratically elected councillors in what they considered to be their field of operation; the Forum was killed off in the year 2000.

Light industry was also undergoing a renaissance in the town: commercial property specialists Hall, Pain and Foster announced that they had 55,000 sq ft of distribution and light industrial space changing hands in 1993, an indicator of the new accessibility and attraction of Petersfield to distribution companies, thanks to the bypass. The former Southdown bus depot in Station Road and properties in Penns Road and The Avenue were being converted to accommodate new firms, as well as space at Bedford Road being developed for larger industries, such as the Danish Bacon Company.

CRIME AND PUNISHMENT

The historic police station in St Peter's Road – dating from 1858, the second oldest in Hampshire and one of the only surviving stations in the county designed by Thomas Stopher – still bears some of the features of its long history: the stable block (now a garage), the Victorian cells (now decommissioned) and the upstairs living quarters which, in pre-war days, housed the superintendent in charge. During the Second World War, there were more than one hundred special constables working here – all volunteers – mostly gentlemen over the age of 60!

During the 1960s and 1970s, most police officers lived locally, until it became commoner for them to commute – thanks, in part, to the high cost of housing in Petersfield. This immediately brought the now commonly heard complaint that few officers from the community were visible within it. It was during the 1970s that Petersfield was downgraded from a superintendent's to a chief inspector's station. Nevertheless, the station thrived on its complement of 4 sergeants and 26 constables, with extra forces available for traffic patrol and CID work. In those days, traffic was a major problem for the town, with the A3 tailbacks stretching from Adhurst Hill in the north to Butser in the south.

Until the early 1980s, police had very limited access to firearms and one revolver – under strictest control – was kept in a safe in the chief inspector's office. The availability of alcohol and the rise in affluence took their toll in the town centre during the 1980s and, with the licensing of the nightclub in Swan Street, public disorder rocketed, especially at weekends. The 1990s brought administrative and logistical changes, reducing the station's importance and self-sufficiency.

Three hundred and fifty years of local justice came to an end with the closure of Petersfield's autonomous Magistrates' Court in 1995. For the previous four years their bench had been amalgamated with that of Alton, where there were twice the number of magistrates sitting. Prisoners are now taken directly to Alton police station. The effect of this is that the Petersfield police can no longer prosecute minor cases on site and, after the final local sitting in May 1995, the town mayor, Bert Perry, was prompted to bemoan the fact that Petersfield was losing one of its functions as a town and that justice itself might be the loser, as local miscreants would no longer fear being named and shamed before a court in their own community.

Of course, cost and efficiency was the twin mantra used to justify the closure, but the new, larger and underused courthouse in Alton also played a role in determining it. The seventeenth-century royal coat of arms which was displayed above the Petersfield bench until 1966 was recently restored and again hangs in the Old Courthouse building (now the museum), probably the third courthouse to be built in the town and dating from the late Victorian period.

TWO CENTENARIES

Two old-established Petersfield firms celebrated their centenaries in 1995: Jacobs and Hunt, and Rowland, Son and Vincent.

William Percy Jacobs started the firm which bears his name at a small office in Lavant Street in 1895 and Frank Hunt joined him soon afterwards. The company's staple business has always been auctioneering and property, but, equally, it was always connected with Petersfield market. Jacobs and Hunt were responsible for the pigs and sheep, and Frank Hunt also conducted the sales in the poultry market. In the postwar years, the firm's furniture salerooms and valuation department (for antiques, porcelain, silver and pictures) increased in importance and new departments dealing with estate agency, letting and property management, and professional services have been created.

One of the most central and commercially historic buildings in Petersfield is that of Rowland, Son and Vincent in The Square, with a façade dating back to the eighteenth century and roof beams in the attic suggesting a Tudor origin. This roof space was used as a refuge by Portsmouth people fleeing the Blitz in the Second World War. The building underwent a four-year renovation programme in the 1990s. When Charles Rowland founded the firm in Victorian times, it was a haberdashery; the family later turned it into a furnishing store which it remained until the end of the twentieth century.

THE CAUSEWAY SITE

The third attempt by developers to build a major controversial housing and golf course complex at the Causeway Farm site was made in June 1991. This 131-acre site had been farmed by the Palfreys (father and son) for forty years and was now used for cattle grazing and haymaking. The PTC voiced their strong opposition to the plan, as it would breach the development plan and could open the door to large-scale development to the south of the town. A packed public meeting elicited equally strong objections and, after going to a government inspector for a decision, the proposal was finally rejected in 1993. However, another site south of Cranford Road was approved, that proposed by Galliford Sears for 125 houses close to the Jolly Sailor pub. Meanwhile, the Petersfield Golf Club, which had previously been a contender for the Causeway site, unveiled its new plans for an eighteen-hole course and clubhouse on the Liss side of the Adhurst Estate.

In 1994, Bryant Homes announced that they wanted to develop the Kingsfernsden site, but both the PTC and the EHDC preferred to see the Causeway site as a priority for new housing. The same year, the abattoir in the Causeway was closed with the loss of seventy jobs, and Tesco showed an interest in building a superstore on the site. A new controversy was about to begin, with the PTC, the Petersfield Society, the Folly Market and Lavant Street traders, and the public largely against the development. It finished with a government inspector overriding all objections and allowing Tesco to proceed with their plans in 1996.

RECLAIMING A TRUNK ROAD

Once through traffic is removed, many of the former trunk roads can be modified in scale, making their layouts more appropriate to their new role. Providing more space for pedestrians and cyclists and less for motor vehicle traffic can improve safety and the environment.

Dragon Street in Petersfield, formerly the A3, has been completely rebuilt. The bypass removed two thirds of the traffic, allowing the carriageway to be narrowed, footways to be improved and offering space for parking bays and planting. Junctions have been treated with block paving and the perceived width of the carriageway has been reduced by use of blockwork channels and planting. New street lighting appropriate to the new layout has now been installed. The front cover of this report illustrates the dramatic change.

*Dragon Street, Petersfield
before the bypass, before
traffic calming and now*

The Bypass Demonstration Project, 1993. (*Department of Transport report*)

THE DEMONSTRATION PROJECT

The original catalyst for the creation of a new Town Forum had been the completion of the bypass and the simultaneous offer from the Department of the Environment to fund a 'Demonstration Project'. This scheme, offered to six small towns nationwide, was intended to show the environmental benefits for town centres which could result from a bypass; in Petersfield, the first phase of the £2-million project brought an attractive enhancement to Dragon Street, but also included the removal of the mini roundabout at its junction with Hylton Road and Sussex Road. This provoked some consternation among road users, but the officer concerned with the scheme did not agree, stating that a roundabout created uncertainty in drivers' minds. The scheme did produce a visually improved street scene:

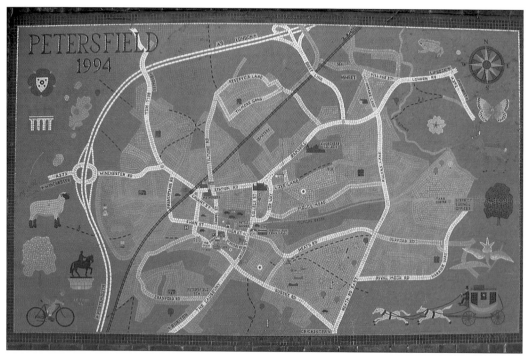

A mosaic, designed in 1994, to commemorate the completion of the bypass. (*Author's Collection*)

pavements were widened with old-style paving slabs, rumble strips were inserted in the roadway to slow traffic down, the war memorial was enhanced as a focal point by creating a new paving pattern, lay-bys for buses and parking were incorporated into the tree-lined pavements and space was created for a town mosaic celebrating the completion of the bypass. This work of art was commissioned by local and county councils and several Petersfield societies and was won by an ex-Bedales student, Rosalind Wates, whose work was unveiled the day the Tour de France cycle race passed through Petersfield in July 1994 – a first for the town, which gave it a pretext for some civic celebration and public enthusiasm.

This first phase of the Demonstration Project was completed in 1993 and the second phase, the remodelling of College Street, began and was completed in 1995. The third and final phase, never to be undertaken, was to have been one of those sporadic attempts to re-route traffic away from College Street by making Tor Way into a two-way road.

PROGRESS ON MANY FRONTS

The town's development appeared to be rampant in 1994 and 1995: St Peter's Church was promised a major £250,000 facelift, the infants' school celebrated its centenary and Herne Junior School had a new extension built, consisting of a hall and improved facilities for drama, music and PE; the home for the elderly at Silverlands in Ramshill was merged with the Ramshill Day Centre to become Bulmer House, thus recognising the efforts of Ken and Elsa Bulmer in providing such excellent care for Petersfield's older residents over many decades; the golf club finally left the Heath in 1997 after an association with it lasting over a century; Frank Westwood's Petersfield Bookshop received Prince Charles's royal warrant in 1995 – to add to that of the Queen in 1988 – for services to picture framing for the Prince's watercolours; a detachment of a flight of the Waterlooville squadron Air Training Corps was set up in Petersfield in 1995; a bid was made by the company owning Oscar's nightclub in Swan Street to open a cinema on the first floor of the building – but, despite the PTC welcoming the project and granting the necessary licences for public entertainment, the project was later abandoned; and the University of the Third Age (U3A) began operating in the Community Centre. Trade was also booming: the Portsmouth

The Petersfield Bookshop's royal warrant, 1988. (*Author's Collection*)

firm of jewellers, Constad, moved into the High Street and felt the town was 'buzzing and humming', while the old Petersfield engineering firm of D.C.M. Tew, having absorbed three other local firms in the period 1984–90, now planned a £1½-million expansion into a new factory in Bedford Road (now Mastec), which it had owned since 1976.

In 1995, Petersfield Housing Association bought 'The Shack' in Hylton Road from the PTC, demolished the youth club, and constructed a small block of low-cost homes on the site. With the withdrawal of the Wadham Stringer garage from behind College Street in 1994, the way was clear to create a new, private, warden-assisted housing development for the benefit of retired people, to be named Cremorne Place. A pattern was thus emerging of the desire to remove light industry from residential streets in Petersfield and to allow people to populate the central area of town, while industrial premises were encouraged to situate themselves on the growing Bedford Road – and subsequently the 'Vision Park' – complex on the western edge of the town.

The Petersfield Society celebrated its Golden Jubilee in 1995. Its influence continued to be felt in the town, whether on conservation and improvement matters (its recent projects included the burying of electricity and telephone cables in Heath Road, designing the Bell Hill roundabout and introducing its annual award – the President's Owl – for good design in the town) or on town planning decision-making, where it acted as a watchdog, detecting and identifying threats to Petersfield's environmental and rural qualities.

DEPARTURES

The death occurred, in June 1992, of Alan Ray, one of Petersfield's leading businessmen and the first town mayor of the new town council in 1974. He was Chairman of Gammon and Smith builders' merchants, having joined the company in 1950 after marrying Mary Pearson, the daughter of the former owner. As well as taking an active role in several town groups, he had served in local politics for over twenty years, both on the old UDC and the new PTC. He was a man of vision, integrity and honour, and was largely responsible for the purchase of the Penns

Farm land. He was for eleven years a governor of Churcher's College, Chairman of the Board of Governors of Petersfield Secondary School and served for eighteen years as a governor of Petersfield Infants' School, as well as becoming president of the Petersfield Musical Festival in 1986. He was a founder member of the Petersfield Round Table and Rotary clubs and an active member of many other organisations. It would be hard to better his record of service to the town.

Just a few months after the death of Alan Ray, another town stalwart died: Edward Grainger, former art teacher at Churcher's College and a great musical influence on the town, passed away at the age of 83. He was a member of many town groups including the Southern Orchestral Concert Society, the Hi-Lights and the Operatic Society. He had moved to Petersfield in 1935 to join Churcher's College as art master, and left it thirty-four years later as Senior Master; while there, he founded the Air Force Section of the CCF and stage-managed performances of Shakespeare plays and Gilbert and Sullivan operas. In the town, he was Secretary to the Arts and Crafts Society and helped found the Petersfield Area Historical Society in 1973.

Plus ça change . . .

'A scheme to ban outsiders from clogging up residential roads in Petersfield town centre with their cars has been put on ice.' (May 1992)

'Police are clamping down on after-hours drinking in town centre pubs after complaints of drunken troublemakers causing weekend mayhem in Petersfield.' (July 1992)

'Petersfield's old Savoy cinema looks set to re-open as a film and entertainment centre.' (November 1992)

'Big cat is spotted as it chased three deer across the old A3 between Hill Brow Road and Rake.' (February 1995)

CHAPTER NINE

Prosperity
1996 Onwards

PROTRACTED ENDGAMES

Several projects initiated in the mid-1990s were to take many years to come to fruition: the grudging acceptance of a Tesco supermarket, the controversial relocation of Churcher's College Junior School, the polemic over the siting of a McDonald's fast-food restaurant and the rival schemes for new housing developments on the Causeway or Ramshill sites all created fierce debate between protagonists and antagonists within the town or between the residents and government inspectors from outside.

Few plans sparked such vocal and overwhelming objections as those to build a superstore and a (later abandoned) filling station on the old abattoir site in the Causeway; Tesco had originally bought the abattoir and the old Grange sites, but the EHDC insisted that they also purchase Mint House (at the junction of Hylton Road and the Causeway) and the former gasworks site in order to bring the new store closer to the town. This, they hoped, would also ensure that Tesco's customers would take the path to Hylton Road and, via the lane past St Peter's Court and the museum, frequent other shops in the town. Another trade-off with the company enabled the historic Grange site (dating from the sixteenth century) to be tastefully refurbished as a doctors' surgery and bus services within the town to be improved. After much legal wrangling, the superstore finally opened in 2000. The sale of a strip of land by The Petersfield School to Tesco for £500,000 not only allowed the superstore to create the link to Hylton Road but it also financed the school's fine new performing arts centre.

The relocation of Churcher's Junior School, forced upon it by the imminent termination of its lease at Moreton House in 2003, was another intransigent problem in the later 1990s. The school's first attempt to buy ground at Penns Place in 1996 was rejected, as was its revised application a year later; it then beat a retreat to its own site at Ramshill (thereby reducing its sports capacity for the senior school) but, despite planning consent – with stringent conditions attached – being granted, the proposals again met with local opposition. Serendipity finally rescued the school from its predicament two months after its latest attempt to build on the Moreton House site when, in February 2003, Littlefield School in Liphook announced its imminent closure. Churcher's purchased the site and their junior pupils moved into the premises the following January.

Planning permission for a motel, restaurant and filling station at the Buckmore Farm site had existed since 1987 and it was therefore only a question of time before sufficiently interested parties filled the space between the farm and the A3, and all three projects were completed by 2006.

The same inspector who had permitted Tesco to build on one side of the Causeway rejected any housing development on the other side: instead, the Ramshill site was preferred for the 278 homes proposed by the Taylor Woodrow company.

EXPANSION

The growing population of Petersfield brought repercussions for its schools: new science blocks were built at both Churcher's College and The Petersfield School, and the latter announced plans to abandon its sixth form but to expand to 1,200 pupils by 2000. Herne Junior School had also added two new classrooms and grown to 480 pupils by 1998.

The imminent competition from Tesco prompted Waitrose to add 20 per cent to its sales area (diverting and reculverting the Drum Brook in the process), but it also forced the closure of the Co-op food store in The Square. On the industrial front, there were signs of a new confidence in the town: the old Bedford Road estate began to expand considerably in this period. The newly named Vision Park saw some speculative office blocks occupy the space beside the council depot and a new Petersfield business park began to take shape on the triangular 10-acre site between the A3, the depot and the railway line.

Interior of St Peter's Church after the renovation of 1995. (*Author's Collection*)

In 1996, responsibility for council housing had been transferred from the EHDC to the East Hampshire Housing Association (EHHA), itself part of the Drum Housing group. When the old Cottage Hospital was finally demolished in 1996, Drum developed the site and installed its own headquarters there. It was the EHHA which was responsible for the redesigning and conversion of the old (1836) workhouse and its chapel in Ramshill into ten houses and two flats, renamed Rookes Mews, which received an East Hampshire Best Housing Design award in 1997.

A good number of other building conversions and refurbishments took place around the turn of the twenty-first century: the familiar Donkey Cart restaurant at 1 The Square, the roof and first floor of which had suffered badly from a fire in 1996, was reopened after extensive and sympathetic rebuilding in 1998; the old Magistrates' Courthouse was reborn as the Petersfield Museum and opened in 1999; the long-awaited replacement sports pavilion in Love Lane was completed in 2000, just in time for use by the Town Juniors football teams which were celebrating their twenty-fifth anniversaries. The original pavilion had been built during the early 1950s and was in very poor condition. Construction of the new building was delayed while funding was sought for a combined youth and sports pavilion, including a sunk concrete BMX bowl, but despite significant efforts by the local community to raise cash, the project unfortunately failed. With the support of Petersfield Area Churches Together (PACT), the police and youth leaders, the King's Arms youth centre opened in the converted former lampshade factory near the Festival Hall in 2001 and has become the most popular and successful of any youth centres attempted in Petersfield. Finally, the statue of William III was (again) refurbished in 2000, when he was given a new set of reins and retrieved his scroll.

The most impressive of the refurbishments during this period was the 2000 Project at St Peter's Church. The most comprehensive alteration since the major restoration undertaken in 1873 brought a new stone floor with under-floor heating, a new podium and altar, a small chapel and meeting rooms behind an oak and glass screen at the west end of the church, and the old, immovable pews were replaced by individual light-coloured chairs. The Methodist Church also underwent improvement. The chairs replaced the old pews and new community rooms and a kitchen were added to the west end of the church. Petersfield Methodists celebrated the centenary of their church in 2002. Both St Laurence's Catholic Church Hall and the Salvation Army Hall in Swan Street underwent refurbishment at this time as well.

The new café culture in the Square, 2006. (*Author's Collection*)

DISAPPEARING BUSINESSES

In contrast to these visible signs of progress in the town, some familiar names disappeared from among local businesses: Martin and Triggs shut their shop in Lavant Street after sixty years' trading; Corrall's coal yard by the station also shut after fifty years, when the site was sold by Railtrack (now the site of the Focus DIY store); Bassett's the ironmonger's in Swan Street closed in 2004, when there was no successor to the owners, the Ismay brothers, to take it on.

Willis, the organ builders, who had had difficulties in recruiting staff to Petersfield because of the high cost of living and housing, relocated to Liverpool in 2001. Attempts to turn their Rushes Road factory into an arts centre failed, the building was demolished and the site has been awaiting housing development for several years.

It was with a clear sense of a passing era that two neighbours on the east side of The Square also vanished in this period, both having traded there for nearly a century, both victims of social changes. The Co-op had been overtaken first by the super-market revolution, then by the prosperity and changed shopping habits of the public, more and more of whom were turning to the Internet to shop. Meanwhile, Rowland, Son and Vincent, another old Petersfield family firm, have succumbed to the emerging café culture and Caffè Nero, with its outdoor seating, has replaced the former furniture firm. Petersfield's commercial transformation from a reliance on its old, local, family firms to a dependency on multiples was more or less complete by the end of the twentieth century.

THE HEATH IS REJUVENATED

The jewel in Petersfield's crown, its 95-acre Heath incorporating a 22-acre Pond, home to badgers and voles, migrating birds from colder climes and the largest Bronze Age burial ground in the south, benefited from the efforts of the PTC and local volunteers in the 1990s. After the dredging of the Pond had been completed in the late 1980s, a Millennium Walk was created around it by the PTC, in collaboration with the Rotary Club, in 1990. The boardwalk was built in 1991 to keep the public clear of dangerous mud, the silt bunds were removed and the ground below them returned to heathland. When the golf club finally vacated the seven holes of its old course on the Heath in 1997, after an association with it lasting over a century, one section of the course was laid out as a wildlife area and other areas became wildflower and grass meadows. A voluntary group, the Friends of Petersfield Heath, was set up in 1999 to promote, but also to protect, the natural heathland, grassland, woodland and the Pond, and to manage this exceptional area so rich in archaeology and natural history.

For some time, the PTC had felt increasingly powerless to cope with the problems of litter and bad behaviour around the Pond. It decided to invite the Angling Club to manage the water, while allowing a small daily charge to cover the expenses of bailiffs, litter picking and administration. The Club also ensured good angling practice and safeguarded the waterfowl, fish stock and vegetation of the Pond. By the end of the century, there were as many as 5,000 visits made by anglers to the Pond annually and this in turn created new problems: erosion of the banks, reed bed damage and the supervision of night-time fishing. The Club also fenced off the 'bird cage' (at the south-east end of the Pond) to protect nesting birds from people, dogs and boats.

THE DEATH THROES OF PROVINCIALISM

The half-century which has elapsed since the end of the Second World War has brought with it the virtual elimination of a provincial ethos: Petersfield in particular, has, to all intents and purposes, lost its rural identity and (unavoidably) succumbed to the

Rt Hon. Michael Mates MP.

Joyce Perry MBE.

homogenisation of British society. At the start of the new millennium, it finds itself prone to many of the ills associated with British life in general: the need for CCTV cameras in the town centre to combat crime; the continually changing measures taken to alleviate traffic chaos; the constant battle to prevent vandalism; the drink- and drugs-related petty crime witnessed at the weekends, to name but the commonest.

Petersfield's response has always been to adapt cautiously to its changing circumstances, while retaining as much of its character as possible. On a human scale, it has aimed at being all-encompassing. For the very youngest in our society, the Grange Birth Centre at the hospital ensures a local provision for a local need (although currently this is in jeopardy); for school-age children, sports and leisure facilities, an Air Training Corps (with new premises in 2004) and the King's Arms are fulfilling a useful role; for families, Petersfield's long tradition of amateur entertainment and numerous hobby groups bring an enviable vitality to the town; for the older residents, adequate housing, health care, a Shopmobility scheme, the Winton House Centre and a well-established support network for the elderly are in place.

Elsa Bulmer MBE.

Socially and politically too, we have moved a long way from the conservative and somewhat hidebound society of the immediate postwar days, and transparency and accountability are the order of the day. Two ladies, Elsa Bulmer and Joyce Perry, have recently been awarded MBEs for their services to the community, Mrs Bulmer particularly for her work on behalf of the elderly, and Mrs Perry for her work at the Petersfield Voluntary Centre, which she co-founded in 1980.

We have matured politically and become confident as a town: consensus politics, demonstrated by collaborative surveys such as the Petersfield Area Transport Strategy of 2000 or the formation of the Petersfield Torrow group (becoming the Petersfield Town Partnership of 2006), have supplanted the parochial, and frequently tendentious, decision-making processes of the past.

YOUNG PEOPLE'S VIEWS

We should perhaps conclude with the opinions of the younger generation, for it is to them that Petersfield will turn to maintain and secure its future identity. Perhaps it is natural that they would like to see more facilities for young people, such as a cinema, a skatepark, or a (non-alcoholic) nightclub for young teenagers, but they also recognise that what already exists is commendable: the Penns Place and Taro Centre sports facilities, the numerous cafés and bars around the town, the Folly Market shops, the variety of music and drama venues, and some attractive clothes shops for the younger generation.

But realism also plays a part in their appreciation of the town and frequently corresponds to the wishes of older residents: they would also like better bus links to outlying villages and towns, more visible policing to stop vandalism and weekend disturbances, and an accident and emergency department at the hospital.

Young people's views on the town's heritage are all positive: Petersfield, they say, is a town for families and is congenial, (relatively) safe and stable; it enjoys a strong tradition of cultural activities, boasts some interesting buildings, and has a tangible community spirit; it is beautifully situated in the Downs, is easily accessible to larger conurbations, and has markedly improved with recent developments in the town centre.

With the opening of the highly successful youth centre, the multitude of sporting activities for young people and the huge success of the SNAP (Say No And Phone) discos which started in the year 2000, Petersfield may perhaps pride itself on some success in satisfying the new, emerging generations of its citizens. Given the enormous changes in society in the past decade, it is salutary to note that our teenagers can feel able to flock in their hundreds to anti-drugs discos run by the police; an offshoot of the Crimestoppers national campaign, the SNAP discos subtly combine the attractions of pop music and prize competitions with an educational approach to alcohol, smoking and drugs.

If the satisfaction quotient among the young in Petersfield is at least adequate, then perhaps those concerned with the town's welfare can congratulate themselves on their achievements.

DEPARTURES

Elsa Bulmer, awarded the MBE in 1996 for her work with Age Concern, Hampshire, and having had the residential care centre in Ramshill named after her the same year, finally retired from local government after thirty-five years' service in 2003. She had fought St Mary's Ward as an Independent candidate, concentrating her efforts on obtaining affordable housing for local people, but also championing the Citizens' Advice Bureau, the open-air swimming pool, the RSPCA and the Winton Players, where she was an active member in their pantomimes. She cannot be remembered without mention being made of her husband Ken, himself a community stalwart and Petersfield's representative on Hampshire County Council for twelve years, who was made an honorary alderman in 1997.

Peter Jenkins, described as 'one of life's perfect gentlemen' who served the town for forty years, died in 1999. He was the housing manager for the Rural District Council from 1946 until 1974, then Town Clerk to the PTC from 1974 until his retirement in 1985. He had a tremendous knowledge of Petersfield and also of Liss, whose Historical Society he helped to found when he retired. An Old Churcherian, he served in the RAF during the war and became involved in radio communications, including code breaking.

John Thomas, surveyor and engineer to the old UDC and a senior officer with the new EHDC after 1974, died in 2002. He was responsible for a wide range of local government services, including housing, car parks, lighting, sewerage and refuse collection. He was also involved in designing the open-air swimming pool and the Weston House sheltered accommodation for the elderly in Borough Road. Few can match his contribution to the physical development of Petersfield in the postwar years, nor his dedication to the community.

Frank Westwood, a veritable institution within, but also well beyond, Petersfield, died in 2006 at the age of 76. He was the natural successor to Flora Twort in Petersfield, having worked with her for two years at 1 and 2 The Square before setting up his own bookselling business in Chapel Street in 1958. He expanded the shop little by little into adjacent buildings (including an old abattoir) and introduced subsidiary services such as picture framing and book and print restoration. He was widely respected for his knowledge and expertise in the world of bookselling, and was awarded royal warrants by the Queen and Prince Charles for the supply of artists' materials and picture framing.

CONCLUSION

There is no doubt that today's Petersfield is still recognisable as the town it was fifty years ago, with some additions and subtractions more or less acceptable to its older citizens. Its physical and spiritual hub is still the Square, its radiating streets remain those of pre-war days, its newest developments are, for the most part, on the periphery of the town, and the countryside is still within easy walking distance.

How, then, has it changed? The steep rise in population has brought the supermarkets but taken away some individual traders; the by-pass has eliminated through traffic but problems remain in the shape of traffic congestion and parking; developers have been, and still are, a threat, but the largest of the postwar estates (Herne Farm) has met with approval by the majority.

Less tangible, but probably more significant, are the changes seen in local government and in wider society. The old UDC contained indigenous people of experience in the fields of town planning and civil engineering; there were home-bred businessmen, accountants and solicitors, for example, who took pride in serving their community. With the greater politicisation of local government since the 1970s, however, fewer such candidates have stood for election and this has weakened the clout and the expertise of the councils. Secondly, where members of councils have been elected to both the PTC and the EHDC (due to a shortage of candidates standing), this has resulted in divided loyalties and a certain democratic deficit. Thirdly, the recent rise in the number of commuters appears to be in inverse proportion to the number of Petersfield residents committed to the town's welfare and development. The effect of these political and demographic changes is that councillors are now more distant from their electorate, although there is of course no doubt as to their commitment to the town's best interests.

In society at large, the growth of affluence has brought with it different expectations of the townsfolk: more and larger shops and car parks, a greater variety of cafés and restaurants and improved recreational facilities. We have become victims of our own success, and this has brought its own problems: there is continual pressure from exploitative developers to expand at our expense and to their profit; Petersfield has a constant requirement to attract light industry and build low-cost housing for its inhabitants if it is not to atrophy; furthermore, it is impossible to ignore or deny the emergence of a commuter counter-culture in our midst, which is gently but perceptibly eroding some of our sense of community.

However, over the past half-century, Petersfield has, chameleon-like, adapted to most of these pressures, and general public services such as health, education and housing are immensely superior to those experienced by the immediate postwar generation. The town has maintained its tradition as a centre of culture (music, drama and local societies are all very buoyant), we enjoy a stable society (few of the older generations or the original Herne Farm residents have moved away), and Petersfield is fast becoming a thriving focus for visitors to the soon-to-be-designated South Downs National Park. The recent success of farmers' markets might even be a sign that we are returning to our rural origins, conscious of the agricultural wealth and the visual beauty of the countryside which surrounds us. In short, Petersfield's heart still beats.

We can, therefore, legitimately end on an optimistic note. If the past fifty years have borne witness to an extraordinary increase in Petersfield's population, but without any significant deterioration in its innate character; if development has been dictated by restraint and a care for the town's architectural heritage; if we retain a proper sense of scale and an awareness of the spirit of Petersfield in planning the future, then we should not fear the consequences of an inevitably expanding town.

Plus ça change . . .

'Proposals for the creation of a South Downs National Park were said to be "unworkable".' (October 1999)

'The Countryside Agency is to go ahead with a consultation process – the first step towards the creation of a new South Downs National Park.' (April 2000)

'The government has given the go-ahead to build a bypass and tunnel under the A3 at Hindhead.' (April 2001)

Petersfield Urban District Council Chairmen and Town Mayors since 1945

URBAN DISTRICT COUNCIL CHAIRMEN

1942–7	George Bailey
1947–50	Solly Filer
1950–4	Keith Gammon
1954–7	Mrs A.A. Hayes
1957–9	J.G. Vince
1959–62	H.C. Jacobs
1962–5	M.R. Urquhart
1965–8	C.J. Bassett
1968–71	K.A. Oates
1971–4	A.J. Ray (transition to town mayor 1973–4)

PETERSFIELD TOWN MAYORS

1974–6	Kenneth Hick
1976–8	Elsa Bulmer
1978–80	Nickey Edwards
1980–2	David Lancaster
1982–3	Jim Challen
1983–5	Beryl Jones
1985–6	Gordon Clare
1986–7	John Sinclair-Willis
1987–8	Kenneth Hick
1988–9	Elsa Bulmer
1989–90	Nickey Edwards
1990–1	Beverley-Anne Silk
1991–2	Eric Goffe
1992–3	Liz Mullenger
1993–4	Teresa Jamieson
1994–6	Bert Perry
1996–97	John Holt
1997–98	George Watkinson
1998–99	Katie Pitt
1999–2000	John Crowhurst
2000–1	Chris Jenner
2001–2	Kenneth Hick
2002–3	Mary Vincent
2003–4	George Watkinson
2004–5	Brian Dutton
2005–6	Vaughan Clarke
2006–7:	Bob Ayer

The Town Mace. (*Author's Collection*)

CONTRIBUTORS

David Allen
Sheila Barge
Robbie Barratt
Roy Barrow
Kathy Bell
Jennifer Bennett
Alan Billenness
Doreen Binks
Trevor Boyden
Shirl Boyle
David Brooks
Donald Brooks
Norman Bryant
Elsa Bulmer
Ken Burrage
Geoffrey Buttle
Bob Carter
Churcher's students:
   Alice Barton
   Alice Cairns
   Nik Fletcher
   David Morgan-Owen
   Peter Musker
Richard Corrie
Derek Cosham
John Crowhurst
Douglas (Dusty) Davis
Gwen Dennis
Nickey Edwards
Clive Ellis
Brian Frost
Jean Gard

Eric Goffe
Eric (Buster) Hampton
Peter Hann
Charles Hardy
Brenda Heath
Rod Herdman
Kenneth Hick
Richard Holder
Bob Holland
Geoff and Marianne Holmes
Rodney Hubbuck
Eddie Hunt
Derrick Ismay
Chris Jacobs
Teresa Jamieson
Beryl Jones
Thomas Kebbell
Mary Kelsey
Geoff King
The King's Arms members:
   Ben Atkins
   Toby Austin
   Michael Cook
   Stefan Robinson
   Jason Scott
Stephen Massey
Michael Mates
John and Margaret Maybury
Dorothy McGinn
John Mepham
Sylvia Mesher
David Money-Chappelle
Liz Mullenger

Alan Passingham
Bert Perry
Margaret Perry
Christopher Pickett
John and Vivien Pike
Katie Pitt
Mary Ray
Michael Reeves
Kathleen Rowswell
Linda Sallows
Jennifer Sandys
Steve Sargent
Andy Shotbolt
Frank Short
Beverley-Anne (Bubbles) Silk
Neil Slatter
Barbara Smyth
John Stabb
David and Beth Stevenson
Tony Struthers
Sophy Tatchell
Richard Thomas
Trevor and Jill Towner
Graham Triggs
Eveline Underwood
Sue Upton
Ian Walder
Margaret Walker
Doris Wall
John West
Frank Westwood
Norm White
Gill Wicksteed

Bibliography

BOOKS AND PAMPHLETS

Farnham, D. and Dine, D., *Petersfield seen and remembered*, Hampshire County Library, 1982

Gard, J. et al., *High Street, Petersfield* (Petersfield Monograph no. 2) 1984

Hick, K. *Petersfield Then and Now*, Frith, 2004

——, *Petersfield – a history and celebration*, Frith, 2005

Inns of Petersfield, The (Petersfield Papers no. 3) PAHS, 1977

Jeffery, D., *Petersfield at War*, Sutton, 2004

Leaton, E. et al., *A History of Christianity in Petersfield* (Petersfield Monograph no. 4) 2001

Lunt, M. and Ray, M., *Petersfield Music Makers* (Petersfield Monograph no. 3) 1986

Munro-Faure, *Flora Twort, A Petersfield Artist*, Hampshire Papers, 1995

Payne, P., *Voices of Petersfield and District*, Tempus, 2003

Petersfield – The Future, The Petersfield Society, 1981

Petersfield Area Historical Society (PAHS) bulletins

Petersfield Area Transport Strategy, Hampshire County Council, 2000

Petersfield Community Association – the first 20 years, 1984

Petersfield Perambulation, A (Petersfield Papers no. 9) PAHS, 1996

Petersfield Planning Policy, Hampshire County Council, 1969

Petersfield Place Names, PAHS, 3rd Edition, 2000

Stamp, W., *Doctor Himself, an unorthodox biography of Harry Roberts*, Hamish Hamilton, 1949

Sheet News, The Sheet Village Association

Street, S., *Petersfield, a pictorial past*, Ensign Publications, 1989

Vesey-Fitzgerald, B., *Hampshire and the Isle of Wight*, Robert Hale, 1949

Wall, D. and Ralton, P., *We had so much pleasure*, Phyllis Ralton, 2004

NEWSPAPERS AND MAGAZINES

The Churcherian

East Hampshire Post, 1976–86

East Hampshire Post, Centenary supplement, September 1983

Hampshire Life

Hampshire Magazine

Hants and Sussex News, 1945–62

The News, Centenary edition, 27 April 1977

Petersfield Official Town Guides

Petersfield Post (and Hants and Sussex News), 1962–3

Petersfield Post, 1963–76
Petersfield Post, 1986–2006
The Rock (St Peter's Parish Church magazine)

ARTICLES

ITS Rubber Ltd, Open Day programme, 28 May 1977
'My Time at Churcher's College (1949–54) and beyond . . .', Adrian Fray, 2001
'The Story of Petersfield Housing Association 1973–2004', Bert Perry, March 2004

OTHER ARCHIVES CONSULTED

Hampshire County Council Minutes
Petersfield Senior School Managers' Meetings, 1952–8
The Petersfield Society Annual Reports
The Petersfield Society Minutes
Petersfield Town Council Minutes

Index